The Passion Trap

The Passion
Trap

How to Right an Unbalanced Relationship

Second Edition

Dean C. Delis, Ph.D.
with Cassandra Phillips

FENESTRA BOOKS™

Formerly published as *The Passion Paradox*

International Standard Book Number: 1-58736-108-6
Library of Congress Card Number: 2002105717

Published (2002) by Fenestra Books™

610 East Delano Street, Suite 104, Tucson, Arizona 85705, U.S.A.
www.fenestrabooks.com

Publisher's Cataloguing-in-Publication Data

Delis, Dean C.
    The passion trap / by Dean C. Delis with Cassandra Phillips. — 2nd ed.
      p. cm.
    Includes bibliographical references.
    ISBN 1-58736-108-6
    1. Marriage.   2. Love.   3. Interpersonal relations.
4. Communication in marriage.   I. Phillips, Cassandra.   II. Title.
HQ734.D455 2002

rev201301

To my parents, Leftare and Irene Delis

Contents

Contents

Acknowledgements

Many friends and colleagues shared with me their intimate lives and their thoughts about love and relationships. Our lively discussions helped to shape my ideas about the passion trap. I especially thank John Fleer, Mark Zaslav, Mat Blusewicz, Edith Kaplan, Alan Fridlund, Corinne Grieco, and Nick and Chris Lowe. Dan Wile and Hilde Burton have had a major influence on my approach to psychotherapy, and I thank them for their valuable insights.

My therapy clients have taught me much about facing and overcoming relationship problems. I am grateful to them for their courage and wisdom. Several of their stories are presented here to illustrate key points; their identities, of course, have been disguised.

Cassandra Phillips is more than a gifted writer. She is also an astute observer of human nature. Her intuitions about people and relationships enhanced the book immeasurably. I will fondly remember our creative struggles and great joy in bringing this book to fruition.

Sandy Dijkstra, our agent, first spotted the book's potential. She has been a vital source of encouragement at every stage. She also had the wisdom to know that Cassandra and I would form an ideal working partnership.

Toni Burbank, our editor, always brought a calm, reassuring voice to our work. Her ideas on the organization, style, and substance of the book were nothing short of brilliant. Fran Fisher's editorial contributions and Nancy Dimsdale's graphic work were greatly appreciated.

I have learned much about life and human nature from my parents. Their deep love for me has always given me the courage to strive for higher achievements. My mother helped research the book, and her reactions to various drafts were deeply influential. My father's guidance and critiques have helped me grow as a writer.

Finally, I wish to thank my most important collaborator, my wife Meg, who was my chief consultant on the book. I am lucky to be married her and to have our three boys, Patrick, Drew and Miles.

Acknowledgements

The coauthor wishes to thank Sandy Dijkstra for her perspicacity and faith; Dean for being wonderful to work with; and her husband Bob Burkey for his insight and love.

HERMIA: I frown upon him, yet he loves me still.
HELENA: O that your frowns could teach my smiles such skill!
HERMIA: I give him curses, yet he gives me love.
HELENA: O that my prayers could such affection move.
HERMIA: The more I hate, the more he follows me.
HELENA: The more I love, the more he hateth me.

William Shakespeare

Introduction

Several years ago I had an impromptu client on a transcontinental flight. She was well dressed, attractive, clearly a professional woman. I put her age at about 37. As she sat down next to me, I noted the distracted, troubled look of someone who "needed to talk."

I was on my way to New York to lecture about a psychological test I'd developed. I'd saved some last-minute preparation for the flight, so I was pleased that "Liz" wasn't fishing for conversation. Instead, she pulled out of her travel bag a popular paperback about relationship problems. I was intrigued, as this subject had become of special interest to me.

During lunch we chatted. Liz was a financial analyst whose work involved much travel to the West Coast. I'm always interested to see how people react to my profession. Sometimes they clam up, sometimes they get a little feisty, and sometimes they open up. Liz was in the latter camp. Specifically, she wanted to know if I was familiar with the work of the author whose book she was reading. I told her I was and that I'd like to hear her impressions of it. Then began a conversation that proved pivotal; it was to send me into the trenches.

Liz said of the book:

I feel like it was written just for me. It's uncanny.

I asked her how so. She raised the book and said:

I'm in the middle of an honest-to-God relationship crisis. I'm caught between two men, my husband . . . and a man I work with on the Coast. And it's got me climbing the walls. My husband, Nate, is the nicest man alive. He's a doctor. He'd do anything for me. After twelve years of marriage, he still brings roses for no reason at all and remembers all these special occasions like the anniversary of the day we met. It's very guilt-making because even though I love him, I get impatient with him very easily. And it makes me feel worse that he takes whatever I dish out and just gets nicer and nicer, especially lately, when I least deserve it.

Introduction

I'd noticed that her voice tensed up as she talked about her husband and marriage. But when she spoke of her lover, her manner changed abruptly. Suddenly she was animated and involved with what she was saying — at least at first.

> I met Doug about a year ago. He's our West Coast consultant. He's younger than me, and very hip, I guess you'd say. At first I was skeptical when he started making overtures to me. I mean, I'm not the type you'd think he'd go for. But he seemed very sincere. I realized I was growing more infatuated with him, but I was hoping that's all it was. Anyway, this went on for about four months. I'd never been unfaithful to Nate, and so finally I thought, what the hell, I'll just have something light with Doug, a fling. But after getting together with him on a couple of trips, I knew something more was happening. He was constantly on my mind, and I was calling him all the time from work. There's a young woman analyst in our office, a comer. She was sent to the Coast and I went insane with jealousy, thinking she'd fall for Doug too.

I offered the obvious: that it must have been a trying time in her life. She smiled ironically.

> Well, my jealousy proved groundless, and Doug and I started getting very close. It was scaring me to death. I was feeling so awful. I mean, here I have the kind of husband women dream about, and look what I was doing to him. I'd make all these resolutions to end it with Doug, but as soon as I'd see him, I'd go into a kind of amnesia. All I could think about was how much I loved him. This went on for another seven months. Finally, I started thinking maybe Doug and I were really meant for each other. I've never had kids, and so I had nothing tying me to New York. It would have been easy for me to transfer to our California office. Also, Doug had started acting a little distant, so I thought I'd better act fast.

She paused. The troubled look I had seen earlier returned to her face.

> So, this trip I brought him the classic, gold cuff links. I was all prepared to share my new idea with him. But he seemed more distant than ever. Then he asked me what I wanted and I got flustered. All I said was that it would be nice if we could spend more time together. He said, "Sometimes, the greatest challenge is to walk away from something beautiful before it fades." I felt ice water running through my veins. I pretended he was joking. I'm almost positive he's met someone else. I tell you, I'm just about ready to check into Bellevue.

We talked a little more, then I asked Liz if the book was helping her with her situation.

It really shows why I'm so screwed up about relationships. Now I know that it all comes down to my fear of emotional intimacy. That's why I've kept my husband at arm's length all these years. And I also see that I'm addicted to Doug in kind of a sick way. And my parents probably raised me in a way that would cause me to seek out the wrong partners, although I was fairly happy as a child. It all ties in to low self-esteem and a need to punish myself, maybe because my parents were too loving and I couldn't deal with that ...

Looking for Blame in All the Wrong Places

Most people who enter therapy do so because of relationship problems. I'd long marveled at how very difficult it is to find lasting pleasure in love, and how often we find only pain. It seemed to make only a perverse kind of sense that love, the most joyous human emotion, could also be the most punishing.

As I listened to Liz pick herself to pieces, I felt a new sense of purpose. Here she was, a very bright and attractive woman, defining herself as an emotional basket case. On one hand, she sounded like a "commitmentphobe," afraid of real intimacy in her marriage. But on the other hand, with Doug she behaved like a "woman who loved too much," addicted to an uncaring man. In other words, the self-help books were offering her contradictory diagnoses. From her statements about her parents, I concluded that she'd been blessed with an unusually supportive family, not the type of dysfunctional unit that can cause one to carry bad relationship patterns into adulthood.

I certainly empathized with Liz. Love really *can* make you feel crazy. And it doesn't matter if the relationship is new or long-term. Fear of rejection, for example, can cause low self-esteem, extreme anxiety, over-reactiveness, and an obsession about the loved one that can surpass that of new love.

On the other hand, if *your* feelings of love start to fade, you may go emotionally numb, you may worry that you're incapable of love, or you may experience a severe sense of guilt.

I'd felt all those feelings, just like Liz, and *just like everyone I'd ever talked to who'd been in love.* Apparently, these very intense feelings were quite normal.

Because of her situation, Liz was experiencing both sides of love at the same time. No wonder she felt emotionally fractured. I was struck by how her whole demeanor changed dramatically from one moment to the next, depending on which man she was talking about. *Relationship dynamics are so powerful that they can literally transform us.* The nature of the transformation depends on which side of love you're on—that is, if you feel in danger of rejection, or if you feel rejecting of your partner.

I had concluded that because of their force and predictability, the emotional dynamics of romantic relationships should be dealt with *on their own terms.* Yet, the literature about love and relationship problems indicated that no one had ever held this view. Our behavior in intimate relationships is always seen as a barometer of something else, usually of how we were treated as children. For example, Liz was blaming her relationship problems on personal inadequacies originating in her childhood. But there was nothing "wrong" with her. What seemed wrong was her eagerness to blame herself. And even wronger, to me, was the support the book was giving her for doing so.

I told Liz that there are simply some *built-in* problems with love, problems that bring out certain kinds of behavior that can easily be labeled pathological, but that are entirely normal, predictable, and universal. Liz had made me realize that it was vital to get this view widely known. What she helped crystallize in my mind was:

- We in the "therapeutic" community shouldn't automatically view relationship problems as symptoms of emotional dysfunction rooted in childhood. More and more I felt it was unconscionable to allow people to feel that they were "sick" because they were having relationship problems.
- Pathologizing the normal, universal problems of love can be very destructive. It makes us pessimistic about being able to change or finding a satisfying relationship. It makes us feel stuck in bad relationship ruts. Pathologizing fails because it doesn't take into account the reality of unrecognized relationship dynamics.
- It was more important now than ever before that we deal effectively with relationship problems. Never has there been such a psychologically literate population as ours, due to the

countless self-help books of the last decade. But I was growing more convinced that many of these books were doing
more harm than good with their pathologizing and often
contradictory stances. The fact that relationship books were
being read so avidly suggested that we've never been so lost
in our dealings with romantic partners, or so hungry for
guidance.

The Passion Trap

When I first began to question the prevailing approach to relationship
problems, I went back to basics. I described for myself in the plainest
terms possible what was causing the most trouble in my clients' relationships (and, admittedly, in my own). It boiled down to this: *One
partner is **more** in love (or "emotionally invested" in the relationship) than
the other. And the more love the loving partner wants from the other, the **less**
the other partner feels like giving.*

I had described a state of imbalance, in which the more-in-love
partner was in what I term the "one-down position," while the less-in-
love partner was in the "one-up position." I knew from experience
that both men and women occupied the one-up and one-down positions at various times. So it seemed to me that the contemporary pre-
occupation with women as victims of male mistreatment was causing
us to lose sight of an important fact: that women can be heartbreakers
too.

I'd also concluded that virtually everyone experiences love's two
sides in the same way. It doesn't matter if your mother adored you or
ignored you, or if your childhood was happy or miserable. No one —
even the "emotionally healthy" person — is exempt from the pain of
love when it tips out of balance. The troubled individual may, of
course, more frequently wind up in unbalanced relationships, and the
healthier person may recover more quickly and learn more from
them. But love can go out of kilter for *anyone*.

Having gotten this far, I realized that there was some "missing
link" between this imbalance of emotional involvement and dysfunction in relationships. What I found at this emotional pivot point was a
paradox, a contradiction, what I call the "passion trap," that explains
why it's been so difficult for us to recognize this problem.

Let's return to Liz's situation. With her husband, Liz was the one-up. The expression of the imbalance was Nate's increasing "courtship behavior" and Liz's equal and opposite reaction of wanting to withdraw from him—to the point where she wondered if she loved him. She knew she no longer felt "in love" or had any sexual desire for him.

It was very different when we were first married. Nate was my doctor, and he's fourteen years older than me. He was in a very traditional marriage with a doting wife. I idolized him. After all, he was older *and* a doctor. But after the first couple of years, I realized we had problems. He was used to having a wife on call, and I'd decided to go for my MBA. He didn't mesh with my friends, and I didn't particularly go for his. Then I wanted a child and he didn't. Then he wanted a child and I didn't. And yet he's so loving to me. We have some wonderful times together and there is a definite bond of caring.

I said that it sounded like she'd come to accept her marriage.

Yes . . . Until I met Doug. Now my whole focus has changed. Before, I concentrated on my career and finding just the right linen tablecloth. Now I feel like some lost part of me has been awakened. And it has taken over. I have to struggle to keep up my job performance. And I think Nate is starting to suspect something.

The relationship with Doug was like a mirror image of Liz's relationship with her husband. Nate emotionally revolved around her, while she revolved around Doug. With her husband, she felt restless, detached, and not terribly loving—and she felt guilty for having those feelings. With Doug, she felt passionate, anxious, and very much in love.

I told Liz that when we fall in love, our central experience is a loss of control. And that creates anxiety. She agreed.

You know, the first couple of times with Doug it was just great. I felt completely reborn. Then I got nervous. I started worrying about Doug's feelings for me, and I was afraid of making the wrong move or saying the wrong thing.

Liz's anxiety was rooted in the one-down's fear of rejection. Unlike the other areas of her life, in her new love affair she felt powerless, vulnerable, uncertain, and insecure (as well as madly in love). At the beginning of most romances, both partners feel this way.

One-downs try harder. Feeling insecure and wanting to regain a sense of control, they labor to enhance their "attraction power." The basic rites of courtship are about self-enhancement: wearing your most flattering clothes, spending hours at the mirror, thinking up clever things to say, honing culinary skills, spending money freely on gifts, restaurant meals, and romantic diversions—in sum, making yourself as desirable as possible. Liz joked that she must have spent a month's salary on expensive cosmetics and creams since she'd started seeing Doug.

The goal of all this effort is to gain *emotional control* over a loved one so that we don't have to worry about rejection. That means winning his or her love.

But there's a catch.

If you prove too appealing to the one you want—to the point where he's clearly more in love with you than you with him—your relationship will fall out of balance. You've become the one-up. Or, if you're frightened by your partner's distance, you become the one-down. And herein was the missing link I sought:

The very urge to attract someone, to bring another person under your emotional control, contains the potential for upsetting the balance of the relationship. And that is because the feeling of being in love is biochemically linked to the feeling of being out of control. Once you feel completely in control or sure of another person's love, your feelings of passion begin to fade. Gone is the challenge, the emotional spark, the excitement.

Of course, we all know that the dizzy, delicious feelings of new love can't last forever. In a balanced relationship, after the initial passion fades, the partners move into a phase of enduring intimacy and warmth. But when one partner falls more deeply in love than the other, it can trigger harmful patterns between them. Such was the case with Liz and Nate. As Liz's initial awe of him faded, she began to pursue other interests rather than center her life around him. So Nate began to feel his security in the relationship slip away. And that made him feel less in control of and more in love with Liz. His very loving ways were attempts to win her love and to free himself from rejection anxiety. But his "hypercourtship behavior" backfired by making Liz feel even more in control of the relationship, less excited by it, and eventually less loving toward him.

However, if your lover is more successful at winning your love than you are at winning his, as Doug was, you'll feel more insecure and more in love. Then you'll strive for more closeness and control.

But that will cause the one-up to emotionally back away from the relationship. And this reaction increases the one-down's insecurity and need for closeness and the one-up's security and feelings of discontent.

As Liz's predicament showed, passion trap dynamics can crop up anytime in a relationship. They may abort a new romance or hobble a long-term relationship. They may be caused by various sources of imbalance: attraction power, situational factors, gender role-playing, or personality-style incompatibilities, all of which we'll examine. But no matter the sources, and no matter how overt or covert they may be in a relationship, passion trap dynamics exact a toll by preventing true intimacy.

The Passion Trap Crisis

Obviously, the paradox of passion has always been with us. Perhaps the best example was offered by *Anna Karenina,* Tolstoy's great novel and my favorite work of fiction. The adulterous lovers, Anna and young Count Vronsky, reach amazing heights of passion partly because their circumstances prevent them from truly possessing one another. But once Anna becomes pregnant with Vronsky's child and leaves her husband, Vronsky's passion begins to ebb.

This creates in Anna a gnawing insecurity that turns her passion into jealous obsession, to tragic end.

These universal dynamics have always been with us and always will be. But now, as we live in an age of deferred marriage, we tend to have many romantic relationships—and that means many brushes with the passion trap. I was seeing clients who'd been hurt one too many times turning into chronic, emotionally insulated one-ups. I was seeing career women postponing marriage until their mid thirties, then panicking and positioning themselves as one-downs in the marriage market. I was seeing tremendous cynicism in both men and women about ever finding a fulfilling, lasting relationship. And between the extremes of neediness and cynicism were ambivalence and confusion. People don't know why their loving and unloving behaviors cause particular results in their relationships. They don't know why they're having certain feelings about a partner or relationship. Or, worse, they pathologize themselves and their relationships using the latest "pop psychology" buzzwords.

Not only was the pathologizing message of relationship books disturbing to me, but I knew from my own experience in treating couples that the traditional procedures could prove dangerous in problem relationships. For example, a couple comes in for help. One partner feels emotionally neglected and wants more intimacy from the other, but the other feels emotionally crowded and wants more distance. The standard line is to urge the couple to do more loving things together. But urging closeness on the distant (or one-up) partner makes him feel even more crowded, and also subtly puts the blame on him (he *should* feel more loving). The results of this approach to therapy are often short-lived or countertherapeutic.

On the other hand, I was convinced that working on these problems within the right framework could leave a relationship far stronger than it had ever been. My clients were responding well to the idea that the passion trap was the real culprit in their relationships. As I explained it, *neither partner was to blame* for the imbalance that existed between them. We could work together to discover the source or sources of the imbalance, and then we'd use techniques I'd developed to correct it.

Are You in a Passion Trap Relationship?

We may be brilliant at diagnosing the problems of other couples, but when it comes to our own relationships we're not so perceptive. To determine whether you're caught in the passion trap, answer the following questions.

- Is one partner more jealous than the other?
- Is one partner typically waiting for the other to call or return home?
- Is one partner typed the "good guy" and the other the "bad guy"?
- Does one partner make a bigger effort to generate conversation and communication?
- Does one partner say "I love you" more than the other?
- Is one partner more attractive to the opposite sex than the other?
- Is one partner less affectionate after sex than the other?

- Does one partner want to "work on the relationship" more than the other?
- Does one partner tend to feel neglected at parties while the other feels constrained (or temporarily liberated)?
- Is one partner's career much stronger than the other's?
- Does one partner tend to feel anxious and insecure about the relationship while the other takes it for granted?
- Does one partner express annoyance or embarrassment over the other partner's behavior in public?
- If you're not married, does one partner bring up the subjects of commitment and marriage more than the other?
- If you're married, does one partner bring up the subject of having children (or more children) more than the other?
- During fights, does one partner get labeled "self-centered," "selfish," and "inconsiderate," while the other is accused of being "possessive," "clingy," and "demanding"?

If you answered yes to several of these questions, your relationship harbors elements of imbalance. The more yes answers, the greater the imbalance.

Of course, even balanced relationships have episodes of imbalance and brushes with the passion trap. But balanced couples have a pretty much equal emotional investment in the relationship. That keeps them from getting too far out of sync with each other, except in extremely unbalancing situations.

Let's now turn to the root causes of relationship problems. We'll begin to understand how the powerful dynamics of love can trap us in the one-up and one-down positions, often making us behave in ways we dislike and that seem beyond our control. As our plane started its descent, Liz offered a comment I found to be intriguing:

> I think what you're talking about is something so common, in a way so obvious, that it's been invisible.

The stakes are high. Success in love is one of the great determinants of a happy life. This book is designed to make that happiness more attainable.

Part I

The Painful Patterns that Create Unequal Love

Chapter 1

Falling in Love

The Pleasures and Perils of Passion

When we fall in love, our lives go from black-and-white to Technicolor overnight. New love transforms the way we think and feel and perceive. It scrambles our thoughts, upends emotions, beautifies all we see, and cues the release of strong, pleasure-giving chemicals in our brains.

I always ask my couples clients to talk about how they felt when they were falling in love. It's a valuable exercise because it reminds them of an important fact that's easily forgotten in bad times: that they are capable of giving each other great joy and pleasure. I like to turn a microscope on courtship because it reveals so much about why two people are together, and also because it so often holds the seeds of what is pulling them apart. In most of my cases, we find early signs of imbalance. It's a crucial discovery because, as physicians say, "diagnosis is half the cure."

Three Courtships

I've chosen the following couples to present their courtships here because they disclose so much about the dynamics of attraction.

Paul and Laura

Paul, 35, is an attorney who specializes in tax law. He speaks very precisely, as if to mask the emotional tumult he felt while he was falling in love with Laura, a woman who had caused him extremes of happiness, despair, and confusion.

I met her when she first came to the firm. She was so attractive that it didn't even occur to me to be seriously interested. I actually recall the first moment romance seemed possible. She was sitting next to me in a staff meeting, and another attorney and I were arguing about strategy in a corporate case. Afterward, she leaned over to me and whispered, "Way to go, Becker." Her looks, her perfume, her support, her humor, her natural friendliness . . . they all seemed to reach me at once. I hadn't been in a relationship for a while, and it was like some barrier just crumbled.

Laura, 28, a tall, strikingly pretty woman with shiny dark hair, had planned it that way. She had set her sights on Paul because she liked his air of authority and the way he seemed

... not the wolf type. I don't want to sound vain, but I'd gotten a little tired of men coming on to me. But Paul clearly wasn't about to do that. It intrigued me to imagine what he'd be like in love. I'd singled him out because he was so smart, confident, and respected by the rest of the staff. I even liked his looks. I mean, he looks professorial and a little sedentary, but that had a certain charm.

Like many new couples, Paul and Laura didn't know each other very well before their attraction developed. But their images of each other were well defined and romantic.

Deborah and Jonathan

Deborah, 33, a sandy-haired high school art teacher who dresses with an artist's flair, met Jonathan at a mutual friend's party. A veteran of several "serious and semiserious" relationships, Deborah didn't like the way she always seemed to "lose herself" in her love affairs. She had resolved to be on her own for a year, funneling her energies into painting, with hopes of getting a show.

Jonathan, a carpenter-contractor, had several employees in his small, thriving remodeling business. In his early forties, he had been married once and had a B.A. in philosophy. Deborah recalled of their courtship:

I wasn't particularly taken with Jonathan at first. Physically he wasn't my type, too tall and thin, and I don't like beards. But something appealed, the fact that he seemed very thoughtful and sincere. I told him up front I wasn't interested in dating, but he persuaded me to have "a friendly dinner" with him. He told me then about his devastating marriage—his wife had left him for another man—and how I was the first woman who had interested him in several years. I was flattered, but I still didn't feel strongly attracted. But he seemed so nice and safe that I agreed to see him again.

I asked Deborah if I might invite Jonathan to speak with me separately. She agreed. In one of two sessions with Jonathan, I asked what had initially drawn him to Deborah.

> I'm not much of a partygoer, and in fact I was about to leave when I saw Deborah. I liked the way she dressed, very creatively, and I sensed a kindred spirit. She had a wariness too, but that was fine. I *don't* like women who come on too strong or seem needy. I was excited after we had dinner, because my initial impressions were holding up. And I was ecstatic when she agreed to see me again, because she'd said she didn't want to date.

It's not uncommon that a one-sided interest, like Jonathan's, will stir romantic feelings in someone who was initially indifferent, like Deborah. That's because the prospect of emotional fulfillment through romance can be so compelling.

Beth and Miles

Unlike the other two couples, Miles and Beth were married when they came to see me. They had met four years earlier, shortly after Miles was hired to manage a grand but fading restaurant. His overhaul of the decor and the kitchen staff was dramatically successful. Part of the turnaround involved a carefully mounted publicity campaign, masterminded by Beth, a public relations executive. Beth, 35, had left a serious long-term relationship a year earlier, and was casually dating. Miles, 32, was a noted bachelor around town. Beth recalled their first meeting, which occurred in her office.

> Miles knocked my socks off. He was a little brash, but his mind seemed to work on about six levels at once, and his feel for trends was uncanny. And I loved his looks—handsome, but slightly offbeat. Like his tie had little boats on it. Best of all, and this surprised me, he seemed very grounded. He insisted I come to the restaurant after work to discuss the campaign, and by the end of the night we were making mad love on his office couch. I assure you, this is not my typical behavior with clients.

Miles said of Beth:

The attraction was instant, mutual, mental, physical, and everything else. Beth was all business at first, but her sense of humor emerged as we got to know each other. I really liked the way it contrasted with her prim little business suit. There were lots of interesting contradictions, and her ideas were great too. After I left her office, I couldn't stop thinking about her.

My clients may be depressed, anxious, angry, even bitter when they first walk into my office. But when they talk about those early moments of attraction and excitement, voices and eyes seem to come alive with new hope. They know with greater conviction why they're there and why it matters.

Attraction

Why are we attracted to one person over another? If we reduce this terribly complex question to basics, we must first look at *needs*, specifically *interpersonal needs*. Interpersonal needs can be met only through our interactions with other people. The satisfaction of these needs is crucial to our sense of emotional well-being, and the urge to get them met is a driving force behind much of human behavior.

We have two types of interpersonal needs. First are *the basics*, which include companionship, intimacy, sex, and acceptance. The basics urge us to connect with other people, with the underlying goal of assuring survival of our species.

The second type are our *special needs*. Each of us has a unique, detailed mosaic of special needs. Special needs give us parameters in our search for a mate who'll truly complement us. These needs create preferences in everything from value systems, reading tastes, and acceptable occupations to hair color, sense of humor, and athletic leanings. They determine what sort of emotional ambience we want in a relationship—maybe energetic, maybe placid—and steer us toward people who could help create this ambience.

Special needs can be traced to a variety of sources. Parents and other childhood influences powerfully shape them, as do later experiences and relationships. Our needs change as we grow and change. Even the cultural era has a role in defining our special needs. In the sixties, for example, the image of a successful young stockbroker was a romantic turn-off; now it's a turn-on. If you've ever read the "personals" in a newspaper or magazine, you know how seriously we take our special needs ("SWF seeks vegetarian, Jewish, feminist male . . ."), as well as the basics ("who is warm, giving, and ready for commitment").

The Infatuation Threshold

Everyone has what I call an *infatuation threshold*. We reach it when two forces converge. First, we must be in a state of neediness. That means we're not in a fulfilling relationship, and we're not happy with our lives. Sometimes, someone's interest in us awakens dormant needs that then seek fulfillment.

Second, we must come into contact with someone who appears capable of meeting a critical combination of our needs. If our basic needs are very strong, we may be less choosy than we'd normally be. And if we're very lucky, we come across someone who appears to meet a vast number of our special needs, and we experience the fabled "love at first sight."

We all have different infatuation thresholds, predispositions that determine *how* we fall. Some people fall in love all the time, others do only once; some fall quickly, while others can't until they've gotten to know someone very well.

When someone crosses our infatuation threshold, we experience a sudden and dramatic emotional transformation. Intense hopes and desires are suddenly fixed on this one person, and we feel a new sense of excitement about life. It's like a gate has opened and our pent-up emotions are flowing. As Paul, the lawyer, said of his attraction to Laura, "some barrier just crumbled." Our hunger to satisfy our needs explains how we can fall in love with people we hardly know.

In Love, Out of Control

When attraction triggers infatuation, passion quickly overtakes us. The dictionary definition of passion is "emotion over reason." Passion crosses the wires between our hearts and minds, making it easy for us to confuse infatuation with true love at the beginning. The two feel the same, and our excited brains cannot discriminate one from the other.

However, whether our feelings turn out to be a passing fancy or deep and lasting, the primary sensation is the same: a plummeting, *out-of-control* feeling. Paul felt completely out of control as his infatuation with Laura grew.

> I was thinking of Laura to the exclusion of everything else. It was frightening how little control I had. My work suffered. I was becoming a joke at the office because I kept misplacing important briefs. You have to understand that I'm the one who knows where everything is. Most of my energy was spent on contriving ways to run into Laura and rehearsing things to say to her.

When he finally asked Laura out to dinner, she readily accepted. She cooked for their next date, and instead of eating the peach tart she had prepared for dessert, they made love. Laura reported that they

> ... let everything go. We actually missed two days of work. My mother, whom I talk to most days, thought I had died in an accident with no I.D. I began wondering if I'd ever feel normal again.

Virtually all new lovers find that their "normal" ways of thinking and behaving go haywire in a pleasant but truly frightening way. The fear exists because you feel out of control. And in a very real sense you *are* out of control when you fall in love, because falling in love entails an emotional dynamic called *cathexis* by Freud. Cathexis occurs when your emotions become so totally focused on your lover that you lose control of them.

Falling in love is like investing in the stock market. Just as you temporarily lose control of your money when you invest it, you lose control of your emotions when you fall in love, because you've invested them in your lover. And just as you can't control the fate of your stock market investment, you can't possibly know the outcome of a new relationship. This is the risk factor, the scary part of falling in love.

How Can Something So Scary Feel So Good?

As Deborah found her attraction to Jonathan deepening, she felt surprised and frightened, but also euphoric.

> I wasn't expecting to start feeling "smitten," but I did after about the fifth date. He was acting like I was the answer to his dreams, but he

kept deferring sex. Our good-night kisses were getting longer and more passionate, but that was it. It made me feel uncertain about what was going on, and I found myself wanting him more and getting seductive with him. I'd been around enough to know that someone who's been hurt really badly, like him, can have problems with intimacy. So on one hand I was really anxious, but on the other I felt I was starting to fall. When we finally slept together, on our sixth date, I was in heaven. So much for the "vow of celibacy."

The risks of love—like any other fear—trigger the release of powerful, amphetamine-like biochemicals in the brain. These chemicals spur us to perform optimally with the goal of maintaining survival. In truly life-threatening situations, they help us run faster, fight longer, hit harder, cope with pain, and stay focused on the source of danger. This is known as the "fight or flight" response. But these powerful stimulants have a tantalizing side effect: they create unusually pleasurable sensations. This is why so many people court challenge and danger: to generate natural highs for themselves.

When you fall in love, you pulse with sensations that are the romantic equivalent of "fight or flight": you tremble with anticipation, your palms moisten, and your heart seems to hammer in your chest; you are physically energized, capable of making love all night and feeling fine the next day; you are intensely focused on your lover; your senses seem sharper; you give dazzling displays of charm and wit; and you're anesthetized to unpleasantness in other parts of your life. You even look better. You're reaping the euphoric, biochemical benefits of losing control.

Rejection Anxiety

Rejection anxiety is a major cause of our feelings of danger and passion in love. When we've just fallen in love, the last thing we're likely to worry about is feeling too secure. We're afraid of losing love, not getting too much of it. Miles was expressing pure rejection anxiety when he said:

> Beth was seeing a corporate VP and an internist when we met, so I was sweating nails that I'd seem like a lightweight to her or be just a fling.

Beth's rejection anxiety centered around the almost four-year age difference between her and Miles.

I suddenly became very conscious of my age and the little lines around my eyes and all that. It was hard for me to believe those things made no difference to him, especially when beautiful young women were flirting with him — which happened a lot.

Rejection anxiety opens us up to feelings such as jealousy, obsessiveness, and self-doubt. It can be extremely threatening to lose control to another person, to feel so exposed and vulnerable. As Freud put it, "We are never so defenseless against suffering as when we love."

It's a cold fact of life that a lover may lose interest in you or find a more desirable lover. Most of us know from experience that being "dumped" is painful in a way that penetrates and demoralizes like nothing else. Before we're deeply certain of a partner's love, the possibility of abandonment makes us feel especially powerless, and all the more passionate.

The Defense: Reading Our Partners

Falling in love may make us crazy, but it rarely erases our basic emotional survival instincts. These instincts make us avid to know how our lover is feeling about us at any given time. So we develop ways of reading a partner's words and actions, looking for telling clues. Often we don't heed the data we gather, but rarely have I met a rejected partner who hadn't "seen it coming" in retrospect.

Assessing and Decoding

During courtship we try to protect ourselves by constantly *assessing* and *decoding* our lover's romantic behavior. Deborah described this process when she was falling in love with Jonathan.

I was very confused by his mixed signals and spent a lot of energy trying to sort them out. On one hand, he was always bringing me flowers when we got together, but on the other, he was in no hurry to jump into bed. Then we plateaued at seeing each other about three times a week. At first, he seemed so enthusiastic about me, and us, that I thought I'd be faced with deciding whether or not I wanted to stay with it. But when it didn't evolve the way I'd expected it to, I found myself constantly weighing his affectionate behavior against his cautious behavior.

New lovers reflexively run checks on each other's romantic behavior. They gauge how much time elapses between their last moment together and the next phone call, listen for mentions of future plans, judge whether a partner is getting more or less attentive. When we're in love we're highly alert to these shadings of behavior because what matters most to us are signs of distance or closeness in our partner. We're so focused on our lover that few behavioral nuances escape us. So at any given time, we have raw data for calculating the odds for rejection. It's a technique that gives jittery lovers a small but reassuring sense of control.

The Bug in the System

There is, of course, one flaw in our assessing and decoding system. It works fine as long as we haven't gotten too deeply involved. If we read growing detachment in our partner, we should logically begin to step away from the relationship to avoid getting hurt. But once we've invested a large part of our emotions in another person, a sign of withdrawal will trigger even greater passion in us. And passion has a way of filtering out the bad signals and processing only the good.

The "First Strike" Defense

Sometimes a partner who's terrified of rejection and the uncertainty of new love will choose to end a relationship very early. A person who does this is usually at an insecure time in his or her life or is still hurting from a previous rejecting relationship. By seizing the pivotal role of rejecter, you instantly gain power *and* relief from rejection anxiety. You also cut off the possibility of finding true intimacy.

The Offense: Courtship Behavior

Usually we think of courtship as a collection of "rituals" designed to seek and express love. I believe that courtship serves another crucial purpose, and that has to do with interpersonal power.

I've described the way our loss of emotional control to a new partner creates both anxiety and passion. Now we need to understand how these feelings get funneled into a campaign to bring a new partner under our emotional control. Our most potent tool in this campaign is our ability to *attract*. Both consciously and unconsciously, we employ myriad tactics to make ourselves seem as wonderful and irresistible as possible. Staging performances worthy of Olivier, we offer gleaming versions of ourselves to our lovers.

The Enhanced Self

Separately, I asked Laura and Paul if they were conscious of trying to make themselves attractive to each other.

Laura:

> When I first got interested in Paul, I'd really do myself up on staff meeting days. I'd leave three instead of two buttons undone on my blouse, wear an extra dab of perfume, and mess my hair up a little. Then I'd "position" myself next to him or directly across the table. I'd be *very* attentive to his remarks, nodding when he made a point, smiling when appropriate. I was shameless! [She laughed.]

Paul:

> When it seemed Laura actually had an interest in me, I started worrying about my appearance. This is *not* something I usually pay much attention to. My receding hairline really started to bother me. I tried combing my hair in different ways, moving the part around. I actually began reading hair-growth ads in magazines. And I bought a new Italian suit that was more fitted than my usual baggy Brooks Brothers numbers.

Looking good, or, more precisely, looking the way you think your lover would like you to look, is a basic courtship ritual. If Laura had set her sights on a different type of lover—a hard rock musician, for instance—she might have opted for leather pants and a punk hairdo. The point is that we try to tailor our attractiveness to people we desire to show them how compatible we are.

The Enlightened Self

Deborah practiced another classic courtship ritual.

> Existential philosophy was a special interest of Jonathan's, and I didn't want to seem totally ignorant about it. So I bought a few books about contemporary philosophy and did some boning up. It was tough going, but worth it. When Jonathan started "talking exis-

tential" during one of our dinners, I casually dropped a few comments about Sartre and Kierkegaard and the "authentic life" and so on. He couldn't believe it. In fact, that was the night we first made love.

When we set out to win a lover, we identify his or her deepest concerns and interests, then show that we can share them too. It doesn't have to be something intellectual. Expressing fascination with a person's work or hobbies is essentially the same thing. Falling in love makes chameleons of us; unconsciously we take on our lover's coloration so we'll seem capable of satisfying many of his or her particular needs.

The Self a Mother Would Love

We also attract and charm our lovers by suppressing bad habits and controlling negative behaviors. Miles told of his efforts to accommodate Beth's distaste for cigarette smoking.

> I'd been a die-hard smoker, but cigarettes were a major turn-off for Beth. At first I used a lot of mints and breath sprays, but it wasn't working. So after twelve years of smoking, I quit cold turkey. I guess that's love.

If we're naturally messy, we suddenly get very neat; our homes are never so immaculate as when a lover visits for the first time. We don't lose our tempers, show anger, or act petty with a new lover. Instead, we turn on our wit, charm, and humor, and we show support, sympathy, helpfulness, and approval at every opportunity.

Gift Giving and Free Spending

Beth recalled what she enjoyed most about her courtship.

> Miles and I got into this little game of gift giving. I was giving him little plastic foods, like the kind in the windows of Japanese restaurants. He was giving me "sensible" things, but in a joking way. Like a paperweight from the fifties with a man at a desk inside it. I especially cherished the unicorn lunch box.

From the humble box of candy to the expensive diamond bauble, gift giving is one of the most familiar rituals of courtship. Typically, the gift is something precious, romantic, sentimental, or cute. Rarely do new lovers give each other mundane or practical things, such as an electric can opener. Through gifts, new lovers send the unspoken message: "Give me your love and I'll always make you feel special."

In tandem with gift giving comes the courtship practice of free spending. Courtship makes us act like millionaires on holiday. Jonathan was surprised by his free spending habits early in his relationship with Deborah.

> As I rule, I'm very thrifty. I'm a fan of Thoreau and live by his advice: "Simplify." But when Deborah and I started seeing each other, it was like money was no object. We had some expensive dinners, and I was always going for the best wines. Then we went away for a weekend to Big Sur. Normally I'd stay at the campgrounds, but this time only the best inn would do. I felt like I'd been holding back for so long that it was time to let everything go.

People who are normally sensible about money learn that passionate love can turn their priorities inside out. The new highest priority is attracting and pleasing the lover, and money's only value is in helping to reach that goal.

The Greatest Gift:
Three Big Little Words

For Paul, the prospect of saying "I love you" to Laura for the first time raised his anxiety to new heights.

> I was feeling a great amount of internal pressure to tell Laura I loved her after several dates. But it seemed too soon, and I was convinced she'd say something like, "Oh, how nice," then disappear. When we made love, not saying it started seeming painfully unnatural. Finally, there was a time when she was holding me very tightly and it just seemed to spill out of me. To my relief, Laura seemed thrilled to hear it and said she loved me too.

Professing love is a major milestone in most relationships. It is also a major risk. Usually we won't take the plunge until our partner has offered a body of encouraging cues. The chance that a lover won't reciprocate makes saying "I love you" a moment of maximum vulnerability — and passion. When those three words are mutually tendered, the lovers find themselves at an exhilarating emotional apex. The moment when you draw an admission of love from a wanted partner can mark the start of real intimacy and the gradual easing of rejection anxiety.

Gaining by Giving

The gifts we give and the money we spend so freely during courtship make us feel like models of generosity and altruism. But of course we're gaining something as well: the joy of giving pleasure to someone we love. Still, there's nothing very selfish about that.

However, the excitement, fear, and altruism of courtship tend to cloak a crucial underlying motive for our pleasing and giving behavior: *to gain emotional control over our lover through attraction.* It's very much in our psychological interests to find a reliable, steady source of fulfillment for our needs. No less, we wish to protect ourselves from the trauma of romantic rejection. We try to reach these goals by exerting a kind of spellbinding force over our lover, hoping he or she will be so thoroughly enraptured that rejecting us would be unthinkable.

This isn't to say that lovers are cynical manipulators. Our attempts to gain a sense of control over people who can satisfy our needs are normal and necessary. Courtship rituals are designed to recruit the person we hope will best fill the job. Once we've succeeded in securing the right person's love, we can reclaim our emotional control, settle down, and get on with life—something that's hard to do when we're madly in love or desperately seeking it.

The Delicate Balance of Love

In balanced relationships, *both* partners have secured the other's love. They're more or less equal in several ways: in their attractiveness to each other, in their emotional investment in the relationship, and in the number of needs each will fill for the other. Neither one feels suffocated or emotionally shortchanged, and neither is inclined to take the other for granted. Their intimacy is rewarding, and the autonomy they retain is healthy. They are balanced.

With the recovery of emotional control and the ebbing of passion, balanced lovers find something vastly more manageable, and deeper, to replace the emotional riot of courtship. Ideally, passion fuses two people in a kind of emotional alchemy, bonding them in an intimate, nourishing, comfortable, and often exciting emotional partnership.

But there's a hitch to this best-case scenario: love relationships are so charged with the wish for pleasure and the fear of rejection that it's almost impossible to keep them on an even keel. Now we'll examine the forces that most commonly upset the balance between romantic partners.

Chapter 2

Balancing Acts

Power Shifts in Relationships

Every relationship is a balancing act. In the beginning, the uncertainty, insecurities, and novelty of new love tend to keep both lovers equally invested in each other. But as a relationship matures, the balance can shift in the twinkling of an eye. Or, it can undergo a gradual change that escapes detection until unmasked by the special problems that signal imbalance.

In my therapy with couples, I've identified three of the most common causes of imbalance in relationships. Some imbalances are easier to treat than others, but all can be treated more effectively when the partners are aware of the forces behind them.

Imbalance in Attraction Power

Paul's enthrallment with Laura was complete. In a separate session, I asked him to describe how he felt other people perceived Laura.

> I think she would be perceived as something close to the ideal woman. Not only is she lovely to look at, but her intellect and professionalism are impressive. She's athletic — more so than me — and she has a way of generating an excitement that tends to make her the center of attention in a gathering. I think a lot of women are jealous of her, and a lot of men are intimidated.

I asked the same question of Laura, about Paul.

> Well, I think people are impressed with Paul's mind, and the fact that he's so dedicated to his work. He's not the most ambitious attor-

ney in the firm, but he's carved out a niche and doesn't need to toot his own horn. People appreciate that, and they respect him.

Tellingly, Paul's description of Laura was longer, qualitatively stronger, and more enthusiastically delivered than Laura's description of Paul. Even allowing for personal differences in Paul's and Laura's styles of expression, these descriptions indicated that Laura was more attractive to Paul than Paul was to Laura. Within this relationship, then, Laura had the greater "attraction power."

What Is Attraction Power?

Power is something we all want, although we don't like to admit it or may not even realize it. Particularly in loving relationships, trying to gain power seems negative and destructive. However, it's normal to strive for power and control in our intimate relationships, and to do so in ways that are healthy and positive.

Most of us don't try to control others but rather to control elements of our emotional environment so that the greatest number of our needs can be met. That means attracting and then forming bonds with people who complement us. As we grow up, we learn that certain qualities are appealing to certain kinds of people. We also learn what kinds of people are most likely to meet our particular mosaic of needs. So we cultivate specific attractive qualities in ourselves, such things as appearance, intellect, humor, charm, sexiness, career success, and talents. Of course, we develop ourselves to please ourselves, and that alone is important. But a major motivation behind our efforts at self-improvement is the desire to gain "social power" — leverage for ourselves in the world. Once we've assembled a personal arsenal of attractive qualities, we're able to draw to us people who both arouse and satisfy our desires.

Deeper into Attraction Power

Cosmetics-company revenues place them near the top of the Fortune 500 industries. Billions are spent each year on everything from diet books and health clubs to perfumes and plastic surgery. No one can dispute how seriously we take the business of making ourselves attractive.

Looking good is important. It helps us feel confident about ourselves and in control of the impression we make on people. But studies show that beauty is most important only in initial attraction. Other qualities that can attract and, more important, *sustain* romantic interest are *character attributes* such as warmth, liveliness, empathy, spontaneity, honesty, intelligence, confidence, and creativity. And, of course, it doesn't hurt to have *image qualities* such as wealth, success, power, fame, talent, youth, social prominence, and sexiness. Those who have an abundance of these traits sometimes have more attraction power than they can handle, as supermarket tabloids attest.

What Causes Two People to "Click"?

I believe that partners who have very similar levels of attraction power are the ones who "click," who feel "chemistry" between them, who may even sense they've been searching for each other all their lives. Beth, the PR executive, and Miles felt that way when they met. You may recall that Miles said their initial attraction was "instant, mutual, mental, physical, and everything else."

For a fascinating lesson in attraction power, go to a public place where couples tend to gravitate (a zoo, beach, or amusement park, for example), then sit down and watch. You'll see how remarkably well matched the partners appear. Their levels of physical attractiveness will be about the same, and they'll even dress similarly. A striking disparity in surface attractiveness between two people should alert you to less visible compensating factors. A classic example of this is an average-looking or older man with a beautiful young woman. The man is usually rich and successful.

When we think about couples we know, we automatically weigh their levels of attraction power. You've no doubt heard such assessments in casual conversation: "She's so much smarter than he is"; "He's better-looking than she is"; "She makes more money than he does." We instinctively worry about partners who aren't equally attractive, sensing that this kind of imbalance spells trouble. Or we begin to look for those hidden attributes in the less attractive partner that might compensate for the surface imbalance. And there is also a part of us that believes surface differences shouldn't matter. Of course they shouldn't, but experience tells us that they usually do.

It's easy to understand how negative power tactics such as physical or psychological abuse can hurt a loving relationship. But what the passion trap teaches us is that *an imbalance in attraction power can lead to a loss of love.* Lovers who seemingly clicked during courtship often stop clicking when such imbalances come home to roost.

Balancing Acts

Tipping the Scales

I asked Paul when he first sensed problems with Laura.

> I would have to say at the firm's Christmas party, when Laura and I "came out of the closet," so to speak. We had been involved for about three months, and the rumors were flying around. Interoffice romances are frowned on, but we'd already talked about marriage, so it seemed okay to go public. It turned out everyone knew anyway, of course. At first, I had this funny sensation that this was my moment of triumph. Here I was with the most desirable woman at the party. But a little later, my mood changed.

From the beginning, Paul had sensed an attraction-power imbalance between himself and Laura. You may recall that when he first met her, he felt it would be unrealistic to consider her a romantic prospect. But her attraction to him seemed to invalidate his initial impression, until that evening.

> We were talking to a group of associates, mostly men, and Laura was, as always, the center of attention. She was laughing and talking with them in her usual charming way. It seemed she was flirting, even though she was still holding my arm. Suddenly I had this sinking feeling. I started having thoughts like, "These guys make more sense for Laura than I do. They're better-looking and more social and I'm sure they're more athletic." I couldn't shake the feeling Laura was about to get bored with me.

This was Paul's first taste of the one-down position of love. At the moment when he should have been feeling most secure about Laura, during their debut as a couple, he was filled with anxiety and pessimism. The reason: Laura's greater attraction power was starting to make Paul fall more deeply in love with her than she was with him.

The One-Down Clutch

When a lover feels that his partner is more attractive than he is, the pleasure-coated anxiety of courtship takes on an unpleasant edge, as Paul learned at the party.

> I started feeling so anxious that I couldn't think of anything clever to contribute. I wanted to be a part of the conversation, but all I was doing was standing there like a moron who, by some fluke, happened to be with the best-looking woman at the party. If the discussion had been about the fine points of tax law, I would have been

fine. But they were talking about going to rock concerts in high school. In high school, I was into chamber music. In fact, I tried to make that into a joke, which got one of those horrible "polite" receptions.

Paul suddenly found himself swamped with feelings of inadequacy. His perception that he wasn't attractive or socially graceful enough to hold Laura's interest amplified his natural dread of romantic rejection. Paul was overloading on anxiety and feelings of powerlessness. In this state, he found that his social skills actually seemed to wither. Later that night, back at his place, he experienced his first problem in making love to Laura. Victims of the one-down "clutch" generally stumble when the occasion requires a smooth performance.

Rescue Attempts

In some new relationships, the one-down will be the first to perceive the shift of power in the relationship and to panic about it. In the grip of the passion trap, he then intensifies his efforts to win his partner's love. But he undermines himself by being so openly needy. As Paul described:

> All I could think about was leaving that party so I could be alone with Laura. Finally, I took her hand and suggested that maybe we ought to be going. She looked a little put out, but went along. I thought maybe she was upset with me, so the next day I bought her a solid gold key chain with a heart. I thought it might say better than I could how much I loved her. She really liked it, but she was a little reserved.

People usually sense when their relationship has started to tilt out of balance. It begins with a little anxious clinging on the part of one partner, and a little resistance on the part of the other.

The One-Up Reacts

Laura's perception of the point when the relationship started changing paralleled Paul's.

> When Paul first told me he loved me, I was in absolute heaven. I thought, this is it. Look no further. He was a doll, and it was like he couldn't do enough for me. But then it started to feel like he was doing a little too much. Like he was always buying me expensive little gifts and dragging me off to another fine restaurant. And he

started seeming a little possessive, like at the firm Christmas party. I was having a great time, but he wanted to leave about an hour or two after we arrived. I felt a little resentful, but also guilty. Like maybe I'd been making a fool of myself.

Then two things happened that brought new definition to Paul and Laura's relationship problems. Laura was assigned her first court case, a complicated stock fraud defense. And at about the same time, Paul started trying to move marriage plans from talk to the drawing table. Laura recalled:

> Suddenly my focus had to shift to the court case, and all the little things that had been bothering me about Paul seemed to get a little worse. That's not to say I wasn't feeling committed to him. My attitude at the time was that we had things to work on. I think because he was feeling insecure, Paul tried to get me to decide on a wedding date, but it was just more than I could handle at the time. I knew Paul would make a wonderful husband, but my feelings seemed to be getting more affectionate than romantic. I wondered what was wrong with me. I should have been happy he was so committed to me, but I was, I guess, uncertain about what I was feeling.

More than anything, the new one-up feels confused. His or her heart and mind aren't operating in unison anymore.

The Passion Trap Takes Hold

As Laura's feelings grew cooler, Paul's heated up. He became intent on setting a wedding date. But Laura . . .

> would start teasing or change the subject. About this time, I was bothered by a noticeable change in her everyday behavior. She'd forget to call or would work late, for example. I realized she was anxious about her first case, but she'd go a week without seeing me, except at work. She didn't seem to want my help. In my mind I was telling myself that things were the same, it was just my morbid imagination saying things were going downhill. Finally, I confronted Laura with my worries and fears. She reassured me, but in a placating way. She seemed a bit more irritated than concerned about my feelings. She said, and I believed her, that she had a classic fear of commitment, but that she was "working it through."

Ironically, one of Paul's prime attractions to Laura had been his seeming so emotionally self-contained. But when Laura proved very successful at captivating Paul, he forfeited this attractive quality. His tremendous emotional investment in the relationship endowed Laura with an unexpected and unwanted sense of control. She had, in fact, come to feel so safe and secure with Paul that she no longer felt even a faint biochemical buzz of passion for him. Paul's overcompliance as a lover empowered Laura within the relationship in an unwelcome and unbalancing way.

Why didn't Paul rein himself in? Because at this point he was deep in the grip of the passion trap. Had he been aware of it, he could have helped himself and the relationship. But as it was, his lack of control in the situation was making him miserable. It was also making him feel very passionately in love, due to the biochemistry of romance.

In this crisis, Paul's reasoning power had seriously declined. For example, he'd chosen to misinterpret his healthy doubts about Laura's commitment as projections of his "morbid imagination." One-downs are being told emphatically by their fear-sensing unconscious minds to beware. But commonly these messages aren't properly decoded by the love-drunk one-down brain.

Had Paul not developed feelings of insecurity about Laura's attractiveness, the two might have reached a satisfying harmony. But the imbalance created an opening just the right size for the passion trap. Paul began to pursue, Laura began to withdraw, and the two reactions fueled each other. By polarizing the partners, the passion trap actually widens the imbalance between them.

Situational Imbalance

Beth and Miles described the first two years of their marriage as "ecstatically happy." Their friends were always telling them what an ideal couple they made, and they had to agree. Both were outgoing, ambitious, smart, and attractive. They bought a house and fixed it up beautifully. The icing on the cake was two wonderful surprises toward the end of the second year: Beth became pregnant, and Miles was approached by a group of investors who wanted to give him carte blanche in creating a new restaurant. They also offered him co-ownership. As Beth described that time:

> We did have to put some fairly serious thought into the restaurant part. Miles knows better than anyone the amount of work that goes into starting a restaurant, and it seemed to be timed such that it

would open shortly before my due date. But the backers were offering Miles a considerably higher salary and the co-ownership part was just too good to pass up. We felt the temporary sacrifice of him having to work so hard at that time would be worth the ultimate gain. It also meant we'd be financially secure during my maternity leave.

The reasoning was sound, but the reality of the situation that came to pass bore little resemblance to what the couple had imagined. Miles offered his version.

I'm the kind of person who puts everything into what I do. With so much money riding on the new restaurant, I felt incredible pressure to make it a success. I was working twelve to fourteen hour days, and I missed a couple of the Lamaze classes with Beth. That created tension. I *did* make it to the birth, but I kept falling asleep while Beth was in labor. Then, motherhood hit Beth like a ton of bricks. She couldn't believe how much she loved Chloe, but at the same time, she couldn't believe how strange it was to be stranded with a tiny infant twenty-four hours a day, day after day. I couldn't be there for her, but at the same time, I was going through a lot and she wasn't there for me either. She was getting resentful, and so was I.

The emotional energy Miles was pouring into the new restaurant had to come from somewhere, and the chief source was his relationship with Beth. Meanwhile, Beth was feeling unusually needy. She had left her high prestige job and was now faced with the dilemma experienced by so many women of her generation. Should she compromise her career, or hand her baby over to an outside caretaker for much of the child's waking day? Before giving birth, Beth had resolved to spend three months at home, then return to work. But now she wanted to stay home with Chloe for a year and have *another* baby as soon as possible. "After all, I was thirty-seven," she said.

Like many of my clients, Beth and Miles entered their relationship with a firm commitment to equality: neither partner would be dominant or passive, both would pursue their ambitions outside the relationship with enthusiastic encouragement from the other, and all unpleasant household chores would be shared fifty-fifty.

But as is usually the case, it was the woman, Beth, who ended up carrying the household and childcare responsibilities. Because of Miles's involvement in the restaurant, he shared none of Beth's dilemma about Chloe's care, nor did he feel the guilt, anger, and frustration created by this dilemma. But because Beth opted for the role of mother/housewife, Miles, like most husbands, ended up with the more socially powerful, attractive position of high-gear career man. As Beth lost much of her independence and self-esteem, Miles gained more autonomy and social power.

This persistent inequality in lifestyle options between wives and husbands creates a breeding ground for the passion trap. The low status of motherhood in our society, coupled with social pressure on men to be superachievers, frequently offsets the balance between two otherwise equal partners.

Beth started feeling the impact of her loss of power in the relationship soon after she began her maternity leave.

> I was completely unprepared for the shock of leaving my job. I started my leave two weeks before my due date, then I was almost two weeks late. By the end of the second week, I was going nuts. I'd put on fifty-five pounds and looked like a whale.

> When I showed up at the restaurant, all conversation seemed to stop. I was feeling a kind of double-whammy loss of status. Not only was I functionally unemployed, but I looked puffy and haggard. It made me feel very vulnerable and insecure. Seeing all the pretty waitresses didn't help my self-esteem. Neither did Miles's uptightness with me there. To compensate for all this, I decided I would write "my novel" during my leave. What a laugh. I could barely keep up with the housework.

An Emotional Chain Reaction

Miles began to use work as an excuse to avoid facing a needier and more demanding Beth, and Beth turned to Chloe to satisfy her needs for love and closeness. Loving an infant can be deeply gratifying, but it can't fill the whole spectrum of an adult's emotional needs. Beth grew hungrier for Miles's loving attention, but her methods for getting it had become dysfunctional. The passion trap sabotaged Miles and Beth's ability to communicate, and the polarity grew.

Times of transition make everyone vulnerable to imbalance. Moving to a new town, getting a new job, losing an old job, going back to school, having children, even getting married are stressful times that often unbalance even very stable couples. When two or more of these events coincide, as they did for Miles and Beth, the consequences can be challenging in the extreme.

Imbalance in Personality Styles

Among the things Jonathan first noticed and liked about Deborah was that she seemed as private a person as he. She wasn't the type of woman who'd throw herself at him or show overt neediness. I asked him to elaborate.

> Well, Deborah at first seemed somewhat aloof and reserved. I was intrigued by her. I enjoy my own time alone, and I just can't relate to a woman who's always wanting to talk about things and feelings and so forth. But Deborah had her art and she read a lot too, so I felt we had the makings of a good team. She also didn't seem preoccupied by commitment, or at least she didn't mention wanting to settle down in the beginning. Ironically, I was the one who probably had more of those feelings.

I asked him why he hadn't initiated sex earlier.

> That's something I had to ask myself too. I was very attracted to Deborah, and I wanted to sleep with her from the beginning. But something seemed to hold me back. I think it was a fear, knowing that once something really got started there, it would be major. And that was a little frightening to me because of what happened in my last major relationship—with my ex-wife. And with Deborah acting somewhat distant at first, I didn't want to make a move and then get rebuffed.

Jonathan liked Deborah because he thought her personality style meshed perfectly with his. Her early detachment fed both his rejection anxiety and his passion, because he didn't think she was very interested in him. He saw in Deborah a relationship tailor-made to his needs: with generous portions of privacy and independence.

But I knew from my sessions with Deborah that Jonathan had seriously, and understandably, misread her. She was holding back not because she was an especially private person but because of several other factors.

> First, I probably seemed aloof to him because I wasn't all that attracted to him in the beginning. Talk about irony. Second, I really was serious about not wanting to be involved for a year. Naturally, if the perfect guy had come along, I would have gone for him, but Jonathan didn't hit me that way. And third, when I started getting hooked on Jonathan, I was terrified of showing too much. That hap-

pened with the men I cared about most, and I was trying not to let it happen again. Jonathan evidently thought I was just a cool kind of person. But nothing could be further from the truth. When I fall, I fall really hard. I'm just a good actress, to a point.

In many ways, Jonathan and Deborah were well suited to each other. Their attraction-power levels were about the same—even if Deborah didn't at first feel that Jonathan was her "type"—and their situations in life were compatible. But, as I learned, there was a fundamental difference at the core of their personalities: Jonathan enjoyed solitude, while Deborah valued emotional closeness.

During their courtship, Deborah didn't see Jonathan's true colors because his fear of rejection compelled him to pursue her ardently (for him). Deborah said:

> There were inconsistencies in Jonathan's behavior from the beginning. I knew for certain he was into me. He kept wanting to see me and was creative about what we did. Like he took me to a planetarium show and afterwards pulled out a picnic dinner we could eat under the stars. He would talk about how I was so much more attractive to him than other women he'd met, so he seemed like someone who was looking for emotional closeness. I kept expecting it to happen, but it didn't.

Jonathan and Deborah each had different methods for defending their vulnerabilities, and these methods sent misleading, yet attractive, signals to each other. Inadvertently, Jonathan *had* made himself irresistible to Deborah, just as she had made herself irresistible to him, at first. He tantalized her with the prospect of emotional closeness but kept her off guard with his elusiveness. Unable to get her bearings with him, she felt increasingly out of control, anxious, and passionate.

A Precarious Balance

These two kept a precarious balance as long as they continued to hide their deepest needs. But that balance was lost when Deborah's anxiety grew too strong. The culmination occurred on a family holiday.

> I invited Jonathan to my parents' home for Thanksgiving. I thought it was strange that he seemed very uncomfortable. My family is very friendly and warm, but he was almost standoffish. Afterward, we spent that night at my place, but he seemed distant. I was feeling very strange, because by this time I was crazy about Jonathan, having marriage fantasies and the whole thing. But he'd never told me he loved

me, and I was going nuts. So I decided to put it to him, figuring I had nothing to lose. I said I thought I was falling in love with him, hoping he'd been waiting for an opening. But he replied that he was starting to feel a little confused, and could we talk about it later because he needed some time alone. After he left, I felt very, very lost.

To Jonathan, Deborah's invitation was an intrusive appeal for closeness and commitment. It was then that his solitary personality style won out over his courtship warmth.

> It came as proof that Deborah was wanting more and more of me. When she actually invited me to Thanksgiving dinner with her family, I realized it was getting too heavy for me. I was honest with her afterward and said I'm just not into those kinds of things. It felt as if everyone was sizing me up as a potential family member. Then, the next morning, she was pulling for me to say I loved her. If I love somebody, I'll tell them, but I don't like to say it on cue. I think it's hypocritical. Anyway, I sort of went into shock, and I needed some distance.

When their personality-style differences did emerge, they mandated that Jonathan, the naturally distant one, would be the controlling one-up, and Deborah, who yearned for closeness, the one-down.

Had both been aware of how their true needs were triggering the passion trap, they might have been able to negotiate mutually satisfying terms of relating. Or they might have elected to be friends rather than lovers. But without that knowledge, their reactions to each other began to be patterned by the passion trap.

In later chapters, we'll examine more closely different personality styles, how they mesh or clash with one another, and how to balance them. Next, however, we will look more closely at the one-up and one-down positions of love, and how you can gain more power in your dealings with them.

Chapter 3

One-Ups

The Burden of Power

The one-up holds executive power in a relationship. By this I mean the one-up determines whether the relationship survives or ends. One-downs do sometimes leave — but it's bound to be because the one-up has emotionally pushed him or her out.

I'm sure you've been a one-up at some point in your life. Almost everyone knows the contradictory, confusing feelings of being wanted by someone you don't really want. It's flattering but frustrating, ego boosting but emotionally draining, and it's almost always a situation that forces you to act in ways you'd rather not. You expect a sense of pleasurable relief when it's over, but you don't get it. Now we'll find out why, and how the passion trap engenders emotional no-win situations.

The One-Up Is Not a Monster

Because one-ups have power, it's tempting to label them callous heartbreakers or intimacy cowards. However, the fact is that most one-ups truly want their relationships to work. Just like one-downs, one-ups are victims of powerful interpersonal forces that push people apart when relationships get unbalanced.

In this chapter, we'll explore one-up patterns of behavior and set them against a paramount human need: not to feel emotionally confined by another person.

It's true that the one-down suffers the deepest pain of all, the pain of rejection, but the one-up feels tremendous distress as his relationship tilts out of balance. He will suffer acute guilt, anger, confusion,

29

self-doubt, and frustration. If he tries to deny his unhappiness, it will grow all the faster. He may conceal as long as he possibly can the diminution of his loving feelings toward the one-down. Because he's probably been a one-down himself, he knows how devastating rejection is and he'd rather avoid dealing his partner a killing blow. And he will experience fear of the loneliness of life beyond the relationship and the risks involved in finding someone new.

At first the one-up feels joy and relief when he wins his partner's love. Then he begins to feel confused. He knows he's feeling less loving, but he doesn't know why. He assumes it's a temporary condition, and his mind works hard to create explanations for it. But once the passion trap takes hold, no amount of thought or worry will stop the behavior that reflects his shrinking emotional investment in the relationship.

You Don't Bring Me Flowers ...

An early sign of imbalance in a relationship is the easing of courtship behavior by one partner and not the other. The new one-up no longer feels compelled to give gifts, spend freely, suppress bad habits, or enhance his looks and charm. Jonathan gradually abandoned an affectionate "tradition" as his feelings toward Deborah began to cool.

> In the first couple of months of our affair, I always brought Deborah a flower when I arrived. I like gardening and there's always something blooming in my yard. It was our little tradition. But I started tapering off after Deborah complained that I spent more time with my plants than with her.

In any successful relationship, courtship behavior relaxes into normal behavior in a mutually desired long-term commitment. But Jonathan's return to normal behavior was premature, signaling a weakening emotional investment in the relationship. What he didn't realize was that his pulling back was pulling Deborah more deeply into the relationship.

Laura began to show Paul what she termed her . . .

> true colors. I'm a quick person and I tend to get impatient with people who aren't. It's just the way I am. Paul takes his time, and it wasn't long before I started getting testy with him. When he pointed it out, I blamed it on all the work pressure I was under.

Many one-ups like Laura veil their normal behavior with excuses, and work pressure is the one most often used. Blaming one's work tends to head off unwanted confrontations about relationship problems. Also like many one-ups, Laura wanted to believe her excuse was true, that her stress was only job-related.

In Long-Term Relationships

In long-term relationships, "you don't bring me flowers" takes the form of a one-up being less affectionate to the one-down. Sometimes the change is small but significant; at other times the change will transform a couple's very way of life.

My client Peg, a thin, attractive woman in her midforties, had been married for twenty-three years when she realized a cherished dream. She was an avid collector of American crafts, and with some inheritance money and her sons away in college, she opened a shop offering these wares. The business took off with unexpected force.

Peg's success began to unravel what had seemed a reasonably solid marriage. She told me in our first session:

> About a year after the shop opened, Bill was passed over for a promotion to executive VP. It was management's way of saying he just wasn't "inner circle" material. He resigned, thinking he'd be able to improve his position at another company. He was offered one job, at a lower level. Then he had the idea to help expand my business. It seemed a good solution until I realized Bill expected to take over. And he didn't understand that most of the work I do is really very pedestrian, ringing up sales and such. It just wasn't working out, and he seemed just to give up after that.

Peg knew that her and Bill's career positions had more or less reversed in the space of a year, but she hadn't realized how deeply their relationship had also changed.

> I used to pore through cookbooks and spend hours cooking gourmet meals. I'd monogram his shirts and starch his collars. I had to cut down after I opened the shop, but I still made a real effort to keep him happy. I didn't want him to think he came second. Now it seems like a dream, that attitude of wanting so desperately to please. He noticed I'd stopped doing the "little things" and was surprisingly hurt. I said it was the time factor.

In happy, balanced relationships, the "little things" are the currency of affection. But when giving, or withholding, is lopsided, so is the relationship. For twenty-two years, Peg had been the one-down in their relationship, but now Bill's career setback and her own success had dramatically switched their positions.

The Reverse
Frog/Prince Syndrome

During courtship we're not so blind that we fail to see flaws in our lovers. But passion overlooks shortcomings and even turns them into charming quirks.

Eventually, the one-down's confining love will bring a different bias to the one-up's perceptions. The one-up begins to overlook what's attractive about the one-down and to focus on physical imperfections. It doesn't matter how handsome or beautiful the one-down may be in the eyes of others. For the one-up, the prince or princess has turned into a frog.

Laura had this to say about her changed perceptions of Paul:

> One of the problems I had with the idea of marrying Paul was the fact that I stopped finding him physically appealing. In fact, some of the things that seemed so charming at first — his total lack of vanity and that rumpled professorial air — started turning me off the most. I'd look at him, and then at other men, and wonder what I could have been thinking.

The idealized partner invites closeness during courtship, but the denigrated one-down offers the one-up a reason for emotional withdrawal. Because men generally place more importance on looks than women do, the decline of a female one-down's physical appeal can be deeply disturbing. Often it is a prelude to, and rationalization for, infidelity.

The Ornament Solution

Solutions are the coping methods most often employed by the one-up. But they're the least effective, because they actually fuel the passion trap. Solutions seem beautifully logical, with their intent to restore the one-down's initial luster, but they often backfire.

The Ornament Solution has the one-up offering "beauty tips" to the one-down. He may be direct or subtle, but he'll get the message across, suggesting changes of hair, clothes, makeup, body weight, or whatever one-down feature seems least alluring. Miles tried the Ornament Solution with Beth.

> Beth was really thin when we met, but she was having a hard time taking weight off after Chloe was born. It got to the point where I really preferred making love in darkness. So for our anniversary I bought her a gym membership. She started going and I could see that she was looking better. But then I was turned off by the way she seemed to crave my approval. The expectation was that I'd want to make love more often, but I didn't. Gradually, she stopped going.

The Ornament Solution backfires because the one-down's eagerness to comply reinforces the one-up's feelings of control. And as one-ups feel more in control, the passion trap makes them feel less in love.

The Incredible Shrinking IQ

Not only does the one-down lose his looks. He also starts losing his smarts. No one has presented this phenomenon more vividly than Marilyn French in her best-selling novel *The Women's Room*. After describing the rapture of new love and the idealization of "beloved," she writes:

> Then one day, the unthinkable happens. You are sitting together at the breakfast table and you're a little hung over, and you look across at beloved, beautiful golden beloved, and beloved opens his lovely rosebud mouth showing his glistening white teeth, and beloved says something stupid. Your whole body stops midstream: your temperature drops. Beloved has never said anything stupid before . . . You ask him to repeat. And he does. He says, "It's raining out," and you say, "No, it isn't raining out. Perhaps you'd better get your eyes checked, or your ears . . ."

Sexual attraction is notorious for causing people to overlook intelligence in a new partner. Later, this can be a powerful source of imbalance. But even when a couple's intelligence levels are well matched, imbalance rooted in other areas can make a one-down *seem* less bright than he really is.

The unfortunate fact is that the extreme tension of the one-down position actually *can* drain away the one-down's creative thinking, and also his charm and spontaneity, which we tend to view as corollaries of creativity. The one-down acts stiff, inhibited, self-conscious, like someone in a job interview that's going from bad to worse. When this happens, the one-up feels trapped with someone who bores, annoys, irritates, or embarrasses her. This feeds her desire to gain emotional distance.

The Academic Solution

When a one-down's IQ starts shrinking, the one-up may try the Academic Solution. A perfect illustration of this came from my client Scott. A bookstore manager and writer, Scott became infatuated with a beautiful, lively waitress at a coffee shop he frequented. But the relationship quickly developed imbalance-rooted problems.

> Alana's cultural tastes ran to *Police Academy, Wheel of Fortune,* and Danielle Steele. At first I thought her preferences were charming because she had amusing things to say about them. Then they started seeming very juvenile. I encouraged her to take extension courses. Philosophy and literature seemed like good starting points. To her credit, she worked very hard, but her fear of failure was really oppressive. She was trying to use big words and talk about the sorts of things she thought *I'd* like to talk about. It was embarrassing around friends. I was actually relieved when she got quieter.

Alana was trying desperately to please Scott by molding herself to his specifications. By trying so hard, she drew attention to the gulf between them and fell into the one-down trap of overcompliance. Alana's retreat into silence brought suppression of her natural, attractive spontaneity.

The "Why Can't You Be More . . ."
Solution

A critical part of any relationship's evolution is the partners' gradual acceptance of each other's everyday, non-courtship self. But when a relationship tilts out of balance, the one-up will be disappointed by the "real" version of her partner. In fact, she'll often find him lacking in the basic personal qualities she expects in a partner.

For one-ups, "Why can't you be more . . ." is commonly completed with such words as:

- outgoing
- confident
- interesting
- spontaneous
- successful
- independent
- entertaining

The one-up doesn't always confront her partner with these words, but she'll often use them with friends to describe her relationship problems. Such words show how a one-down's confining love can cause so much resentment that the one-up finds fundamental fault with *who he is*. This fault-finding translates to greater detachment, and aggravated polarity.

When Laura found herself getting restless in her relationship with Paul, she attributed it to her and Paul's lack of socializing. She was beginning to miss the night life she used to enjoy with friends, since Paul was an admitted stay-at-home type. So she organized an outing to a new night spot with friends from the firm. Paul was resistant but relented when Laura threatened to go without him. The experience reminded her of their "debut" at the firm Christmas party.

> Paul was alternating between being overly affectionate and sulky. I finally took him to the back of the club and asked him what was going on. He said the place was too noisy and he wanted to leave. I said fine. He said *with* me. Then he started getting amorous again, as if that would persuade me. I kind of pried him off and went back to the table. I was disgusted and embarrassed and angry that he was so . . . inept.

Laura wanted one simple but impossible thing: that Paul be the person she wanted him to be. This is the one-up wish behind all the solutions. But, as we know, it defeats itself, because it invites one-down overcompliance and all its complications.

The Thrill Is Gone

Gradually, the one-up's sexual interest in the one-down will dwindle. Sex itself becomes a passionless release of tension, or, as women clients often tell me, something to be endured or avoided. For the one-up, the thrill seems gone.

Woody Allen's movie *Annie Hall* contains my favorite example of how differently the one-up and one-down view sex. Once Annie becomes the one-up to Alvie Singer's one-down, a split-screen scene shows her and Alvie in simultaneous therapy sessions. On one side, Alvie complains to his therapist that he and Annie hardly ever make love, maybe three times a week. On the other side, Annie moans that Alvie wants sex constantly, at least three times a week. Annie feels trapped and increasingly put off by Alvie's sexual interest, while Alvie wants her more and more. In real life, of course, this is hardly a laughing matter.

The Eroticism Solution

Eroticism may be introduced to lovemaking by *either* partner in an effort to revive the one-up's desire. A couple may try to enhance lovemaking with erotic props, fantasies, X-rated material, drugs, or even additional partners. Of course, eroticism is not exclusive to unbalanced relationships. However, in unbalanced relationships eroticism often becomes a necessary crutch.

In the case of Peg and Bill, Bill was the one to introduce eroticism after two decades of straightforward sex. Peg, nonplussed, sensed that it was because he was feeling insecure about the changes in his life.

> It was as if he had to prove his manhood and value, to me and himself. I was really channeling my energies in other directions, and I wasn't all that interested. But Bill started bringing things home. Like X-rated videos. I went along with it because it seemed to mean so much to him and I didn't want to hurt his feelings. But it was hard, and he knew I was acting.

The Eroticism Solution may also take the form of a trip to a romantic locale where passion can temporarily be rekindled. The hope is that the revived feelings of passion can be brought home. Unfortunately, romantic vacations usually give a temporary boost and no more.

Another form of the Eroticism Solution is when the one-up simply closes her eyes during lovemaking and pretends she's with someone else. Afterward, lying in her partner's arms, she may feel guilty for her fantasies.

In slightly unbalanced relationships, erotic strategies may be beneficial, giving the one-up at least one good reason to stay. You've probably heard a friend say of a problem relationship, "It's hard to leave because the sex is so good." But if the imbalance is great, there will come a time when no amount of eroticism will revive feelings of love. The problem with calculated eroticism is that it is calculated.

Keeping Secrets

Two people in a new, exciting relationship, or a close, balanced one, tell each other everything. They talk about their feelings, share experiences and theories, and they gossip.

But when the passion trap sets in, one-ups lose their desire to communicate spontaneously with their one-down partners. As with so many of their behaviors, one-ups may not fully realize that their tendency to withhold communication is a sign of growing emotional detachment. But the one-down often does, and will try to draw out his or her partner. This is what happened to Peg and Bill.

> I would come home from a busy, interesting day at the shop, and Bill would want to know everything that happened. But I just felt too tired to go through it all with him. So I'd tell him maybe one thing, and say nothing much else happened. But he'd press me and I'd feel the irritation rising in me.

Notice that Peg attributed her unwillingness to communicate to fatigue. She didn't want to admit that she simply had no desire for conversational intimacy with Bill. Silence is one of the strongest barriers to closeness that the one-up constructs. Because the one-up is feeling so emotionally smothered by the one-down, such a barrier seems necessary for survival.

The One-Up Feels Trapped

Eventually the one-up's confusion about her feelings will crystallize. When they do, she'll realize that her overriding feeling is that of being trapped in a relationship with someone who loves and needs her very much but whom she is not sure she loves or can love.

One-Ups

LAURA:
The thing I disliked most about my relationship with Paul at this time was the feeling that I'd never again be able to experience passionate love. It was hard for me to believe Paul was having such intense feelings for me, because mine were so . . . flat. I resented him for not being capable of keeping my excitement.

JONATHAN:
Deborah's an either/or person. She expected total submersion in a relationship, or nothing. She couldn't accept the middle-ground I needed, with some good times together but also with plenty of space. Once I figured this out about her, I started feeling like I was getting sucked down by quicksand.

MILES:
It's funny. Here I achieved everything I wanted in life—a terrific wife, a beautiful child, a nice home, a successful restaurant and I felt so unhappy. It got to the point where I dreaded going home. Beth had gotten into such a dependent state that it seemed there was no way out.

The one-up may turn to another group of coping strategies, hoping to take pressure off his or her feelings of imprisonment in order to avoid having to go through the pain of a full-fledged escape.

Girl-Watching and Boy-Watching

At the beginning of courtship, lovers have eyes only for each other. But when a one-up starts feeling trapped, he or she may escape *visually* by watching attractive members of the opposite sex—often in the presence of the one-down.

It's only human to enjoy viewing another person's beauty, and many happily partnered people indulge in this behavior from time to time. In a sense, girl- or boy-watching is a safety valve for monogamous people—a benign way of dealing with the fact that monogamy goes against some human instincts.

But when it reaches the extreme, such behavior can be very hurtful and symptomatic of real problems. This was the case with Beth and Miles.

On one of our rare family outings, we went to the beach. I packed a beautiful picnic, got my first new swimsuit since I started at the gym, and really planned to make it a good time. But all Miles did was look at other women. It was almost like he couldn't help it. I'd be talking to him, and his eyes would focus on some point over my shoulder. And I'd turn around and it would be two girls in bikinis. And not necessarily *that* good-looking!

There is no need for the watched person to be better looking than the one-down. Of greatest importance is that he or she is someone *other* than the one-down, someone who's not emotionally controlled by the one-up.

Blatant staring will usually provoke the one-down to make a pained, angry, or pseudo-joking comment. The one-up may even try to break the habit, but it won't be easy: girl- or boy-watching is an involuntary and compelling psychological response to boredom, a way for the brain to find stimulating escape. But once caught in the act, the one-up may adopt sneaky tactics, as did one client who took to stealing glances at pretty women while his wife inspected produce at the supermarket.

The Party Solution

The next time you go to a party, carefully watch the interactions of the couples. You may see a woman flirting her way through the crowd, and a man in her shadow, looking glum. Or a man who is dancing with every woman except the one he came with; she's talking to friends, but her eyes follow him.

Parties can be like relationship parole for restless one-ups. They appreciate the excuses parties offer for unseemly behavior. "I'd had a few too many," is one, and, "But he (or she) threw himself at me," is another.

Typically, the one-down tags after the one-up, hoping for an early departure from the threatening situation. Afterward, each partner suffers: the one-up feels more trapped after the brief taste of freedom, and the one-down feels more anxious about rejection.

The One-Up Feels Anger

We naturally feel anger when we can't get what we want. The one-up's resentment and anger are proportionate to his feelings of being trapped. He's angry at the one-down for disappointing him, and he's angry at himself for getting into a situation he feels helpless to alter without emotional firestorms. Of course, anger further diminishes the one-up's feelings about the one-down.

The One-Up Can Be Mean

The one-up may control the relationship but feel out of control of the *situation*. This is an important distinction and frequently causes a turn of emotional events. One-ups who feel powerless often lash out at their partners and afterward feel shocked and dismayed by their own behavior. When the one-up is mean, resentment and frustration have overflowed from emotions into behavior. Laura discovered that her irritability gradually grew into verbal outbursts at Paul.

> I react unreasonably to snoring because I have a brother who snored like a foghorn when we were kids. I'm a light sleeper, and Paul's a world-class snorer. There was one night when it really started driving me up a tree. I finally woke him up and kicked him out of bed, after having a fit. He slept on the couch. I felt horrible afterward, but I noticed that after that incident, I was expressing more irritation about more things. It was like it opened the floodgates.

The one-up easily displaces her anger onto smaller issues, such as snoring, because she would rather not discuss the larger problem — her sense that she's falling out of love. As Laura did, the one-up will often begin picking on the one-down almost constantly. This meanness is not only an expression of anger but an unconscious method to drive away the one-down without having to confront the real issues.

Good Guys, Bad Guys

The one-up's anger seems to turn her into a villain. The mechanics of the passion trap allow her *safely* to vent her anger without fear of negative repercussions from her compliant partner. As we'll see, the one-down also feels anger, because *his* needs aren't getting met by the relationship. But he *can't* safely express that anger; his fear of rejection scares him into silence.

So, the angry one-up slips into the role of the mean, aggressive bad guy, while the one-down often plays the part of the devoted, victimized good guy. This particular configuration of the passion trap fuels imbalance in an insidious way. It makes the one-up feel worse and worse about herself and more inclined to blame the one-down for turning her into an ogre. And it turns the one-down into a "relationship Joan of Arc" whose greatest virtue is enduring the one-up's unloving behavior. But labeling the one-up "bad" makes her solely responsible for the relationship's problems and denies the one-down's very real co-responsibility.

The One-Up Can Be Abusive

Feeling anger and expressing it, even indirectly, are normal reactions to the one-up's sense of confinement. As I tell my clients, those reactions *don't* make you a bad guy. But unfortunately some people handle anger in very destructive ways.

Some clients have come to me on court referral, most of them one-up men who had physically and psychologically abused their mates. Although treatment is very difficult and not always successful in such cases, those clients who respond best are encouraged to believe that their *feelings* of frustration and anger in the relationship often were *justified*. However, violent behavioral reactions to those feelings are *never* justified.

Finding validation for their frustration and anger represents a huge ego boost for these men. Instantly they feel better about themselves, which makes them more likely to learn to manage their anger effectively and nonabusively.

Anger as Solution

Another fascinating function of anger rooted in the passion trap is its use as a solution. By venting anger, the one-up sometimes tries to provoke an overly compliant one-down into fighting back and breaking a pattern of passivity. The one-up correctly senses that a more equal expression of anger between the partners will help balance the relationship. Many one-ups, like Laura, start thinking that their one-down partners are weak or bland.

> Paul seemed to be able to take anything I dished out, even when I'd be critical of really basic things. Sometimes I just wished he'd explode at me, you know, show some spine. I would have respected him more.

The Anger Solution usually backfires because it makes the one-down feel even less secure. Remember, a one-down has to feel intense anger, or have unusually strong self-esteem, before he or she will express anger.

The One-Up Feels Guilt

Most of the one-up's reactions to the one-down provide fodder for guilt. The one-up feels guilty for losing his love, feeling or acting disloyal, not wanting sex, criticizing the one-down, being embarrassed by the one-down, being dishonest with the one-down, and so on. Above all, the one-up feels guilty about nursing so much anger toward the one-down.

Anger urges the one-up to leave the one-down, but guilt (and fear) inspire him to think about the good things in the relationship. Insidiously, guilt can make a one-up feel so bad about himself that he will stay in an unbalanced relationship to punish himself for his awful behavior and unjustifiable feelings.

The Anger/Guilt Spiral

The relationship between anger and guilt is very close, so close that a one-up sometimes feels both emotions at once. Not only does his anger make him feel guilty, but his guilt can make him feel angry. On one explosive evening, Miles vividly experienced the Spiral in his relationship with Beth.

> I'd had this horrendous night at the restaurant. The chef called in sick and a food critic showed up. When I finally got home, I walked in and tripped over Chloe's walker. The place was a mess. It just set me off. I started shouting about what a pigsty we were living in and Chloe started crying. Beth woke up and yelled at me about that. Then I got nasty. I accused Beth of having lost it. Not only was the place a mess, but I didn't see her accomplishing *anything*. That really got to her and she started to cry. Then I felt really bad and guilty about making *her* feel so bad. But then I thought, I'm *stuck* with this. I don't have to feel guilty.

The Anger/Guilt Spiral absorbs a great deal of the one-up's emotional energy. The Spiral itself can be like an emotional trap for the one-up, because it's a self-perpetuating dynamic that fuels the one-up's feelings of being trapped.

What's Wrong with Me?

One-ups often feel that their anger at and resentment of their partners are beyond reason. When they try to explain to themselves why they're feeling so angry and resentful, they're apt to use a certain "logical" progression.

1. My partner loves me and would do anything for me.
2. My good and loving partner richly deserves all my love.
3. But I feel more resentful than loving toward my partner. Therefore:
4. Something must be wrong with me.

The one-up often believes that the "something" wrong is no less than a profound character flaw, a fundamental selfishness and cold-ness that makes her incapable of loving. Laura practiced just this type of *self-pathologizing*.

> The way I treat Paul makes me think, "God, I'm such a bitch." It wor-ries me because when I can't start building something with a man like Paul, I have to wonder if I'm even capable of loving anyone for more than a couple of months.

Self-pathologizing is a form of self-punishment, and by punishing ourselves we work off some of our guilt for having hurt someone. It's much like penance.

There's a very real danger in this. One-ups often feel totally responsible for losing their feelings of love for the one-down, as if lov-ing feelings could be turned on and off at will. This can spawn such strong self-contempt that they will do almost anything to escape this feeling. That usually means pulling further away from the relation-ship. One of the hardest parts of my job is persuading one-ups to release their tenacious grips on guilt and blame for their relationship problems. I remind them that the one-down shares equal responsibil-ity and that strong relationship dynamics are the true culprits.

With an easing of guilt, one-ups feel less burdened by their rela-tionships, and more hopeful. Paradoxically, then, their best chance for reviving their love occurs when they stop blaming themselves for los-ing their love.

Please note, however, that I am not saying that one should *never* feel guilt. If your frustration toward your partner has led to abusive *actions*, then your guilt is trying to tell you an important message: *Stop that behavior.* But for the vast majority of my clients — and for people who read books like this — the problem is usually one of feeling needlessly guilty for having "bad" feelings and thoughts. (I'll discuss helping strategies for dealing with guilt in Chapter 10.)

Guilty Women

Some of my most difficult work as a therapist is trying to get women one-ups to feel less guilty. From childhood, women are taught that being feminine means being helpful and supportive. Anger is considered an aggressive, male, negative emotion. As such, it isn't part of feminine behavior. While these expectations have weakened, they still hold sway, especially among pre–baby-boom women. So, when these women become one-ups, they're highly prone to hiding their anger behind guilt, turning it inward, where it has corrosive effects. Many of these women feel threatened by the idea that they control their relationships or have more power than their husbands. Like Peg, whom I classify as a "disguised one-up."

Peg had very rarely expressed anger to Bill while she was the one-down in their relationship. But when she became the one-up she still internalized most of her anger. Her constant guilt was making her depressed, hopeless, and at one point even suicidal.

> At one point I even felt that I was too evil a person to deserve to live. Can you believe I've had fantasies that Bill has a heart attack and there I am at the funeral, dressed in black, and everyone is feeling sorry for me. But what's really despicable is that deep down I'm actually happy about being free at last. When I have these thoughts, I just want my car to swerve off a cliff.

Peg's anger emerged as self-hatred and depression. She was beginning to have physical symptoms as well, headaches and appetite loss, which had led to an almost gaunt appearance.

The Widow/Widower Fantasy

At the core of Peg's depression was what I call the Widow/Widower Fantasy, a common coping strategy for one-ups prone to suppressing anger with guilt. If the one-down were to suddenly die, the one-up would be *free without guilt*. In fact, people would feel sorry for the one-up rather than cast her as a heartless villain. It was hard for Peg to accept that such fantasies are like warning signals from our unconscious minds when we've overloaded with guilt and shame. I told her how common this particular fantasy is and suggested that instead of adding it to her self-hate (which would only make her feel guiltier and more in need of such fantasies), she should view it as a barometer of her unhappiness and frustration in her marriage.

Some one-ups instinctively know exactly what's going on when a new relationship starts to show signs of the passion trap. If a lover seems wrong or starts coming on too strong, the one-up will withdraw as swiftly and gracefully as possible. But if imbalance has been cloaked by strong needs and passion since the outset of the relationship, and the relationship itself sinks roots, something else happens. Many—maybe most—one-ups become mired in what I call CAS, the Commitment-Ambivalence Syndrome.

Chapter 4

The Commitment-Ambivalence Syndrome (CAS)

When the One-Up Is on the Fence

When I see a couple in therapy for the first time, both partners will usually say that they want to save the relationship. However, as therapy progresses it becomes clear that only the one-down is unequivocal about this goal. The one-up will be confused about what he or she wants, hopes, or can expect from therapy. Can therapy turn the one-down into a new, exciting lover? Will it offer an easy way out of a stifling relationship?

I've come to realize that what one-ups really want from therapy is an end to ambivalence. They can't decide whether they should stay in the relationship, so they hope the therapist/arbitrator will cast the swing vote.

Jonathan expressed classic one-up ambivalence when he described his feelings just after he had told Deborah he needed time away to think.

> On an emotional level, I was really disturbed by the way my feelings for Deb went from hot to warm so fast. But objectively, I knew I wasn't going to meet anyone who had more to offer than she did. I imagined how I'd feel if Deb were to start seeing someone else. Not good. So in some ways it seemed stupid even to consider ending the relationship. It was a rough time for me. I felt reluctant about going ahead and trying to make something with her, but damned if I didn't. And the stakes were high.

Ambivalence is a maddening emotion. By definition it means "simultaneous attraction and aversion to an object, person, or action." The ambivalent person finds the arguments for and against a particular action to be evenly balanced and therefore irresolvable. Perhaps the most frustrating thing about major relationship decisions is that you want so badly to make them with knowledge of the future. You want to know if leaving a one-down would turn out to be the biggest mistake of your life, or if a much better partner for you is waiting just around the corner. It seems that there is a right and a wrong decision, but no one's revealing which is which. You don't want to burn your bridges on either side, but you know that this is one case where you can't "have it all."

Almost everyone experiences some ambivalence when making a big relationship decision, because no relationship is perfect and, as Jonathan put it, the stakes are high. But for a one-up in an unbalanced relationship, ambivalence can lead to prolonged emotional torture. As we'll see, one-ups use a number of strategies to help tip the scales one way or the other, to end the painful limbo of ambivalence.

I call this behavior the Commitment-Ambivalence Syndrome (CAS). It's a label I coined to describe the dilemma of unmarried but seriously involved one-ups, but it equally describes the situation of married one-ups who must decide whether to stay with a one-down spouse. As we'll see, CAS can be experienced with varying degrees of intensity.

Mild CAS

For many one-ups, the decision not to get married is privately made early in a relationship. For Scott, the bookstore manager, this was the case with Alana, the waitress.

> I was completely obsessed with getting together with her, but commitment wasn't something I was thinking about. There was so much momentum from my initial attraction that *maybe* I thought for about two seconds that things might work out. But deep down I knew she just didn't have the right mindset for me. I really liked the way she seemed to want to take care of me, though, and I didn't want to hurt her. I think that's why things lasted longer than they should have.

A relationship like this is often inspired by the one-up's needs of the moment. Frequently, the one-up is going through a rough time or a stressful transition; he feels a need for coddling. Students in demanding graduate programs often find themselves in unbalanced, nurturing relationships, as do people whose careers are rocky or who hurt from failed relationships. Scott, in fact, had just finished his first novel and gotten two lukewarm readings from friends when he became infatuated with Alana.

This type of one-up usually doesn't let on that he's put a ceiling on the relationship's potential. He doesn't want to needlessly hurt his partner's feelings or plunge a stable arrangement into turmoil and drama. Instead, he remains vague, making no vows, withholding true feelings.

These one-ups may end a relationship for any number of reasons. They may be drawn to someone new. They may feel too much commitment pressure from the one-down. Or the hard times in their lives may abate, leading to changed needs. Often these reasons occur in combination. And though they may feel very certain that they should move on, ambivalence can suddenly shake their resolve at the point when they reveal their intentions to the one-down. Then the one-down's woundedness and protests may converge with the one-up's compassion and anxiety about leaving a safe situation, convincing him to rethink his plans. Thus, ambivalence can cloud even a seemingly clear picture.

Serious Commitment-Ambivalence

One-ups seriously afflicted with CAS are typically warm to the idea of marriage until their relationships start wobbling out of balance. CAS can also occur within an unbalanced marriage, but the form is slightly different: the one-up begins to entertain the idea of divorce.

Debating Marriage

Ambivalent one-ups find themselves turning to the old Ben Franklin technique of ticking off the pros and cons of the situation. What's unique and especially tormenting about CAS is that the pros look very much like the cons:

Good Things about Marriage	Bad Things about Marriage
a devoted spouse	a smothering spouse
end of singles' "meat market"	missing out on singles' fun
safe, available sex	boring, routine sex
close companionship	old friends more distant
puttering around the house	boring chores
emotional security	feeling trapped

With such evenly balanced pros and cons, one-ups can obsess endlessly about which course of action to take. And as they do, their anxiety increases. No matter which way they turn, they face a painful loss. It feels like a genuine no-win situation.

Mind Says "Yes," Heart Says "No"

CAS opens a debate between the one-up's mind and heart. His mind rationally tells him that he'd be a fool to leave such a loving, devoted partner, but his heart heatedly demands more than it's getting. So, the one-up *thinks* he should stay in the relationship but *feels* he should leave.

The one-down's debate is just the opposite. Her heart wants to hang on to the relationship no matter what, but her mind perceives the one-up's detachment and cautions her against staying.

What Kind of Love Is This?

Most one-ups have positive feelings toward the one-down, but they don't know whether the feelings are "true love." It's a question that vastly compounds ambivalence. Even when Laura was having her gravest doubts about spending the rest of her life with Paul, she never stopped feeling affection for him.

> I was so confused. Even when I was getting irritated with Paul, I had many positive, loving feelings for him. How could I not? He was so sweet and generous and supportive, and I admired him in so many ways. And we knew each other so well. He was like the best friend a person could ever have. The disappointment was coming from a relatively superficial source—that lack of excitement. I suppose I was taking him for granted. But I'm not so naive that I expect excitement to last forever. Maybe I was feeling what people in long-term relationships are *supposed* to feel. I honestly didn't know.

The Commitment-Ambivalence Syndrome (CAS)

The English language, so rich in meaning and nuance, falls flat in the arena of love. We know that the feeling we have for a parent is qualitatively different from the feeling we have for a new lover, let alone the feeling we have for a favorite food. Yet we're stuck with the same overburdened little word to describe each emotion. No wonder Laura, and so many other one-ups, felt confused.

I explained to Laura that the feeling she had described was what psychologists call "companionate" love, as opposed to romantic love. Paul had evolved into a "very special friend" who no longer sparked romantic feelings. Many happy and enduring relationships are grounded in companionate love. But Laura's doubts clearly signaled that her needs for passion and romance were strong.

I urge one-ups like Laura to accept the validity of wanting romantic feelings in a long-term relationship. Once they stop denigrating themselves for having this perfectly natural need, one-ups are in a better frame of mind for working on the relationship. And as the relationship inches back toward balance, romantic feelings really do have a chance to resurface.

As Peg attested, sometimes there's confusion between feeling sorry for someone and feeling love.

> It was really very strange. I still felt a strong bond with Bill, because of our history together, and the boys and all the rest of it. But when he stopped working, I almost began to pity him, like he was a wounded bird or something. I wanted to take care of him, at first, but feelings of romance simply weren't a part of the picture.

Pity is a natural enemy of passion. The pitied partner by definition has suffered a loss, and losses almost always change the balance of positive power between romantic partners. A vital goal in Peg's therapy was to help her help Bill grow in response to his double challenge of being passed over for promotion and having such a successful wife.

Riding the Pendulum

It's the Edgar Allan Poe way to be in love. The CAS victim feels trapped in a pit of indecision while ambivalence causes her emotions and desires to sweep back and forth like a pendulum.

On the downswing, everything about the relationship seems bad, wrong. The one-up tries to force herself to look at all the good things about the one-down, but now they seem to count for nothing. The prospect of commitment has all the appeal of life in an emotional Alcatraz.

Sometimes her daytime dread will permeate nighttime dreams. Laura had a dream shortly after the club episode that graphically expressed one-up dread. She was wearing a beautiful wedding dress and walking toward a chapel where Paul awaited her. But the organ music wafting from the chapel sounded somber and foreboding, and as she drew closer, she saw a "bottomless pit" gaping before her. Unable to avoid the pit, she fell in, a sensation so terrifying that she woke up in a cold sweat. Her unconscious mind was sending her a clear, strong message to run from Paul.

As negative pressure builds, the one-up becomes convinced she must leave the relationship. There must be someone righter out there, someone smarter, funnier, better-looking, sexier and more accomplished, someone who will inspire lasting passion and who won't confuse her emotions. She mulls possible candidates, and the thoughts are very pleasant, too pleasant . . .

So pleasant that the one-up is suddenly gripped by strong feelings of guilt and disloyalty. As Miles remarked:

> The thought of making love to another woman had more and more appeal, and I probably would have acted sooner if it hadn't also made me feel like a worm. I'd think about what I'd be jeopardizing, the trouble it would cause, the complications, the devastation to Beth. And little Chloe . . . My heart would almost start to ache.

When the one-up visualizes the real consequences of rupturing the relationship, she lapses into sentimentality and nostalgia. Whenever Peg thought about divorcing Bill, memories of their special times together would flood her thoughts.

> I'd start thinking about how happy we were when we bought our first house. He was so proud of being able to move me out of that apartment. Or about the difficult delivery I had with our second son. I woke up from the anesthesia, I was surrounded by bouquets of flowers and there was Bill, holding Bobby and smiling through tears. Those times were very special.

Guilt, compassion, and nostalgia collude to push the pendulum toward the positive side of commitment. Sometimes the change of attitude comes so swiftly and dramatically that the one-up can hardly believe she even considered leaving the one-down. Now she focuses on the cozy warmth of the relationship and the desperate insecurity of the single life. She thinks about the very real risk of AIDS. She wonders if there really is anyone out there better than her partner. If so, will she wind up with him? Probably not. She warns herself not to be so greedy when it comes to love. She could so easily lose *everything*.

Now the pendulum stalls on the pro side of marriage, priming the one-up for commitment. The lifting of guilt brings such welcome relief that she might even experience moments of genuine, spontaneous happiness. She wants nothing more than to hold on to these positive, loving feelings.

But soon another dynamic comes into play. Now the one-up is free of the guilt and anxiety that accompanied the thoughts of leaving. But the old thoughts gradually creep back. She takes another look at the one-down: he's still the same person with the same qualities that had disenchanted her in the first place. Suddenly she's not so sure she should have decided to commit.

Did she want to stay with her partner because she truly loves him, or because she's trying to avoid guilt and anxiety? By staying is she selling herself short? Now the one-down's shortcomings seem less appealing than ever, and fantasies about leaving him return. The pendulum has swept back to the negative side of marriage. Only now she's deeper into the relationship. She feels more trapped than ever, and the cycle begins anew.

Runaway Ambivalence

When a circumstance like a pregnancy or job transfer forces a relationship decision, the pendulum may swing wildly out of control. For the one-up, it's like a ride on a runaway emotional roller coaster. One minute he's firmly resolved about leaving the relationship: he's packed his bags. The next he's passionately clinging to the one-down, vowing never to leave. Virtually all CAS-afflicted one-ups I've known (including clients, colleagues, friends, and, yes, myself) who had to decide quickly about a relationship experienced a kind of "temporary insanity." It's a state marked by severe mood swings and a tendency to drive friends crazy with appeals for help and support. And when the roller coaster takes off for the one-up, the one-down is right alongside, riding those treacherous peaks and valleys.

Buying Time

Jonathan did what most one-ups do when ambivalence creates an internal deadlock. He negotiated for more time.

> Deborah called me several days after Thanksgiving and asked if I'd come to any conclusions about the relationship. I told her honestly that the conclusion I'd come to was that I didn't know exactly what I wanted. I suggested we play it by ear. We decided to meet for breakfast that coming weekend.

Suggesting that they "play it by ear" was an ideal solution for Jonathan. He wouldn't have to terminate the relationship, and at the same time he set limits on Deborah's expectations. Though hurt by Jonathan's change from ardor to ambivalence, Deborah accepted his reasoning that his disastrous marriage had left him with a deep-seated fear of serious involvements. He wanted to take things slowly, he said, hoping, as one-ups do, that things will eventually take care of themselves.

Many one-ups maintain a "dating" relationship with a one-down for a very long time. There's an assumption that the relationship will progress, but instead it remains curiously static. Many one-downs learn that to press for engagement or marriage is to risk losing the one-up.

There is another way one-ups buy time, a far riskier way than dating. And that is by trying …

The Living Together Solution

When a couple is evenly matched and seriously considering marriage, living together can be a positive step toward intimacy and commitment. Even happily balanced couples have commitment anxiety, and living together can help them ease into the practical aspects of sharing quarters and lives. But I am quite certain that the majority of couples living together without concrete marriage plans have unbalanced relationships.

Living together is another way one-ups buy precious time and put off making an "until death do us part" decision about a relationship. The one-up maximizes his options by holding on to the one-down, who's still meeting important needs, but not totally closing off future romantic possibilities.

Mainly, the one-up hopes that living together will resolve his mounting ambivalence by giving him answers about his feelings. Maybe life with the one-down will be heaven, or maybe it will be hell on earth. He prays it will be one or the other.

Some one-ups try to avoid the commitment implications of living together. The story of Jessica and Philip shows how one-ups often rationalize moving in with the one-down as a practical measure.

Philip produced a television news show in New York. Jessica was working as a writer for the show. Lunches led to dinners, which led, one night, to Philip declaring love. Jessica was touched and flattered. Philip was highly respected in his field, and he was warmly liked by her friends for his intelligence, thoughtfulness, and humor. There was only one problem. Although Jessica felt very close to him, she didn't feel the passion she had known in a few other relationships. She recalled the process behind her decision to move in with him.

> When people become couples in New York, living together is instantly an issue because the rents are so high. I was 32 and still living with a roommate when Philip and I got together. You know how at a certain point you just get beyond roommates? Philip had a great place in the Village. I know that makes me sound like a rank opportunist, but the combination of feeling very good about Philip and his having such a nice place was really compelling. I sometimes wonder what would have happened if we had met someplace other than New York ...

When a partner is so strongly motivated by practicality, it's a good bet that she's an ambivalent one-up in an unbalanced relationship.

After a couple moves in together, the situation's novelty may give the relationship a temporary boost. But when the "honeymoon" is over, the one-up wakes up to heightened ambivalence. The half-commitment of living together naturally tends to solidify the relationship by comingling the couple's lives and possessions. Inevitably, the one-down becomes more emotionally dependent on the one-up, and the one-up feels even more confined. The "big decision" still looms, allowing no relief from CAS.

Letting Fate Decide

CAS-afflicted one-ups sometimes simply abdicate. They avoid decision-making altogether by letting fate decide the outcome of the relationship. This is a solution practiced by the more passive type of one-up, like Jessica.

> I had been living with Philip for several years. He wasn't real pushy about it, but once in a while he'd bring up the topic of marriage. My typical response was, "Not yet . . ." Then my sister had a baby girl. I'd never been around a baby before, and I fell in love. I knew I really wanted to have a child, but I still couldn't bring myself to marry Philip. Then I got pregnant. But I was still on the fence about marriage. I was actually thinking in terms of waiting until after the baby was born to do anything. But my upbringing suddenly seemed to come to the fore, and we married at city hall when I was four and a half months along.

Jessica avoided decision-making to the bitter end by letting biological and social forces push her into marriage. Her only choice was to follow the path of least resistance.

Weddings: A View from the Passion Trap

The wedding is a social institution that has cleverly evolved to deal with the Commitment-Ambivalence Syndrome.

There are two basic ways of marrying, the "low-key quickie," which Jessica opted for, and the "huge extravaganza." In the quickie, the ambivalent one-up elects to go ahead with the marriage—"what the hell"—during a moment when the pendulum has swept to the positive side of commitment. It becomes a spontaneous, relatively painless, even exciting act of impulse, not a decision the one-up has to grapple with through many swings of the pendulum.

The huge extravaganza, on the other hand, makes the ambivalent one-up feel helpless. It simply rolls over him in all its magnitude. Even when the extravaganza is not so huge, the planning, spending, invitations, and expectations of everyone involved all function to bully the one-up into toeing the line. Wedding extravaganzas fill the one-up with a special kind of dread, but like a rabbit frozen in the headlights, he rarely has the courage or presence of mind to break for the open plain.

This isn't to say marriage is always a bad idea for unbalanced relationships. I would far prefer that unbalanced couples work on their relationships *before* they marry, but marriage itself can actually help the balancing process.

The Marriage Solution

Even in an age of easy divorce, most people are quite serious about the meaning and importance of marriage. Many couples have told me they never would have worked so hard on their relationship problems if they hadn't been married.

But if a one-up expects marriage to confer a magical, pain-free, fairy-tale happiness, as some do, he's in for a big surprise. If he felt trapped before the wedding, he may feel buried alive afterward. And when he realizes he's entered a contractual agreement to remain forever tied to the one-down, and that severing the agreement would be emotionally and financially disastrous, he's tempted to try even more extreme cures for his worsening CAS.

The Forbidden Affair Solution

Sexual infidelity offers a dramatic way for ambivalent one-ups — married or not — to try to break their internal deadlocks. Sometimes the one-up will consciously seek an affair. More often she simply slips into a courting mode with people she finds attractive. Keep in mind that unhappiness in her primary relationship may be only half-acknowledged, and likewise her signals of interest to prospective partners may not be wholly intentional.

Whether consciously or not, she finds herself drawn to the excitement, novelty, passion, and change a new partner would offer. At the same time, guilt, shame, and anxiety tend to hold her in check. There is a crucial moment, however, when the one-up realizes that an affair itself could actually help her make up her mind, once and for all, about her relationship. This is *the rationalization,* and it allows the one-up to set aside guilt and fear in the interests of testing her commitment to the one-down.

The one-up may be amazed by the highly charged eroticism of his first encounter with a new lover. Forbiddenness amplifies the passion. Miles found this to be the case when his disillusionment with Beth drove him to a torrid encounter with the restaurant's pastry chef, an attractive woman in her twenties.

I knew Monica was interested in me, and the feeling was mutual, but I knew any involvement could be very messy. But there was one evening when Beth called several times with trivia and I was getting pretty fed up. After the restaurant closed, Monica brought me a glass of wine and asked if I wanted to talk. Before long, we were in my office making love. I must admit, it was phenomenal.

Unless the affair partner clearly has qualities that would make her a more balanced match for the one-up, infidelity offers no authentic solution and only makes matters worse. Miles's encounter with Monica allowed him to vent pressure from his frustration with Beth, and it satisfied sexual needs that had been building. But it also added immensely to the guilt he was feeling about Beth *and* to his anger at her for failing to meet his expectations. The short-term pleasures of the Forbidden Affair Solution persuaded Miles to persist with Monica, *further* aggravating his guilt and anger. This solution often becomes a habit, and an even bigger problem.

The Trial Separation Solution

When the pendulum sticks on the negative side of commitment, the one-up will probably propose another popular strategy to buy him yet more time: the Trial Separation. The appeal of this solution is that it allows the one-up unbridled freedom in the romantic marketplace yet *still* doesn't lead to the dismantling of the primary relationship.

The one-up proposes the trial separation delicately, emphasizing how it will give them *both* time to think about things. He says he needs some "space," some distance, a chance to sort things out. The one-down may ask what she's done wrong, but the one-up will readily accept all blame. He'll tell her he's "really messed up right now," and often he'll say pressure at work is the cause. The one-up will feel and express a good deal of guilt about the way things have gone, and he'll tell the one-down that she'd probably be a lot better off if he weren't around.

After sleeping with Monica for two months, Miles couldn't stand the "hypocrisy" anymore. He and Beth were barely speaking, and his life was revolving more and more around the restaurant, and Monica, about whom Beth was still officially unaware. Still, it wasn't an easy decision. Miles felt torn between two very different lives, that of a family man and that of the bon vivant restaurateur. He recalled the night when everything changed.

I'd come home from the restaurant late and Beth was up, reading a book. I was still in the thinking stages about a separation, but the schedule kind of got speeded up. Beth came out and accused me of being with Monica. I didn't answer but said I'd been thinking we should have a trial separation. She began to cry and said she really couldn't believe it had come to this. I said I was pretty messed up and that if we just had some time apart, I was sure we'd be able to work it out. She looked at me in this way that made me feel like dirt and then heaved the book at me and sobbed that she hated me for doing this.

For some one-ups, instigating a trial separation is a "kind" way of ending an unbalanced relationship. By implying there's still hope, he exposes the one-down gradually to the anguish and humiliation of rejection. Many one-ups, however, find themselves consciously believing their own words about the separation being temporary. But no matter what preconceptions a one-up brings to a trial separation, the likelihood is that he'll be surprised by the reality. Because when you leave an intimate relationship, a new and forceful set of emotional dynamics is triggered by the passion trap.

When There's Someone Waiting

When the trial separation is spurred by an affair, there are three common outcomes:

New Love: The End of Ambivalence

The affair proves more rewarding and balanced than the primary relationship. Ambivalence may end, but not conflict, guilt, and emotional pain. Especially when the original relationship has a great deal of history, the one-up will feel powerful senses of loss, grief, and often failure. In his mind, the one-up knows that a clean break is better for him and his partner, but that doesn't stop the pain. After the breakup, the one-up hopes his former partner will quickly find a new romantic interest, releasing him from guilt.

Two Loves: Ambivalence Intensified

When the one-up breaks with the one-down and aligns himself with the affair partner, his feelings suddenly go through a strange metamorphosis. Now that the affair partner has become the primary partner, the one-up finds himself longing for the abandoned one-down. Suddenly, she seems far more exciting and challenging than the affair partner, who so recently had monopolized his thoughts and dreams. It's a baffling turn of events, and one that was experienced by Miles.

> I couldn't believe what was happening. Shortly after I moved out, Monica and I went to Palm Springs for the weekend, but all I could think about was Beth. I think I'd expected her to put up more of a fight, and I was getting fixated on the idea that some other guy was going to step in and take over my family.

Typically this transformation occurs when the one-up remains in the one-up position in his new relationship. The affair partner seems more exciting when she is at arm's length—out of reach of the one-up's natural urge to bring her under his emotional control. Until he does, she is, naturally, a free agent, and may become involved with someone else. But once the one-up romantically links with her, his former partner becomes the free agent. When the one-up thinks about his "ex" forming new romantic ties, he's anxious to control her again. This anxiety can become so strong that he will leave the new partner to return to the old partner, thinking he's made a serious mistake. If both one-downs are so in love with the one-up that they're willing to take him back, a shuttling arrangement between the two partners can develop.

The shuttling one-up winds up chasing a feeling—passion— between two compliant lovers, always longing for the one he's just set free. He will decide he must be in love with both partners, and he'll fantasize living with both. Now the one-up has two partners to feel ambivalent about, and his emotional juggling act is liable to compound his anguish.

Usually, one of the one-down partners will reach her limit of tolerance and deliver an ultimatum. And the one-down who does usually winds up with the one-up, because she's the one who's most likely to withdraw from the relationship.

Lost Love:
The One-Up Gambles and Loses

This is the opposite of the second outcome. When the one-up frees himself and joins his new lover, the new lover begins to feel disenchanted. The fact that the one-up was willing to abandon his old partner proves to the new lover that she has emotional control over him. Now he's in the one-down position, and he starts to feel more and more in love with his new partner as she grows more distant. In fact, she's acting toward him very much like he acted toward the partner he just left. The irony probably won't escape him. Typically, this affair will collapse, leaving the one-up wounded, humbled, and alone with the hope that his old partner might take him back.

Almost all breakups generated by infidelity fall into these three categories. But the simplicity of these brief descriptions belies the emotional agony and scarring that accompanies them.

When There's No One on the Side

If the one-up spearheads a trial separation before she's found someone new, she'll tell herself to wait awhile before leaping into a new romance. She wants to savor her freedom. In fact, moving out is a little like going to summer camp for the one-up. At least at first.

Tasting New Freedom

When the one-up breaks free, she feels an immediate rush of euphoria. She revels in having her own place, eating when and where she wants, coming and going when she pleases, and gearing up for her search for a new lover. Her preparations might include joining a gym, enrolling in classes, and shopping for new clothes. Some one-ups continue to enjoy this freedom over time, develop a taste for independence, and decide not to return to the relationship no matter what happens in the search for new love.

The Downside of Freedom

Many one-ups who savor their first taste of freedom find that their euphoric mood collapses after several days. Replacing it is a feeling of desperate insecurity. While he was living with the one-down, the one-up was guaranteed security, comfort, and intimacy, all of which he took for granted. But another lonely night in a new apartment may bring home how deeply isolated and adrift he feels. He fights solitude by seeking out a great deal of social contact, hoping to find romantic prospects, but not really enjoying himself. He may have been unsatisfied with the one-down, but he was not prepared to feel so empty without her.

Jonathan found this to be the case when he withdrew from Deborah.

> I'd had this fantasy of resuming my old life, almost pretending Deborah had never happened. That meant lots of listening to music, reading, puttering in the garden. But when I tried to duplicate my old routines, something had changed. I felt I was going through the motions, not doing things as spontaneously as I had. There was a void. I'd gotten used to being with someone again.

Jonathan had hit on the one-up's greatest surprise: the hole the one-down's absence leaves in his life.

> One night I went out to eat, alone, and I looked around and saw couples leaning toward each other, talking and laughing, which made me feel even more alone. I felt like a loser or some kind of undesirable. It made me think of Deb's and my early dinners out, when we were like those couples and things seemed so promising.

For many one-ups, separation from the one-down's ego nourishment and security brings on emotional starvation. It matters little how trapped and suffocated the one-up may have felt before leaving. Without emotional buttressing from the one-down, the one-up cast free in the world will usually face an unexpectedly tough adjustment.

Looking for New Love in All the Wrong Places

When a newly separated one-up finds himself face to face with new romantic prospects, he may be in for another rude shock. After breaking with Alana, Scott discovered that his attempts to charm attractive women were meeting with failure.

> The bookstore has occasional author receptions. There was one in particular, for an Irish poet, that seemed to draw only good-looking women. Heaven, right? After the reading, everyone was standing around drinking wine and trying to talk to the poet. I picked out one woman who really appealed to me, and I approached her. I introduced myself and asked her if she wanted some wine. She said yes, but when I poured a cup for her, my hand was trembling a little. She

excused herself and joined the circle around the poet. It's ironic, because when I was with Alana, women were always approaching *me.*

To understand this decline in the one-up's appeal we must look at the changing dynamics in his emotional world. While still linked with his old partner, the one-up's primary interpersonal needs—sex, intimacy, and companionship—were always met.

Freed of the urgent tugging of these needs, he was relaxed and charming around other people. The fact that he was officially "taken" heightened his desirability and made him a romantic challenge.

When the one-up leaves the warm shelter of his old relationship, his primary interpersonal needs go begging. As these needs build over time, the one-up's relaxed manner and charm will give way to transparent emotional neediness. Like Scott, the one-up broadcasts neediness through anxious, inhibited, overeager behavior. The women he approaches intuitively know how desperate he is to form a new attachment. Entering a relationship at this point, the former one-up would be an instant one-down, a fact sensed by most potential partners.

Passionate Interlude

Shortly after the trial separation begins, the one-up usually makes contact with his old partner. Often there will be no need for a pretext: there may be clothes or children to be picked up, or vital matters to be discussed. Sometimes the pretext is flimsy. A perfect example of this comes from the movie, *Annie Hall:* Soon after moving out, Annie, the one-up, calls Alvie in the middle of the night. There's a giant bug in her bathroom and she wants him to come over and kill it. He gladly obliges, of course.

Often, the "old" partner will look very appealing, almost as appealing as she did during courtship. The reason is clear. When he instigated the trial separation, the one-up gave up direct control over her. She became free to do what she wanted, just as he did. Because she's beyond his emotional control she regains her excitement and appeal.

Back on his old turf, the one-up often feels a surprising and pleasant sense of arousal. As he carries out his "official business," he may "accidentally" brush up against the one-down. The touch sends waves of desire through his body.

This is what happened the first time Miles returned home, after three weeks.

> Beth had been so upset that she'd lost her appetite and was notice-ably thinner. She'd decided to go back to work part-time and seemed to be getting her life together. Actually, she looked great. I was so happy to see her I automatically tried to give her a hug, but she held me back. She was still very angry. But when I was about to leave, she brushed something off my shoulder. I turned and tried hugging her again, and this time she hugged me back. And then, suddenly, we were kissing each other and heading for the bedroom. Later, I wanted to stay, but she said I had to go.

Most one-downs will harbor love for the one-up for a long time after he leaves, even when they're angry at him. Some will do any-thing to lure him back, but others, like Beth, have too much pride.

Reunited and It Feels So Good

One-ups who fail to find a new, improved relationship during a trial separation may suffer a sharp and bruising decline in self-esteem. This plunge in confidence compounds their neediness and sense of insecurity. Estranged one-ups begin to crave the intimacy the one-down used to give and which they blithely took for granted. And when this craving begins, the one-up will feel he has made an emo-tional breakthrough. Gone is ambivalence. Now he has a strong, unswerving desire to return to the abandoned one-down. Excitedly, he prepares to break the news: there will be a happy ending to the trial separation.

Now the fate of the relationship lies in the hands of the one-down.

Making Up Is Hard to Do

If the one-down welcomes the one-up back with open arms, the cou-ple will relive courtship, going through the same developmental steps and stages, but in "fast forward." The trial separation equalized the partners, making the one-up needier and less secure and transforming the one-down into an attractive, free agent.

The reunion is a reenactment of the moment in courtship when the one-up first felt joy and relief at having won the love of his partner. If the couple isn't married, this is often the time when wedding plans are made and carried out. If the couple is already married, they may take a second honeymoon, have a new baby, or buy new furniture or a new house.

But the joy of reuniting is no lasting cure for deep-seated relationship problems. This is in fact a good time for couples to enter therapy, because they're *both* motivated to make the relationship work. But it's also the least likely time, because their problems seem to have vanished. Unfortunately, it's usually only a matter of time before the partners fall back into their old behavior patterns. For one-ups in highly unbalanced relationships, that means the unwelcome return of discontent and CAS. Discontent may return with a vengeance, because the one-up finds himself more confined than ever by marriage, the new baby, or the new house.

Many of these one-ups will leave again. Some realize they simply must overcome their fear of separating in order to have a shot at real happiness. A few will conclude that their leaving will actually be good for the one-down too. Many will enter therapy to gain perspective on themselves and their romantic interactions.

Other one-ups realize that the unbalanced relationship won't work in the long run, but they choose to stay in it anyway. This type uses it as a safe place from which to search for a more exciting and compatible partner. This way, they won't have to deal with their insecurities—or risks such as AIDS—in between partners.

And some one-ups simply give up. Emotionally burnt out by failed attempts to find new love, they choose to stay in an unbalanced relationship, shortcomings and all. Sometimes they turn to workaholism, "TV-aholism," alcoholism, or interests outside the home to fill the emptiness they feel.

The Accepting One-Up

For many one-ups, the trial separation serves as an important and lasting lesson in life. They learn that the loss of passion in a relationship is a small price to pay for the boons of comfort, security, and companionship. They accept their imperfect partner and resolve not to take her for granted again. The agenda of their lives is filled with responsibilities: going to work, caring and providing for children, being a dependable spouse. The accepting one-up will have very real emotional rewards. He will feel deep affection for his partner, and he'll know the comfort and warmth of a very secure and loving relationship. And as his partner feels more secure in his acceptance, balance will naturally grow.

Yet, however this one-up reconciles himself to his unbalanced relationship, he cannot escape a lingering sense of loss, a feeling that he might have had a life at whose center was a joyous romantic union — if only he'd held out for a more perfect partner.

Chapter 5

One-Downs

Love Turns into Pain

When two people fall in love, *both* are in the one-down position. Anyone who feels tremendous passion for another person, regardless of whether it's returned, is a one-down. One-downs are not in control of their emotions.

Newly-in-love one-downs experience one of life's supreme pleasures: shared passion. But being the one-down in a one-way relationship is a very painful experience. I've heard one-downs say that it would have been less painful had their partner died rather than rejected them.

It all starts with a vague unease. Subliminally, one partner is beginning to sense the other's lagging interest.

Sensing Detachment

Deborah said it was only in retrospect that she realized there had been signals.

> I've heard that the three-month point in a relationship is crucial, and I believe it. It was around then that I noticed changes. I'd started out feeling fairly confident that Jonathan was mine for the asking. But then something happened. Or I should say, something stopped happening. We were seeing each other less, not more. For a while we'd been spending our weekends together, but it got whittled down to Saturday night and Sunday morning. He still hadn't said he loved me. I thought it was strange, but I was operating on the assumption that we were on solid ground. Then it occurred to me that a pattern

was forming. That's when I started thinking that maybe I was in trouble.

I explained to Deborah that a lover's first signs of distance *are* very difficult to see. When you fall in love, your natural optimism about the relationship makes it exceedingly easy to miss subtle cues from your partner. And when the relationship first begins to lose balance, chances are your partner isn't sure himself what's going on. *His* emotions include many positive feelings about the relationship along with new feelings of detachment. So, the signals the one-up gives *are* mixed and confusing.

Those first signs of distance may go undetected because they look like normal behavior in any new relationship. As a healthy relationship gets under way, both partners may experience the anxiety of setting sail in uncharted waters. And sooner or later one or the other partner will get home late or forget to call. In a balanced relationship, the infraction will be redressed by a sincere apology or casually dismissed as trifling. But in an unbalanced relationship, one partner will come to monopolize the detached behavior while the other carries all the anxiety.

I tell people who feel very anxious early in a relationship not to discount their feelings. The key is to control the emotional reflex to act like a one-down, *not* to begin pressuring the one-up for reassurances and closeness. Anxiety can be an ally, giving us early warning of the passion trap. And the sooner these dynamics are recognized, the better the chance of controlling them.

The One-Up Is Perfect

Even the earliest, most subtle symptoms of a partner's emotional withdrawal can deepen the one-down's love. And that makes it harder yet to admit that anything might be wrong. With this deepening love comes a strong perceptual distortion. New love may beautify the beloved, but imbalance will turn the one-up into a paragon. Now when the one-down kisses her prince, she finds she is holding a king.

This is an equal and opposite reaction to the one-up's "Reverse Frog/Prince Syndrome," which exaggerates the one-down's flaws and minimizes her strong points.

Deborah's changed perceptions of Jonathan show how imbalance can exalt the one-up.

> When I first met Jonathan, I thought he really wasn't my type. I don't like beards, and he's bearded, and I don't like men to be too thin, and he is. But after a while he started looking better and better to me. I couldn't imagine wanting any other man, even when I reminded myself of my original impression. The men I notice now are thin and bearded.

Paul experienced a similar perceptual distortion of Laura.

> By any yardstick, Laura is an extraordinarily attractive woman. Part of the despair I felt when things were first starting to sour was that I'd never be able to fall in love again. She was my impossible standard against which all other women would have to be measured.

It's a fact of psychology that so-called objective perception depends on the emotional state of the observer. This is especially true when the observer happens to be madly in love. The one-down's positive bias toward the one-up is rooted in the hope that she has finally found the ideal partner. As her passion continues to grow, she feels validated in that hope.

Seeing Detachment

In time, the one-down will no longer be sensing detachment in the one-up; she'll see it. Signs of the one-up's growing need for distance inevitably become overt and undeniable: phone calls not made, dates broken, late nights at work, the one-up's distracted, impatient manner. These will finally penetrate the one-down's awareness. Paul told of a decisive evening for him, when the troubling clues could no longer be dismissed or rationalized.

> Laura really threw herself into the fraud case. It was a big one, with several codefendants and a team of attorneys from our firm and another one. Laura was working up to fourteen hours a day and spending most of that time with "the team." We hadn't spent a night together for almost two weeks because she said she was always too busy or tired. So I suggested we at least have dinner, and she said, no, the team always ordered in. Then my parents came to town, and I took them to a very special restaurant. About halfway through din-

ner, I realized Laura was sitting about six tables away with one of the co-attorneys, Nick. I almost passed out. It was a very embarrassing situation in terms of my parents, who had been wondering about this Laura who I wanted to marry. I was amazed when Laura came over and was her gracious self. She said she was having a "strategy session" with Nick, and she was very convincing. But I knew there was more to it.

Paul was experiencing his first bout with "one-down dread." With all his heart and mind he wanted to believe he was being groundlessly paranoid about Laura's loss of interest. But this episode burst the bubble. He felt less in control than ever.

Fear and Hope

When the one-up's detachment becomes the norm, the one-down enters a twilight existence bordered by fear and hope. Fear engenders anxiety, the one-down's constant companion. Fear also nourishes the one-down's feelings of being out of control and helplessly in love.

Any sign of caring from the one-up brings on a fever of hope. Perhaps the one-up's deepest feelings haven't really changed — only surface behavior is different. Behind hope is the one-down's healthy need to feel at least some power in the relationship. Fear and hope put Beth on a kind of merry-go-round as Miles's homecomings grew later and later.

I'd sit in bed reading magazines, unable to concentrate, yet not able to get tired. It was like my eyes were glued open. I'd tell myself Miles was just held up at the restaurant. Then I'd get this horrible gut feeling, very instinctive and real, that he was with someone. I even knew who, because I had met her a couple of times and sometimes you just know. Then, as if to erase that, I'd feel bad for not trusting him and start worrying he'd had a car accident on the way home. It was like I was on this awful mental merry-go-round that kept going faster and faster, and I couldn't get off.

How the One-Down
Loses Herself in Love

The one-down's passion and pain get fused into one gnawing emotion that begins to take control of her identity. She's acting reflexively when she embarks on a series of maneuvers to rekindle the one-up's love, end her anguish, and bring her a new sense of control. Unfortunately, these maneuvers are compliant behaviors that, ironically, will cause her to lose more of herself and more of the one-up's love.

The Hypercourtship Solution

"I wanted everything to be special," Paul recalled.

> I think what I was trying to do was convey to Laura that no one else would or could love or treat her better than I. I did everything I could to please her, from taking her to the best restaurants to jogging, so I could run with her. I was continually supportive and thoughtful. I'd cut meetings and phone calls short if I was supposed to meet her. I was even picking up her dry-cleaning. I really knocked myself out, and yet she *still* wasn't satisfied. It was beyond me.

In hypercourtship behavior, you use the same attraction techniques you did during courtship, but you intensify them. It's really very logical. If being nice and charming and generous helped win the one-up's love in the first place, why shouldn't that behavior win it back now?

I tell one-downs that courtship behavior succeeds in new relationships because both lovers feel anxious, insecure, and needy. Signs of caring are extremely welcome because they ease anxiety and insecurity. But when one partner starts feeling too much security and control, the other's fervid courtship behavior will seem smothering. The last thing the one-up wants to hear is the one-down vowing to devote the rest of his life to pleasing the one-up. He's actually vowing to sacrifice his identity and life to the relationship. He doesn't know it, but he's guaranteeing imbalance and sabotaging the very qualities that might allow the one-up to regain passion for him.

The Echo Solution

Echo was a nymph in Greek mythology who made the mistake of angering a powerful goddess. Echo was known for her conversational talents, so the goddess punished her by making her only repeat the words of others. This proved a terrible tragedy for Echo when she fell in love with the beautiful youth Narcissus. One day Narcissus became lost in the woods, and Echo had a rare chance to make contact. But she had to let him speak first. He cried, "Is anyone there?" and she responded from the bushes where she hid, "There!" She continued to repeat whatever he shouted, and for a while he enjoyed it. Echo approached him, but when he realized she was helplessly parroting his words, he pushed her away, vowing, "I would die before I let you possess me." Echo could only say, "Possess me!" Devastated, she retired to a cave where she withered away. Only her echoing voice survived.

Greek myths have a way of getting to the core of human nature. The story of Echo illustrates one of the most universal one-down maneuvers. Again, Paul:

> I'm considered a person who always speaks his mind, damn the consequences. But Laura seemed to turn me into a shameless "yes man." For example, *The Firm* is one of her favorite books. I found it annoying, but I actually told her I'd loved it. Same with movies. She was always right ...

Paul noted that around others he still fiercely adhered to his opinions. But with Laura it was different. His fear of displeasing her, or of showing a lack of compatibility, drove him to support her views. He didn't realize that she'd find him far more interesting if he offered bold opinions.

The Anxiety Effect

There is a principle in psychology known as the Yerkes-Dodson Law: We perform optimally in a state of moderate arousal or anxiety. Anxiety in high doses can make it hard for us to perform well or even to function like our normal selves. And a high dose is just what the one-down gets when she sees the first hard signs of the one-up's waning interest. Deborah described how she began to act in ways that were completely out of character as Jonathan seemed to be slipping from her grasp.

> After the Thanksgiving fiasco, days went by and Jonathan hadn't called. I was frantic, and I'd lost whatever pride might have kept me from calling him. So I did, but I got his answering machine. I was all prepared to talk to him, not to his machine. When the beep went off, I panicked. I blurted, "Hi, it's me," and then my mind blanked and I hung up. But I knew that was too bizarre, so I had to call back and leave a real message. Then I was stuck with trying to explain the first "non-message" without seeming too pathetic, and then leaving a second message, and I knew I was sounding looney-tunes. Lord, how I

wished I could have climbed in his window and erased that tape before he got home.

Anxiety was compromising Deborah's performance in all aspects of her life. She told me that she was so distracted at school that the principal called her in and asked if something was wrong. Her visible anxiety "told" Jonathan that she'd lost the cool he'd initially found so appealing.

In Search of the Lost Self

One-downs realize they're "not quite themselves." They wonder where that self went and why it's been replaced by this suffering person whom they don't like or respect. The need to recover the sense of self fuels the one-down's struggle to recapture the one-up's love. That's because if she wins back his love, she also wins herself back in the bargain. But once again, the one-down's efforts turn out to be self-sabotaging.

The "Be Spontaneous" Solution

Deborah was excited about seeing Jonathan again over breakfast at the oceanside cafe where they'd often gone. Her instincts were right: She wanted to act as if she were seeing Jonathan and nothing had changed.

> I vowed to myself I wouldn't carry my pain into this meeting. I'd be my old self — smart, contrary, a little snotty, a little sarcastic. I wanted to tell him about my week as if I'd hardly given him a thought, instead of obsessing about him constantly. I practiced anecdotes.

So far so good. Deborah understood that spontaneity would equalize her emotional leverage in the meeting. But here's what actually happened.

> When I saw Jonathan my heart started hammering so loudly that I couldn't hear myself think. He bent down to kiss my cheek and I sort of halfway got his lips. He'd taken my hand, and I could feel it was clammy. I asked him what he'd been up to, really trying for a bright tone, and then knocked over my water glass. He stared at me for a

moment or two and asked if I was all right. I said I'd had the flu for a couple of days.

The Be Spontaneous Solution requires that the one-down command herself not to be uptight. But, paradoxically, imposing such a demand will only make the one-down *more* uptight. If anyone has ever told you to "loosen up," and you found yourself tensing even tighter, you know the dynamic. If Deborah had told herself it was okay to be upset around Jonathan—after all, it's almost impossible to hide such strong feelings anyway—she would have appeared naturally upset, which is healthier than appearing artificially jovial. Unfortunately, after this breakfast, Jonathan suggested they "take a breather" and see how they felt in several weeks.

The Instant Replay

Like a sports fan watching instant replays of disputed calls, the one-down holds in her mind an afterimage of her "wrong" behaviors with the one-up. She becomes her own harshest critic, ruthlessly assessing her performances and trying to determine what will work better the next time.

Before they separated, Beth felt she was stumbling over her feet as she tried to find ways to please an increasingly critical Miles.

> I never knew what would set him off. He'd come home from the restaurant, and I'd assume he'd want to hear about Chloe's latest feat. But he'd get impatient with the way I was telling the story. I tried to get more economical when I related things, but it didn't feel natural. Gradually, I stopped sharing much with him. He always seemed put out when I asked him to do a favor, like pick up milk. So when I needed something, I'd spend several moments framing the request so it wouldn't antagonize him. But no matter how I did it, he'd get into a snit. I began to think something was *really* wrong with me.

Miles's negative reactions to so many things inspired in Beth a domestic version of performance anxiety. No matter how closely she scrutinized her moves and mismoves, her efforts seemed doomed to failure. Beth hadn't yet realized that the best way to win over a one-up is not to try so hard.

The One-Down's Passion

There's a compensation for the one-down's loss of control, sense of self, and happiness, and that is passion. The one-down feels love more intensely than he has ever imagined possible. That it's heavily laced with pain actually heightens the feeling. Grand, aching passion imbues the one-down's life with drama and danger. His emotions make him feel special, even if the one-up doesn't. And despite evidence to the contrary, many one-downs cling to the belief that love itself will eventually solve the relationship's problems.

The "I Love You" Solution

The one-down may have lost spontaneity in the presence of the one-up, but there is one phrase that seems to spill from him as naturally as breathing: "I love you." He cannot contain his powerful feelings of love. Peg noticed that shortly after Bill stopped working, he became unusually verbal about his love.

> Bill was never the type to talk about his feelings. He used to go for months without telling me he loved me, and only then when I dragged it out of him. But after he left his job, he was always saying affectionate things. Like, "You know, I think you've really turned out to be a remarkable woman, and I love you." At first I teased him about it, but he seemed very hurt.

Saying "I love you" is an emotional step toward another person, an invitation to intimacy and closeness. During courtship, the one-down may have found that saying "I love you" really did bring his partner closer. But once imbalance starts, the words "I love you" come to be dreaded by the one-up. Her guilt and empathy make it hard for her to do anything *but* return the words. However, her response will gradually become perfunctory or evasive. Not wanting to be forced into hypocrisy, the one-up may reply nonverbally, in the form of a hand squeeze or a hug.

The "Do You Love Me?" Solution

When the one-down senses his partner's withdrawal, his tactics may change. He may act assertive, seeking reassurance by asking point-blank, "Do you love me?" What he's likely to hear may not be so reassuring: an impatient "Of course I do," or, even less reassuring, "What do *you* think?" Despite the mixed message, some anxious one-downs come to need a reassurance "fix" on a regular basis. And like all one-down solutions, this one makes the one-up feel more suffocated, more distant, and less loving.

Sexual Passion

The one-down's passion is by no means confined to the emotions. It is very physical as well. Being in the one-down position can be a powerful aphrodisiac. Most one-downs think a lot about making love with the one-up. Many have to force themselves not to apply steady sexual pressure to their partners.

Deborah recalled her sexual feelings toward Jonathan.

> He wasn't the best lover I'd ever had, and he certainly wasn't the sexiest-looking man I'd been with, but he excited me like no other. If we were at the movies and he took my hand, my entire body would start tingling. When he'd come over to my place, I'd steer him toward the bedroom as soon as decently possible. My body had never been so responsive. He hardly had to do a thing.

For Paul, Laura had offered no less than a sexual awakening.

> I never knew the difference between "sex" and "making love" until I fell in love with Laura. She's more creative than any of the women I'd been with. I'd simply never had some of those sensations before. My wanting sex more than she did got to be a problem. I got so anxious and desperate for her that I was having trouble performing. That only made things worse, naturally.

One-down sexual passion is both symptom and solution. It's a symptom of how out of control the one-down feels, because losing control cues the brain to manufacture the "in love" sensations of arousal and euphoria. It's also a solution for the one-down's desperate need to gain control over the one-up, because sex is a way of possessing another person. For the one-down, lovemaking symbolizes his greatest desire: to fuse with the one-up. And on a purely practical level, sex allows the one-down to have the one-up all to himself, and in the closest of ways.

As we've seen, one-ups try to use good sex to justify a relationship they feel ambivalent about. One-downs are more ambitious: they hope sex will reignite the one-up's love and redeem the relationship. However, the one-down's hunger for sex, and the closeness it entails, can raise the one-up's feelings of confinement to new heights—especially for women one-ups. But as a solution the one-down is loath to abandon it, because the payoff is so wonderful and self-reinforcing. As the wisdom goes, sex with love is one of the most extraordinary experiences available to us. Some male one-downs will feel so madly in love and so wildly aroused that, like Paul, they'll experience anxiety-induced performance problems. This may be one reason why men tend to strive for the one-up position.

The Painful Part of Passion

By the time the one-down has exhausted the "loving" solutions already mentioned, she is anxious, afraid, and pessimistic for most of her waking hours. Her emotions are grindingly dissonant: on one hand, she's in serious pain; on the other, she's feeling aching love and desire, products of her emotional jeopardy.

The One-Down's Ambivalence

Given all the one-down's warring emotions, it's no wonder that she has her own brand of ambivalence. Recall one-up ambivalence: His *mind* says, "I should stay in this relationship because it's secure and convenient, and my partner loves me so much." But his *heart* counters, "I must break free of this relationship or I'll die of suffocation."

One-down ambivalence is the opposite. Her *mind* asks, "Why am I staying in this relationship? It's causing me pain, grief, and humiliation. My life is a mess. I hardly know myself anymore. I should be out there looking for someone new who'll really love me." But her *heart* pleads, "I can't leave this relationship. I've never been so in love, and I've never been with anyone I wanted so much. I may be miserable with him, but I'd be much more miserable without him."

The One-Down's Anger

If you've ever been a one-down—and most of us have—you know there's more to it than love, passion, and pain. There is also a great deal of anger. The one-down is angry at the one-up for hurting her, for disrupting her life, for making her feel powerless, for not loving her. She may not be fully aware of her first pangs of anger, because they're drowned by her passion. But as an unbalanced relationship goes on, the one-down's love and passion may be worn down by the one-up's unloving behavior. Then, resentful anger may become a prominent feature of the one-down's emotional norm.

I believe all emotions are healthy, including anger. Where we run into problems is in our *reactions* to our emotions. Powerful emotions like anger, fear, and guilt, when we don't deny them or overreact to them, can give us valuable information about our inner world and our outer lives. But when we deny or overreact to our emotions, they almost always multiply our problems.

Buried Anger

Thwarted desire eventually and inevitably generates hostility. But when the one-down begins to feel anger, she also begins to feel extremely vulnerable. Uppermost in her mind is finding a way to recover and secure the one-up's loving interest. The last thing she wants to do is double her jeopardy by voicing anger at the one-up. Anger, she reasons, will drive the one-up away, not foster the closeness she so desperately wants. So she buries it, as Deborah did.

> I wanted so much to tell Jonathan off at that breakfast, about how I felt he'd led me on, made me think it was safe to fall in love with him, then started pulling back. About how he had no right to decide the fate of the relationship. I think if we had been a little further along, I would have. But I still had that tiny hope that things might work out and I didn't want to burn my bridges.

The one-down faces a dilemma: What can she do with her anger that won't alienate the one-up or demolish the relationship? She would like to continue hiding it behind various types of pleasing behavior. But, as Freud first observed, the head-in-the-sand approach doesn't work. You may think you've eliminated a disturbing emotion by suppressing it, but you're actually creating a bigger problem. Anger is especially prone to quietly growing and shape-shifting deep in your emotional corridors, then emerging in altered forms to make trouble. If the core problem isn't tackled, anger will gradually harden into hostility.

Love/Hate

When one-downs bury their anger for too long, they move into a love/hate pattern of relating. Beth told me of an incident that embodied this dynamic.

> I remember cooking a really complicated paella for Miles—his favorite—for his birthday, and trying to make it so perfect that all of our problems would disappear. Believe me, it's not easy to please a restaurateur with food. But that morning we'd had another of our tiffs, and he'd left angry. I was cursing him as I chopped the vegetables for the meal I hoped would make him be more loving to me.

As long as the one-down is hostage to her fear of being left, her main strategy may still be "loving" solutions. However, her resentments will find expression some way, either in other parts of her life, or through double-edged behavior directed at the one-up.

Expressing Hostility

Virtually everyone sometimes has problems expressing anger. But for the one-down, managing her hostility becomes one of life's most energy-absorbing challenges. She cannot risk alienating the one-up, so she directs her hostility away from him and toward other targets.

Displaced Anger

When Miles started coming home later and later, Beth vented her anger by getting mad at his business and even at Chloe.

> I'd rant and rave that the restaurant business sucked and I'd complain about the backers and their outrageous expectations. This was instead of yelling at Miles, demanding to know how he, my own husband, could possibly stay away so long from me and his child. What really upset me was that I started getting short-tempered with Chloe. I think somewhere in my mind I'd reasoned that if it wasn't for Chloe, Miles and I would still be close.

Beth was redirecting her anger to avoid driving a larger wedge between herself and Miles. But when the new target *is* another person, such as a child, even more suffering *is* generated. Meanwhile, the real issues that need so badly to be dealt with remain under cover. By displacing her anger, Beth reinforced the passion trap, because her efforts were being spent on pleasing, not challenging, Miles.

The One-Down Gets Angry at Himself

Bill had had all sorts of ideas for changing the way Peg ran her business, and he wanted to help put them in place. Typical of him, Bill kept insisting, and expecting, that things be done his way. With much distress, Peg had tolerated his takeover, then felt nothing but relief when he eventually became disenchanted and withdrew.

> After that he just let everything go. He'd spend the day drinking in front of the TV, then leave for the bar. He usually wasn't there when I got home. He wasn't bathing much, and I really couldn't stand having him in the same bed. So he started sleeping on the couch, usually in his clothes. One day I went through the classifieds and circled things I thought he'd be qualified for, but when I gave them to him, he looked at me like I was insane. He said, "Who in the hell wants a broken-down, over-the-hill bastard like me in their so-called executive suite." When I suggested he get help, he said what was the use and left the room. It almost killed me to hear those things. I know it hurt him that not only was I succeeding at a time when he felt he had failed, but in a business I had created. He used to fantasize about starting a company, but he never did anything about it.

Bill was expressing his rage in self-destructive ways. This is a common and highly dangerous side effect of the loss of self-esteem one-downs experience. It's very natural for someone whose partner is withdrawing to feel inadequate or unattractive, especially when the loss of power in the relationship is linked to a defeat in the outside world. Self-destructive behavior is a way for one-downs to punish or destroy the self that feels so worthless.

The Jealousy Solution

Jealousy, one of the most toxic, unpleasant, and powerful emotions, is the one-down's constant companion. In balanced relationships, one or both partners may feel an occasional pang of jealousy as a reassuring sign of their importance to each other. But in unbalanced relationships, jealousy belongs to the one-down. Jealousy is a special kind of anger, created by the rage and helplessness the one-down feels when the one-up seems not only distant but interested in someone new. To the one-down, that represents the ultimate rejection and an absolute loss of control.

Paul fell prey to jealousy.

> I was nervous about Laura spending so much time with the three other men on the defense team, but forced myself to be philosophical about it. But seeing Laura with Nick demolished my ability to be rational. When I next saw Laura alone, she still maintained she wasn't involved with him, which may have been technically true. Anyway, I trashed Nick, who has a reputation with women and unfortunately is a very good attorney. I told her what a shallow, manipulative, vain, and corrupt human being I thought he was. From then on I could barely sleep at night thinking of Laura and Nick together.

It may seem odd to view jealousy as a "solution," but it can be another way the one-down tries to channel anger away from the one-up. Paul heaped all his jealous hostility on Nick, but he didn't accuse Laura of trying to attract the other man. At least Paul was able to ventilate his angry feelings without playing adversary to Laura. But the price the one-down pays for letting off the pressure is very high. Jealous behavior is anathema to one-ups because it represents the one-down's emotional clinging and dependence.

The Possessiveness Solution

The one-down's first direct expression of anger at the one-up is often a demand for more togetherness. Since loving and ingratiating behavior isn't working, she's ready to try to coerce intimacy from the one-up. The one-down's persistent insecurities tend to give her demands a whiny tone. Later, the tone may get angrier. Miles said of Beth's possessiveness:

> One of the things I had a hard time handling about Beth was the way she harped on how little time I spent at home. She couldn't understand that I needed more in my life than just the restaurant and home. I needed to see friends, play golf, do some normal things. But if I took any time off to do anything other than spend it with her and Chloe, Beth went nuts.

Even if the one-up complies with the one-down's possessive demands, the victory is false. Possessiveness is a very blatant expression of a one-down's need to monopolize the one-up. This often alerts the one-up, as it did Miles, to the one-down's emotional hunger. And that, we know, will automatically make the one-up pull away.

Possessiveness is hostile in that it expresses the one-down's anger at the one-up for not acting as she thinks he should. She wants him to "be there" for her without having to be told, but he rarely is. Her possessive demands are a way of telling the one-up how to act like a loving partner. It's a lesson that inspires the student's resistance.

Last-Ditch Efforts

The one-down may be miserable and in despair, but his instinct for basic emotional survival remains intact. And while he probably couldn't verbalize the reasons why his relationship is faltering, he now has a keen sense that new tactics must be used if he is ever to reclaim the one-up's love. At this point, the one-down may be willing to risk losing the one-up in his efforts to reclaim her love. The strategies he'll use will be more aggressive and contrived, a kind of last-ditch boldness.

The Playing Hard-to-Get Solution

The heaviest gun in his new arsenal is the classic Playing-Hard-to-Get Solution. The universality of this solution indicates that most people have an instinctive understanding of the passion trap. The one-down who plays hard-to-get hopes to show his one-up partner that she doesn't really have the control over him that she thinks she has. It will go against his grain, and the risk factor will frighten him, but the one-down doesn't have much to lose. This was Paul's thought when he devised a plan to make Laura jealous, after she broke off their tempestuous six-month relationship.

> When Laura finally fessed up about Nick, I decided not to let go without a fight. The librarian in the county law library had always acted interested in me, but I'd never followed through. The firm was having a big picnic and softball game and I asked this woman, Daphne, to be my date. Laura was with Nick, of course. But it was more than a little satisfying to see her double-take when she saw I was with someone.

In balanced relationships, a bit of game playing, including playing hard to get, simply adds spice to the proceedings. But for the one-down, the Playing-Hard-to-Get Solution is very urgently employed. Not only does the one-down wish to startle and impress the one-up with his autonomy; quite often he wants to hurt her too, in punishment for the pain she's caused him. Of course, now there is another vulnerable player in the arena, the third party. The problem with playing hard to get, even when it works, is that it doesn't dissolve the unbalanced relationship's underlying problems. Because of this, its balancing effect on the unbalanced relationship is generally fleeting. Some one-downs, like Paul, don't even get short-term benefits because they can't help showing their hand. As Laura said of Paul's attempt:

> It did shock me to see Paul with Daphne at the picnic. But after a while it seemed he was performing for my benefit. There was something forced about his manner with her, and he kept glancing over at me.

Paul's nonverbal communication worked against him: it told Laura that his interest in Daphne wasn't sincere. Paul felt so frustrated after Laura left with Nick that he took Daphne home early, pleading an upset stomach.

The Pregnancy Solution

For one-downs who want children, and even for those who aren't so sure, the passion trap can trigger a strong urge to have a baby with the one-up. Deborah had such a response.

> At thirty-three I was conscious that my "time" was starting to run out. I suppose that's why the idea of having a baby with Jonathan got to be totally compelling. I'd imagine what our child would look like, and him assisting the birth. I did mention kids to him once or twice, and he seemed pretty averse, but I figured all men are like that at first.

Having a baby may seem the perfect solution to the one-down's problem. Children represent the ultimate commitment, bonding the partners irrevocably in a biological — not just social — contract. And for just this reason, the one-up can be very "averse" to having children with the one-down.

Some women one-downs, married or unmarried, may become relaxed about birth control, hoping consciously or unconsciously to turn their baby fantasy into reality. Of course, this solution is a dangerous one because pregnancy can create a huge leap in the one-down's neediness and in the one-up's feelings of entrapment.

The One-Down Explodes

When one-down hostility finds no outlet, and when frustration is intense, the result may be an explosion of violent anger. Peg gave an emotional account of the incident that prompted her to seek therapy.

> I had come home late one night from the shop, and Bill was sitting on the couch in front of the TV, drinking scotch. I said hello and then excused myself to go to bed. Suddenly he was behind me, grabbing my arm and whirling me around. He said, "Don't you dare be polite with me," and other things much worse. And he was out of control, slapping me and slapping me, and he wouldn't stop. Because he was drunk I was able to get away from him. I ran to the bathroom and locked myself in. He pounded on the door and I thought he was going to break it down and really kill me. But I guess he needed another drink and left.

Physically attacking Peg seemed the only means left to Bill to control her. She had quietly proceeded with the running of her store, by herself, contrary to his wishes, and her withdrawal from him made him feel as if he'd been negated. Communication between these partners had almost completely broken down, so they had no safe or constructive way to vent anger or try to renegotiate the terms of their relationship. Bill's explosion was one of the most overt expressions possible not only of hostility but of horrible emotional pain.

Chapter 6

From Rock Bottom
to Rebirth

The Renaissance of the One-Down

The one-down clings fiercely to her tattered dreams of love. She shouldn't be surprised to hear the one-up suggest they separate, but she is. Deborah's response to Jonathan's proposal that they "take a breather" was physical *and* emotional.

> When I was driving home, I had this very real sensation that the bottom had dropped out of my stomach, leaving a kind of cold, empty void inside. I was crying, of course, but it was the aching, hollow, shaky feeling that was so strange. The coldness made me think I was having real, physical shock. The amazing thing is that I knew it was coming, and it was still so traumatic. I think it must be like when you know a loved one is dying, but you can never be prepared for the actual event.

Deborah was in fact shaken by a kind of death—*psychological death.* Jonathan had become so important to her, so central to her life, that his leaving was equivalent to death—and just as traumatic. Her shock analogy was apt. Physical shock slows the body's processes so that healing can begin. Emotional shock prepares the one-down for the challenging task of self-healing.

It's like a juggling act on a wobbly high wire. The one-down must find a way to fill the gaping hole left by the one-up and at the same time cope with crushing pain. She must learn to let go of the one-up while she's craving him more desperately than ever. It's the ultimate configuration of the passion trap, when one partner has broken free, taking with him the vast emotional investment of the other. But the process of reclaiming her wholeness begins while the one-down still reels from the shock of rejection.

"I'll Never Survive"

Romantic rejection creates such a piercing sense of loss that the one-down may at first feel utterly defeated. Her thoughts are dark. Phrases I commonly hear from newly rejected one-downs include, "I'll never survive," "I'll never love again," "I'll never find happiness," and, "I'll never be myself again." This reaction is powerful, visceral, and defies conscious control, as Beth learned.

> When Miles moved out, I kept saying to myself, "Okay, just be calm. Things are going to work out. I've just hit a low point in my life, but I'll pull myself through this just like I've always done in the past." But the very next minute I'd be sobbing uncontrollably, like it was the end of the world.

Many psychologists believe that romantic loss reawakens the primal fear of abandonment. Babies instinctively fear abandonment because their physical survival depends on having a constant caretaker. In a sense, we *are* like babies when we feel abandoned, only our fears center on *emotional* survival needs. The anguish of romantic rejection tells us something about the strength of these needs.

Beth actually did well to allow herself free expression of her grief while at the same time giving herself pep talks. Pep talks may have little immediate impact on a newly broken heart, but they'll still penetrate the unconscious and help speed healing.

The One-Down Feels Victimized

It's natural for a rejected one-down to go through a phase of feeling victimized. She's offered the one-up the ultimate gift, her vast and undying love, and she's been so good to him in a hundred ways. But he *still* rejected her. It's grossly unfair!

The one-down also feels that anyone capable of rejecting her so cruelly must have something emotionally or morally wrong with him. So the one-down feels not only victimized but self-righteous. She'll pathologize the one-up, concluding that he's devoid of sensitivity or depth, and she'll usually be supported by her commiserating friends. Everyone close to Deborah told her that Jonathan was too "screwed up" for her, including a psychic she'd never met.

> ... not the neon palm kind, but a woman who was recommended by a couple of friends. Before the crisis with Jonathan, I had no interest in psychic things. But I was so confused that I was ready to listen to anybody. First she said some pretty amazing things about my past. When she got to my love life, my face must have given it away. The psychic said the man I'd been involved with was too "selfish" to be a good partner.

The one-up may look like the "bad guy" and the one-down like the "good guy" or innocent victim. And during the first stages of recovery from a rejection, the one-down can derive solace and needed ego nourishment from thinking that the one-up, not she, failed the relationship.

But I try to encourage one-downs to look a little deeper. Instead of seeing only what the one-up has so selfishly taken and she has so generously given, I want the one-down to learn how she may have *enabled,* even fostered, the one-up's hurtful behavior. We discuss why she may have been clinging to a relationship after it stopped giving pleasure and started offering mostly pain. By acknowledging her role, the one-down comes to realize that she had more power than she knew in the relationship. At the same time, I encourage her to shift *blame* from herself and the one-up to the powerful dynamics of the passion trap.

The One-Down Is Sensitized

One of Beth's reactions to Miles's moving out was typical of rejected one-downs.

> I was so filled with self-pity and sadness and moral outrage about Miles's behavior that it was like all my nerves were exposed. It got hard for me to watch the evening news, because everything seemed so sad or corrupt. There was one story in particular about a woman who was losing custody of her children to her ex-husband because of clinical depression. I couldn't stop crying for her.

The spurned one-down often projects her pain and sense of tragedy onto the outside world, much like new lovers who paint the world beautiful with their projected love. She feels an affinity for anyone who has known the tragic side of life. She finds emotional validation in sad music, downbeat movies, and lovelorn poetry. The one-down's new sensitivity may convince her that her suffering has made her a deeper person. In fact, she is often right. The silver lining of emotional loss is the opportunity it offers for personal growth.

Filling the Void

The shock of romantic rejection imbues the one-down with a sense of emotional desolation. One-downs struggle to fill this void with behavior that may be perfectly healthy when practiced in moderation. Many of these behaviors function subtly to begin the process of restoring the one-down's sense of wholeness. In filling the void left by the one-up, most of these "solutions" shift the one-down's emotional focus away from the one-up.

And "filling the void" behaviors are by no means exclusive to newly separated one-downs. They're often practiced by one-downs in ongoing unbalanced relationships.

Spirituality, Charity, Good Works

Many one-downs find solace in a new or renewed sense of spirituality. Spirituality offers a highly satisfying surrogate for lost love, explaining the familiarity of the image of the rejected lover who enters a monastery or convent, or joins the Peace Corps or similar good-works organizations.

We associate spirituality with sacrifice, faithfulness, and devotedness, words the abandoned one-down now sees herself as embodying. In tandem with new self-identification, the one-down finds in religious devotion or charitable service a safe and culturally approved focus for her loving feelings.

Typically, spirituality also offers "a way." Following a set of spiritual beliefs can lend structure to a life that's been thrown into disarray by a failed romantic relationship. After her visit to the psychic, Deborah took a few classes in spiritual self-development.

They gave me a sense that the most important part of life happens outside of romantic relationships. I realized I was putting far too much weight on having a man. I should have stayed with the program, but they weren't quite me.

The Shopping Solution

Deborah felt she'd been unfairly punished by Jonathan and that she deserved something that would make her feel better. She developed a sense of material entitlement.

> I usually shop once a season, but suddenly I was spending whole weekends in better shopping malls. I bought outrageous things, like a $350 leather jacket and a $250 pair of black boots. Me, who always buys on sale or in vintage clothing shops. I almost felt like a new me when I was wearing my new clothes, and that was nice.

In retrospect, Deborah realized she chose the jacket and boots for their assertiveness. Clearly, they were items that compensated outwardly for the powerlessness she was feeling. She was also turning to the well-known psychological boost of buying new things to fight the onset of depression.

Treating yourself well after an emotional loss is a vital part of self-healing. But any strategy, when carried to extremes, can become a vice. Deborah's shopping compulsion subsided, to be replaced by despair when she got her next credit card bills. The high from her new clothes was ephemeral; the $3,000 tab wasn't.

Eating

The practice of eating your way through an emotional crisis may have become a sitcom staple, but recent research suggests that crisis eating shares emotional roots with narcotics addiction. From infancy, feelings of satiation from eating are profoundly soothing. These feelings quell anxiety and negative impulses by creating a strong sense of comfort. Narcotics function much the same way, by blocking both inner and outer pain and producing euphoria.

Paul looked to food to fill the void left by Laura.

> I found myself seeking out the kinds of foods my mother used to make. Things like hot cereal, popovers, creamed chicken, and warm apple pie a la mode. There's a home-cooking place not far from my

condo, and I was going there for breakfast and dinner. And I was gaining weight.

It was no accident that the foods from Paul's youth seemed to offer the most comfort. His childhood had been uncommonly secure and loving, and the childhood foods seemed to resurrect feelings of security and acceptance.

Interestingly, Deborah's shopping enhanced her physical appeal while Paul's eating undermined his. Yet, both "filling the void" behaviors reflect diminished supplies of self-esteem.

Starving

Other one-downs have an opposite reaction to food, shunning it as Beth did.

> I almost started to despise food, partly because my stomach was in knots most of the time, partly because I almost viewed food as the enemy. I know that my having gained weight wasn't the real problem, but it probably contributed. And then there's Miles's connection with food. So it made sense I'd react against it.

While the shock of abandonment still grips the one-down, food may seem unimportant or unappetizing. For some one-downs, however, avoidance of food is part of an overall, punishing neglect of self, a neglect reflecting demolished self-esteem.

And there's another interpretation. Psychologists who specialize in eating disorders say that anorexia is a fairly common reaction to romantic disappointment. Vigorously controlling her food intake enables the one-down to compensate for the lack of control she feels in her emotional life.

Alcohol and Drugs

According to Peg, Bill had always been a moderate-to-heavy social drinker and possibly an incipient alcoholic. The crisis with his job, and then with Peg, pushed him over the edge. While he held off joining Peg in therapy, wanting to do things "his way," he did start attending AA meetings shortly after assaulting Peg.

Bill used alcohol to numb his feelings of failure. The appeal of alcohol, and other popular "problem solving" drugs such as Valium, crystal methamphetamine, and ecstasy, is that they act immediately to ease mental and emotional pain. Such self-medication not only blunts pain but allows a one-down to punish himself for being unworthy. This is why the appeal of dangerous, mind-altering drugs is so strong for a large number of one-downs.

Bill was lucky. His act of violence frightened him into corrective action. I have known many other cases in which shattered, addictive one-downs weren't so lucky. If the abused substance of choice becomes a permanent substitute for meaningful human interactions, the results can be tragic emotionally and physically.

Benign Retaliations

The anger that the one-down feels toward the one-up often spawns fantasies of retaliation. Sometimes retaliatory fantasies are acted on. Some acts of what I call "benign retaliation" can actually help a one-down express anger directly, channel it in positive ways, and reclaim a sense of personal power. Many retaliations also offer last-gasp opportunities to connect with the one-up.

The Letter

Beth felt much better after she wrote what she called a "fuck off and die" letter to Miles at the restaurant.

> There was a lot I didn't get to say, or have the guts to say, when he was actually moving out. That was almost the worst part, feeling intimidated on that level. Plus, the more I thought about things, the more I was able to formulate exactly what went on. That letter was my way of feeling like I had some say in the situation. And I wanted Miles to know I didn't think *he* was any great prize, either—even though I really wanted him back when I wrote it.

The retaliatory letter gives the one-down a forum she was denied if communication between the couple had reached a serious impasse. It may also give her the "last word" and a sense of control from being the one to close all discussion about the relationship. Such letters are filled with barbs intended to puncture the one-up's ego. But Beth also admitted she simply liked the idea of Miles getting the letter and "holding it in his hands the way I wished he was holding me."

The One-Down's
Widow/Widower Fantasy

Often the retaliation occurs only in the one-down's mind — in a fantasy of attending the one-up's tragic funeral. Whereas this fantasy gave the one-up the feeling of freedom without guilt, it gives the one-down the feeling of control without pain.

In Nora Ephron's best-selling novel *Heartburn,* the betrayed heroine expressed this fantasy while telling her therapy group about her husband Mark's infidelity:

> "What do you want?" said Vanessa. "Mark is going to turn up and you have to know what you want when he does."
> I thought about it.
> "I want him back," I said.
> "What do you want him back for?" said Dan. "You just said he was a schmuck."
> "I want him back so I can yell at him and tell him he's a schmuck," I said. "Anyway, he's my schmuck." I paused. "And I want him to stop seeing her. I want him to say he never really loved her. I want him to say he must have been crazy. I want her to die. I want him to die too."
> "I thought you said you wanted him back," said Ellis. "I do," I said, "but I want him back dead."
> I smiled. It was the first time I'd smiled about the situation.

The one-down emotionally slaying the one-up harkens back to her lament that the pain would be less if the one-up had died rather than rejected her. What I like about Ephron's account is that it shows the role humor can play in the one-down's recovery.

The "I'll Show Him" Retaliation

The most productive of the benign retaliations, "I'll Show Him" (or "Her") has inspired more than a few highly successful careers. By besting the one-up in terms of careers, the one-down hopes to endow herself with greater social power than the one-up — not only to redress imbalance, but to create a substantial imbalance in the opposite direction. This is so the former one-up will spend the rest of his life regretting that he didn't hang on to his one-down partner. Displacing romantic disappointment onto career efforts helps the one-down regain autonomy more quickly. Sometimes it even turns retaliation into a successful solution by re-attracting the one-up, or attracting a better partner. I'll discuss the productive channeling of one-down pain more fully in a later chapter.

Extreme Retaliations

In a small but alarming percentage of cases, romantic rejection can catalyze preexisting tendencies toward aggressive behavior. A vivid fictional example of this is found in the popular 1987 film *Fatal Attraction*. For a one-down who feels completely stripped of power by a rejection, hurting the one-up may seem to accomplish two goals: to revive a sense of personal power and to correct the sharp imbalance between the partners. As such, retaliations are closely connected with the dynamics of the passion trap. The more aggressive and hostile the one-down tends to be in other areas of his life, the more extreme the retaliation.

Nasty Rumors

This very common form of retaliation has one-downs spreading rumors and damaging half-truths about the one-up and the relationship. A classic male retaliation is the claim that an ex-partner was "frigid" or was a "tramp." Soiling her reputation buttresses his ego by implying that she wasn't worth having in the first place and subtly hinting that *he* actually did the rejecting.

Women one-downs may accomplish the same ends by dropping hints that a rejecting partner had sexual performance problems or lacked emotional substance. Men and women who retaliate in these ways hope to humiliate the one-up, as they've been humiliated, and to diminish the one-up's appeal in the romantic marketplace.

Job Sabotage

The workplace is a major source of romantic connections, and a place where retaliations can be especially damaging. Paul guiltily revealed that he had contemplated hurting Laura in this way.

> I was on the review committee and Laura was coming up for her first year review. I'd already thought about the implications, and I'd decided I could live with saying maybe one slightly negative thing about her. The word I'd considered was *erratic*. But when Laura's

name came up, I couldn't do it. I simply withdrew. However, I think enough was known about us that it hurt her a little. She didn't get much of a raise.

As new sexual harassment laws attest, there have been far too many instances of women — and men too — who have suffered professionally when office romances went sour or a boss's advances were spurned. Satisfying love and work are considered by most psychologists to be the cornerstones of happiness, so attacking a rejecting one-up's employment can be particularly devastating.

The "I'll Make Your Life Miserable" Retaliation

Some one-downs harass their former partners with uninvited visits at all hours of the day and night and turn the telephone into an incessantly ringing instrument of torture. Sometimes these nuisance one-downs will engage in acts of vandalism on the one-up's car or home. These one-downs won't easily let go, even though they realize they are all but killing any chance for reconciliation with the one-up.

Using the Children

One of the most psychologically destructive retaliations involves a couple's children. Fortunately, the majority of married couples I've worked with have been relatively successful in keeping their children insulated from their marital problems. But some couples turn their helpless children into pawns in a vindictive chess match. The most common move is for the abandoned spouse to "poison" the children against the rejecting spouse. Underlying this strategy is the desire to deprive the one-up partner of his children's love, so that he'll have a taste of "how it feels." The not uncommon felony of parental child-stealing is an extreme form of using children as instruments of retaliation.

The Suicide Retaliation

About a month after her breakfast with Jonathan, Deborah had never felt so desperate or so low.

I hadn't heard from Jonathan in weeks, and I knew calling him would be fruitless and humiliating. *Everything* seemed to be coming down on me. I'd sent slides of my paintings to several galleries and they were all coming back with form rejections. I started a new paint-ing, and I was completely blocked. I had to ask my mother for money to help cover my shopping binge, and we had a fight. When I hung up the phone, I was feeling very unloved, very untalented, and very useless. I drank some wine and cried, really sobbed, about the futility of my life. Suddenly, I was in the bathroom, pouring pills into my hand. At the time, I had this picture in my mind of Jonathan hearing the news and completely falling apart and everyone think-ing he was responsible.

Deborah was lucky. Her best friend called as she was swallowing the third pill.

I couldn't even talk, just sob. Kelly told me not to do a thing or she'd call the police, then rushed over and made me throw up the pills. She gave me a pretty therapeutic tongue-lashing. It helped to hear her say she'd thought from the beginning that Jonathan was a loser, barely worth an affair let alone dying over. She also insisted I enter therapy, which is why I'm here.

One-downs who attempt suicide have come to an intuitive under-standing of the passion trap. They know there's an insidious connec-tion between their desperate, clinging love for the one-up and the one-up's withdrawal. When depression-prone one-downs feel power-less to turn off their passion for the one-up, suicide may seem a bril-liant solution. They suddenly feel quite calm and powerful. With one stroke, suicide will solve all their problems: stop the unbearable pain, free them from emotional bondage, and force the one-up to pay for all the pain he's caused with the worst kind of guilt possible, that of caus-ing another's death.

Although rejected lovers often entertain passing thoughts of sui-cide, most retain the awareness that their anguish will pass with time. Deborah told me later that she felt she would have been too cowardly to take her plan all the way. But she was glad Kelly's call came when it did and she'd never had the opportunity to find out.

The Ultimate Retaliation

It's not uncommon, and sometimes it's even therapeutic, for lovesick one-downs to fantasize horrible fates for their rejecting partners. What's alarming, however, is the number of rejected spouses and lov-ers who murder their estranged partners. According to statistics from the FBI, about 30 percent of all women who are murdered die at the hand of a spurned partner. And although the figure for men—6 percent—is a good deal less, keep in mind that only a small fraction of all murders are committed by women.

Of course, murder is always symptomatic of larger psychological problems resulting in a gross inability to handle rage, frustration, and feelings of powerlessness. When the one-down kills his partner, he is using the only means he has left to control her. In effect, he is saying, "If I can't have her, nobody else will."

While feelings of anger are normal, violent retaliatory actions are never excusable or justifiable. In a later chapter I'll explore healthy outlets for one-down anger.

Hitting Bottom

Like an alcoholic or drug abuser, many passion-addicted one-downs hit rock bottom. Bill's drunken attack and Deborah's suicide attempt were both examples of one-downs reaching dramatic and decisive low points. For both, the experience spurred them toward renaissance. Paul bottomed out in a less dramatic though no less decisive way shortly after the fiasco at his firm's picnic.

> I was at my favorite coffee shop eating biscuits and gravy and drafting yet another letter to Laura, when I happened to look up and see my reflection in the mirror. My face looked puffy and doughy, and I had a dribble of gravy on my chin. I was disgusted. Here I was, thirty-five, fatter than ever, poorer, and my hairline was still receding. And what did I have to show for it? The knowledge that I am capable of acting like a complete jerk over a long period of time.

Paul signed up at a gym that day and resolved to turn Laura into history. That evening, he called Daphne and asked her to dinner and the symphony for the following weekend.

Hitting rock bottom jolts a one-down out of behaving like a one-down. At that point, there is usually only one way for him to go, and that's up.

Of course, many one-downs don't have decisive turning points, but instead experience a gradual—often *very* gradual—easing of pain and shifting of focus away from the one-up. Triumph comes with the first day the one-up doesn't cross the one-down's mind.

Renaissance:
Becoming Whole Again

The first stage of separation is defined by the one-down's narrow focus on the one-up and on the pain she's feeling. Her emotions are still hugely invested in the one-up.

The second stage begins when the one-down's emotional energy starts pulling more strongly toward making a new life than toward winning back the one-up or simply managing the pain of rejection. It is this gradual process of learning to let the one-up go that marks the one-down's struggle for emotional independence. Often the fastest-acting medicine, though not necessarily the best one, is finding a new partner.

When the One-Down
Has an Affair

Newly separated one-downs, or one-downs hooked into one-way relationships, seek affairs for the same reason: to revive their wilted egos. For one-ups, the Affair Solution carries a very different motivation: to re-experience passion and excitement. But one-ups and one-downs share one motivation: the desire, sometimes unconscious, to connect with someone who'll better fit their needs.

Even though a one-down intellectually knows that a new partner could make her happier, she may have a hard time overcoming a natural distaste for anyone but the one-up. Beth had to deal with this reaction when Kevin, the internist she'd been seeing when she met Miles, heard about her separation and asked her out.

> I was a little surprised when Kevin called. It reminded me of old letters to Dear Abby about the vultures swooping in on new divorcees, though I wasn't quite to that point. I'd thought that Kevin and I had had a pretty casual relationship, but apparently he was pretty upset when I broke off with him for Miles. He's always acted a little too important for my tastes. But I knew Miles felt threatened by him, and I think I accepted his invitation mostly because of that—and just because it was nice to be asked. The first date, I could barely bring myself to kiss him goodnight. But the second date, I let myself be seduced. It was hard to relate to Kevin's enthusiasm. Afterward, he said, "You're still a very married lady."

To Beth, Kevin was no match for Miles, but his sudden reappearance offered to satisfy two of Beth's overriding needs: to feel desirable again, and to hurt Miles in a retaliatory way. The one-down hopes the new liaison will derail her one-track thinking about the one-up, but often it won't.

Ironically, a one-down may also grapple with feelings of disloyalty and fear when she embarks on an affair; typically, she'll feel very depressed after the first encounter, as Beth did.

> I know it sounds crazy considering what Miles has done to me, but I couldn't help feeling disloyal to him when I slept with Kevin. Also, I was afraid that if Miles found out, there'd be no chance of us getting back together.

Beth maintained an emotional distance from Kevin. ("I wasn't to the point where I wanted to subject Chloe to pseudo-daddies 'the morning after.'") But after Paul hit rock bottom, his motives for seeing Daphne a second time were very different.

> When I took Daphne to the firm picnic, it was a ploy. But even then I admired the way she handled herself. She understood what was going on, and getting her to see me again did take some explaining and persuasion. But when she said she'd see me again, I felt like a new day was dawning. I had no interest in any more of this emotional roller-coaster business. The appeal of Daphne was that she was fully formed as a person, not still finding herself like Laura. But maybe not as interesting, either.

Although Paul conceded that Laura still had a hold on him, he was determined to break free of his passionate addiction to her. His symphony date with Daphne was balm for his ego.

> The thing that made me happiest was the way she held my arm when we left the symphony hall. It was so natural and uncomplicated and accepting. It made me feel strong again, not like some groveling fool. Daphne was open about not wanting to jump into anything with someone on the rebound, and I respected that. We saw each other several more times, and when we finally made love, Laura didn't cross my mind for a good four-hour stretch.

Paul was in the joyous process of reinvesting his emotions in a new lover. By doing so, he was unknowingly creating the opportunity for a sea change in his relations with Laura.

The Emotional Boomerang

After he started seeing Daphne, Paul avoided Laura at work. But he did hear on the grapevine that Nick had dumped her after they lost their fraud case. So, her visit soon thereafter to Paul's office surprised but did not shock him.

> She was trying to sound chipper, but she really seemed anxious. She asked if she could still consider me a friend, because she needed one now. Someone who really knew her. It seemed she'd fallen very quickly for Nick, but "things just didn't work out." She also said she felt like a jerk for taking me for granted. Then she asked if I wanted to have dinner. I told her I was seeing Daphne, but lunch the next day would be good. She seemed a little taken aback.

Paul felt confused, but not unpleasantly so. He knew Daphne wouldn't be pleased to hear that he was having lunch with Laura, but he really was concerned about Laura's well-being. She seemed genuinely in pain, and that drew sympathy from him. Besides, it would only be a friendly meal, nothing to be secretive about. Still, he thought he'd best not tell Daphne, to avoid needlessly upsetting her.

When the One-Down
Gains Power

What was so baffling to Paul makes perfect sense in light of the passion trap. After a rough start, Paul had fared well during the separation from Laura. He had resolved to put Laura behind him and he'd begun a new relationship that appeared to rest on firmer, if less passionate, ground. He felt in control again, and he was functioning well in all areas of his life.

Laura, meanwhile, had not fared so well. She had sought a more exciting relationship and found one, only the excitement stemmed from her being in the one-down position with Nick—the first man "since high school" to leave her. She'd also suffered a large professional defeat. Emotionally bruised and stripped of self-esteem, Laura limped back to Paul, hoping for comfort from someone she assumed would still be hers. But when she learned of Paul's new relationship with Daphne, the picture changed. Suddenly, Paul presented a challenge as he had before; he seemed romantically interesting again. The only difference Laura didn't take into account was that she was no longer operating on the same level of attraction power as before. In fact, their power positions had undergone an almost complete reversal.

Paul said of his changed perceptions of Laura:

> Laura was mortal! At our lunch, she really seemed like a friend and nothing more, someone who'd gone through a rough time and needed a shoulder to cry on. I tried to imagine having my old feelings for her, but all I could see was her self-centeredness and the mole near her lip. It was amazing to be looking at her through clear, not rose-tinted, glasses. And it was very strange when she seemed to start flirting.

Paul hardly knew what to do with the unfamiliar and undeniably enjoyable sense of control he now felt in Laura's presence. Augmenting this feeling of power was Laura's transparent neediness. At the end of the lunch, Laura told Paul that she thought Daphne "wasn't good enough" for him.

The One-Up's Narcissistic Wound

The discovery of a one-down's affair often triggers a sharp reversal of the partners' power positions. Miles described his reaction when he first learned of Beth's affair with Kevin.

> I went totally loco. I'd really started missing Beth and one night I got it in my head to go see her. So I drove over to the house, rang the bell, and the sitter answered the door. She was surprised to see me and said Beth was out. I told her to leave, I'd stay with Chloe, and the girl got really nervous. So it dawned on me that Beth was with a guy! It was like being stabbed. I drove around for about an hour, picked up a bottle of vodka, then parked a couple of houses down from our place. About twenty minutes later, a Jaguar pulled up. Beth got out and I could see she was with her old boyfriend Kevin. I couldn't believe it! I went back to my place and put my fist through the wall.

Miles was suffering from a narcissistic wound, an ego blow capable of causing animalistic rage even in the most reasonable of people.

Miles had taken for granted that Beth, despite her anger, would take him back with the proper persuasion. Things had been going downhill with Monica—it turned out she had a problem with methamphetamine—and he found himself yearning for "the warm cocoon" of his home and family. Although he knew Beth had always claimed not to be impressed with Kevin, Miles didn't believe it, especially now.

The next day, Miles tried to look on the "bright" side. With Beth romantically involved with Kevin, he, Miles, no longer had to feel guilt about leaving, or about really playing the field. But now his wish for freedom and excitement seemed empty, bankrupt. Beth had slipped from his control, and the paradox of passion had imbued her with the appeal of the challenging prospect. He wanted *her*.

The One-Up Panics

Naively and a bit arrogantly, Laura perceived Daphne as a negligible threat. But she had been more than a little surprised by Paul's new reserve toward her. Especially when she thought about the last conversation she had had with him when she admitted she'd begun a relationship with Nick. Paul had sworn that if she ever changed her mind, he would be there for her, because for him love was forever.

> After Nick dumped me, and that's just the word for it, I felt like a complete idiot. Here I had this great guy, Paul, and I didn't count my blessings. It was the old story of the grass is always greener. But I feel like I've grown up a lot now, and I know what I want and need. And that is Paul. At our lunch he said he felt he couldn't trust me . . . which hurt. But I can't blame him. Now I want to prove that I've changed, show him that we're really right for each other, and that Daphne is someone he's with to be safe. I'm really thinking marriage now. In fact, I think it was my fear of commitment that drove me into the fling with Nick; unconsciously, I was still in love with Paul. There are so few decent men out there, and the idea that I really may have lost Paul is just appalling to me. I'm going to fight for him.

Laura had become the needy one. Now she, after engineering the separation, had demonstrated her seriousness of intent by suggesting they enter couples' therapy. It was an overt challenge to Paul's integrity, because *he* had pushed strenuously for couples' therapy when Laura became involved with Nick.

Learning about Beth and Kevin made Miles feel angry and betrayed. Then another emotion took him by surprise.

> Deep love. We'd slept together once after I left, and I was surprised by how good it felt. Now I was feeling real, passionate love. I'd arranged to see Beth a couple of days after the Kevin thing, not letting on that I knew, and she was looking great. She'd gone back to work part-time, so she was wearing good clothes and makeup. But she acted a little formal, so I didn't feel comfortable about revealing my feelings. In fact, my palms were sweating.

Like Laura, Miles was having a close encounter with "one-down dread," the fear that you've lost a partner through a wrong move or inadequacy. He was feeling constricted in his behavior, just like a one-down, and he was tasting one-up distance in the form of Beth's aloofness. What he didn't know was whether Beth was acting cold to punish him before accepting him back, or if she had really lost her loving feelings for him.

Reverse Hypercourtship: The Former One-Up Tries Harder

Shortly after their "reunion" lunch, Laura issued another invitation to Paul.

> She said she appreciated my reservations about trusting her again, and she respected the fact that I was seeing someone else. But she said I was too important to her to let go of without giving it her all. She invited me to dinner at her house. I went against my better judgment and said yes. She'd had a couple of pretty good setbacks, and I didn't want to hurt her more. She had prepared a dinner almost identical to the one we had the first night I went over there. She looked very beautiful and had on some heavy perfume. The magic of the first time wasn't there for me, but Laura is hard to resist. We wound up making love.

By attempting to replicate the atmosphere of their first sexual encounter, Laura was engaging in pure hypercourtship behavior. According to Paul, she acknowledged the irony of the situation by joking about the meal, saying it was the only fancy dinner she knew how to cook. But she didn't see how similar her behavior was to Paul's when he had first sensed *her* emotional withdrawal. In her mind, she wasn't trying to reverse a rejection; rather, she was humbly admitting her error of judgment in letting Paul go and trying to demonstrate her sincerity and trustworthiness. She thought she only needed to do these two things to win Paul back. But she was operating in ignorance of the passion trap.

Before Miles began to "hypercourt" Beth, he set the stage. He wanted to convince her that it wasn't the true Miles who had behaved so badly before the split-up. Uncontrollable pressures and circumstances were the real culprits. Beth recalled a letter she'd gotten from Miles shortly after he learned about her and Kevin.

> It was almost cute. Miles wrote that keeping such late hours had made him irritable all the time. That, and the pressure from his partners, of course. He also said he was having a hard time reconciling his "two identities," the "partying beast of the night," and "family man." He said for a while there he felt he'd made a mistake in settling down, but now he knew that was the rightest thing he'd ever done.

Then, Beth reported, came the flowers, the silly-cute gifts, and finally a ticket for Hawaii scribbled with the suggestion that they "start working on baby #2" there. Miles was giving this new courtship of Beth his all.

The Ambivalence of the Resurrected One-Down

When a former one-down takes command of a relationship, she inherits the ambivalence of the one-up position. With clear eyes, seeing her partner now as a mere "mortal," she may wonder if she *ever* felt real love for him. Maybe it was just a dependency trap from the beginning. Having tasted and enjoyed freedom, pleasure, and, now, power, she questions whether she really wants to return to her partner. It seems like a step backward.

Her newly negative feelings about the relationship are deepened by previously buried hostility. Now that she controls the relationship, she can express anger free of her old fear of alienating the former one-up. Her wounded pride argues in favor of rejecting him, just to teach him a lesson. The former one-down may also fear that reviving the relationship could lead to her slipping back into the one-down position. Beth harbored this fear.

> I was very tempted to go to Hawaii with Miles, but I was scared too. He was essentially telling me the same things he said before we got married, all that stuff about how important family values really are to him. But what was to stop us from falling back into the same trap? Would he turn into the same monster every time things got rough at the restaurant? I wanted very much to have another baby, but I was really worried it would lead to the same problems.

Beth's fears were quite justified. Many reunited couples do return to the same old toxic patterns of relating. A reunion can, however, be an ideal time for both partners to gain insight into the forces at work between them and for developing more effective strategies for dealing with them. I urge couples who do reunite to enjoy the happiness of their second honeymoon. But I also encourage them not to shrink from the hard work of improving the foundation of their relationship while it's on more equal footing. Strengthened partnerships are better at fending off inevitable visits from the passion trap.

How to Create an Equal Love That Lasts

Chapter 7

Letting Go of Old
Solutions

Now that you know the emotional dynamics that cause love and intimacy to break down in relationships, let's examine some ways to revive them. In the following chapters I'll take you on the same therapeutic journey as I take my clients. Along the way, we'll question some basic assumptions about how best to "save" problem relationships.

Adventures in
Couples' Therapy

I began my work on the passion trap because I was dissatisfied with traditional couples' therapy. Like many quests, mine was inspired by personal experience.

During my graduate training, I had two long-term relationships. I hadn't yet formulated my theories about unbalanced relationships, but in retrospect it's clear to me that in one relationship I was the one-down and in the other the one-up. Not surprisingly, when love turned into pain, we turned to couples' therapy. In both cases, the relationships eventually ended. What later amazed me were the sharp differences between being a one-up and a one-down in traditional couples' therapy.

As the one-down, I loved it. The therapist was working hard to "save" our relationship, a goal that meshed perfectly with my strongest wishes. But my one-up partner soon became as disenchanted with therapy as she was with our relationship (which baffled me at the time, because I'd been so loving to her).

Then I experienced couples' therapy as a one-up. What a difference! I was enthusiastic during the first several sessions as the therapist probed our problems and showed empathy. But in the middle stage, when she initiated interventions to save the relationship, something changed for me. I began to feel subtle but insistent pressure from the therapist to be more loving and intimate with my partner. It was precisely the same pressure I'd been feeling from my partner. Paradoxically, the more pressure I felt to be loving, the more I emotionally withdrew — from my partner *and* therapy.

It wasn't long before I was practicing couples' therapy myself. And I saw a similar pattern in most of my clients: early breakthroughs followed by resistance from the less involved partner.

I gained insight into the failure of my own experience in therapy, and my theory began to crystallize.

Old Solutions:
A Bias Against the One-Up

Consider a popular exercise prescribed by many marriage counselors — what I call the Bubble Bath and Champagne Solution — in which the couple is asked to spend more "romantic time" together. The one-down couldn't be more delighted. At last he'll get the closeness he so wants and needs. His hopes soar. This romantic time is supposed to bring out all the latent love his partner is afraid to express.

Meanwhile, the one-up is game at best, more likely skeptical or resistant. I've found that most one-ups feel exercises like this are forced and artificial, although they sincerely hope they'll make a difference and end ambivalence. Typically, however, they merely go through the motions — acting close, but feeling phony, hypocritical, and coerced. This is not therapeutic.

I believe these unilateral "closeness exercises" usually backfire because they send three unspoken but harmful messages to couples. They imply:

1. That the main problem in the relationship is the distant partner's resistance to intimacy
2. That this problem can be fixed only if the distant partner changes her feelings and makes herself open to love
3. That the needy partner is the "good guy" in the relationship because he's pro-love; therefore, he should get what he

wants—closeness—without having to do any emotional work himself.

Even when they are communicated subtly, these messages make the one-up feel bad about herself, frustrated, excluded, and resentful that she's not understood. Naturally, this sabotages even sincere one-up attempts to recover love for her partner.

Closeness exercises also demand that the one-up do the hardest emotional work. She's the one who's afraid or blocked or hostile, the one who has to "fix" herself. She's the one who's hearing from both therapist and one-down that she *should* be feeling love, which of course makes it harder for her to feel love. Traditional couples' therapy can wind up making a one-up feel more burdened and trapped than she did in the first place.

I learned a vital lesson from my personal experiences and my clinical work: *The distant partner is as much a victim of harmful relationship dynamics as her partner; therapeutic pressure to make her feel closer is an invalidation of her suffering.*

My approach isn't biased *for* one-ups, either. However, the fact is that the one-up is the partner most likely to leave. In my practice, I've found that one-ups feel tremendously unburdened when I define the couple's problems *neutrally* in terms of harmful relationship dynamics. And one-ups *stay* engaged when I prescribe different sets of exercises for the partners; I ask *both* to do hard emotional work. I design these exercises to acknowledge and respect both partners' pain. When a one-up is understood rather than condemned for feeling distant, she feels better about herself—and the relationship too. This is when we can reasonably begin to hope for the rebirth of love.

Old Solutions: Fatalistic Pathologizing

I like to deal mainly in the present with what I call the "core problems" of a relationship—the dynamics that create imbalance. I focus less on the background—including issues from childhood that might have a bearing on the present. For me, treating foreground dynamics has simply proved more effective, except in extreme cases.

Of course, I'd risk my good standing in the American Psychological Association if I claimed that childhood experiences don't deeply color adult relationships. Yet, I believe the therapeutic benefits of analyzing childhood problems are inflated by many traditional therapists and self-help books. Searching for solutions in the past can divert our energies from solving problems in the present. Worse, placing so much blame on the past may instill a sense of hopelessness in both partners. I call this approach *fatalistic pathologizing*.

Fatalistic pathologizing goes something like this: If you have relationship problems, you grew up in a dysfunctional family with dysfunctional parents who gave you a warped model of the way "loving" relationships are supposed to be. You are destined for the rest of your life to find partners who will make you miserable just like your parents did. If you're finally able to break free from one of these partners—sorry—you're just going to run straight into the arms of another one. Your new partner may look like the opposite of the old one, but after a while you'll realize he was hiding behind a clever disguise. (That was your mistake, going for the opposite.)

Sound familiar?

In *Heartburn*, Nora Ephron gives a good example of a therapist who practices fatalistic pathologizing. The book's heroine, Rachel, is told by her therapist, Vera, why she got involved with a husband who was bound to fail her.

> "You picked him," Vera said, "because his neuroses meshed perfectly with yours." I love Vera, truly I do, but doesn't anything happen to you that you don't intend? "You picked him because you knew it wouldn't work out." "You picked him because his neuroses meshed perfectly with yours." "You picked him because you knew he'd deprive you the way your mother or your father did." That's what they're always telling you, one way or another, but the truth is that no matter whom you pick, your neuroses mesh perfectly and horribly; the truth is that no matter whom you pick, he deprives you the way your mother or your father did. "You picked the one person on earth you shouldn't be involved with." There's nothing brilliant about that—that's life. Every time you turn around you get involved with the one person on earth you shouldn't get involved with ... Let's face it: *everyone* is the one person on earth you shouldn't get involved with.

While amusing us, Ephron's passage shows pointedly how overemphasizing childhood experiences can breed pessimism about love. And this focus often diverts us from the normal, predictable problems of love that can be understood and surmounted.

This isn't to say I automatically exclude childhood experiences from couples' therapy. Some couples' problems are clearly caused by defective patterns of relating. Most of these patterns are formed in childhood, and they can predispose a person to be chronically one-up or one-down. When this is the case, we delve into childhood influences to learn how best to improve the client's interactions with his partner and everyone else in his life. I'll discuss this in more detail in later chapters.

Part 2 of this book mirrors my therapeutic approach. The early chapters are devoted to changing present relationship dynamics; the later ones show how specific personality styles may spawn those dynamics and how to balance them.

Women Good, Men Bad?

In another form of fatalistic pathologizing, men tend to get lumped together as unfeeling, hurtful bad guys and women as sensitive, victimized good guys. This is what Beth was doing when I asked her to define what she felt was Miles's greatest problem.

> I think Miles has turned out to be a typical male, and somehow I duped myself into thinking he was different. I've seen it so many times before. A guy acts like he really cares about the same things you do. Then, it turns out what really matters is his own success in the eyes of others, and being able to do what he wants. It really seems to be true; men are incapable of true intimacy.

I then asked her if she'd ever felt distant in a long-term relationship.

> Well, let me see. Not really. Sort of. I was seeing a couple of guys when I met Miles. I think Kevin was fairly serious. We'd been going out almost a year. I never encouraged discussion of a more committed relationship than what we had. And after I met Miles, I was pretty up-front with him about what was happening.

I asked her if she saw a parallel between her behavior and Miles's. After protesting that the "situation was all different," she did allow that women, like men, can "avoid intimacy."

Undeniably, gender stereotyping does bias men to be one-ups and women to be one-downs. We still expect ambition and control in a man, and nurturing and warmth in a woman; in subtle ways we still transmit these expectations to our children. And there are still gaps between the power men and women wield in the workplace and the duties they assume in the home. (The situational and personality imbalances fostered by sex-role expectations are significant, and I'll discuss them in detail later.)

But there are several reasons why the current trend toward "male bashing" is therapeutically dangerous:

Women who do it may view themselves as innocent victims who needn't examine their own roles in unbalanced relationships.

It fuels passion trap dynamics by polarizing the sexes.

It diverts the woman from the most effective means of changing a one-down pattern in her life: assertively facing and exploring passion trap dynamics with her partner.

It promotes self-pathologizing in women. A recent study at Yale University found that 36 percent of women in its sample were the "less involved partner" — i.e., the one-up. (Men were the "less involved" partner in 45 percent of the couples.) Women may be more likely to be one-down, but they often have more power in a relationship than they think. If they readily label men "commitmentphobes," they'll also be more likely to pathologize themselves when they find themselves the one-up in a relationship.

I explained to Beth how important it is to understand how gender stereotypes can penetrate our attitudes toward relationships. But I cautioned her that writing Miles off as a "typical male" was fatalistic and counterproductive. Such an attitude handicaps a woman's ability to gain or regain equality in a relationship because it's equivalent to a surrender of power.

A Hidden Message in the Paradox of Passion: New Hope

When I first began formulating my ideas about unbalanced relationships, I was feeling pessimistic about ever finding lasting love in my personal life. Friends, clients, even myself, were struggling to keep our relationships afloat. And it seemed to me I was uncovering a dynamic that proved why love was doomed to fail.

Initially, I kept my ideas about the passion trap away from my clients. But I did discuss these ideas with friends and colleagues. To my surprise, rather than deepen our depression, my insights about the paradox of passion made us feel better.

The Power of Insight

Jason, a 35-year-old lawyer who's been married to Jane for six years, is one of my best friends. Shortly before I asked him to read an early draft of this book, Jane had received her M.B.A. and landed a prestigious job at a large corporation. I was riveted by his comments after the reading.

> When Jane got her job, I suddenly realized she'd be working around a lot of dynamic executive types, and that made me very anxious. In retrospect, I was feeling the "relationship forces" pulling me to do one-down things in a very tangible way. Like I was calling her at work a lot and trying to get her not to do dinner meetings. I was driving her nuts. We bickered constantly and she wasn't communicating with me the way she always had. I started thinking, well, hell, if she's going to be out cavorting with all those men, I'll strike first and have an affair myself.

> It was at this point you gave me the manuscript. And I couldn't believe what I was reading. I was able to tell myself, okay, just relax, I'm having a predictable reaction to a power shift in our relationship. Don't make it worse by trying to suffocate Jane or punish her by doing something stupid like have an affair. And just saying that allowed me to snap out of that way of acting and give Jane the support and freedom she obviously needed at that time. And what was truly amazing, and I guess predictable, was that when I did that she started acting more loving.

Responses like Jason's helped me grasp the therapeutic potential of the paradox of passion. I realized that my insights allowed partners to manage problems in their relationships that before had overwhelmed them. Suddenly, people who had been controlled like puppets by divisive relationship forces could say, "Okay, I'm having this very predictable reaction to my partner, and it's only making the problems worse. So now let's work on countering that reaction."

My friends and I then discovered that even when armed with knowledge about the passion trap, we could still fall prey to its potent dynamics. But now we could catch ourselves as we were falling. We could spot and objectify the dynamics in ourselves (and even more easily in others; it became a kind of sport for us). Most important, these insights pointed us firmly in the direction of helpful counteraction. In Jason's case, he knew he had to pull back, tolerate his anxiety, and give Jane the support and trust she needed.

Believing in Magic

It's one thing to restore balance and harmony between partners. But can the "magic" be recovered after it seems dead and gone? The paradox of passion suggests that it can.

Romantic love isn't exclusively tied to the novelty of new love. Nor is it an absolute emotion: It's not something you either feel or don't feel for a person. *Love is a relative emotion that can disappear and reappear depending on the relationship dynamics operating between the two partners.*

Both Laura and Miles, for example, found themselves romantically yearning for partners they'd thought they had fallen completely out of love with. Many one-ups—perhaps you yourself—have left relationships only to find themselves longing for the partner they left. (The movie *The Story of Us* gives an accurate example of this emotional phenomenon.) The potential for romantic love had been there all along, but it was buried under harmful dynamics.

Unfortunately, people who don't understand the passion trap may act out destructively, *then* recover romantic feelings for a partner. Miles practiced a destructive one-up behavior—his affair—then felt a resurgence of love for the newly independent Beth. But the affair diminished their chances of reconciling because it damaged the trust between them.

Experience has shown me that when you alter unhealthy, unbalancing dynamics between two people, something remarkable can happen. The one-down becomes more autonomous and attractive to the one-up, and the one-up recovers what turned out to be dormant, not dead, romantic feelings. And while it's true that the heart-racing passion of new love can't be sustained, the feelings shared by newly balanced partners are exciting and fresh in their own way.

My program isn't about "ten ways to increase passion in your relationship." Rather, it's about changing ways of relating and creating the possibility that romance will bloom again.

Can (and Should) All Troubled Relationships Be Saved?

Of course not. And it would be a mistake to believe we have failed if we can't save a relationship. Nature has ensured our survival by making sexual attraction both compelling *and* blinding. Spurred by primal forces, we can easily find ourselves involved with people who satisfy our short-term desires but not our long-term needs.

Even if you and your partner were well matched when you first met, you may have changed in different ways. Sometimes one partner has grown far beyond the other, and that can be a highly unbalanced and painful situation. It's somewhat less painful when both partners have grown equally but in different directions. I see the "growing apart" syndrome most often among couples who married very young, and this is why I favor later marriages. (In chapters 15 and 16, I'll discuss some of the key characteristics of relationships that make it and of those that don't.)

I believe that almost all relationships are worth working on. The goal of this book is *not* to save your relationship per se, but to help you find fulfillment in love. That's a subtle but important distinction.

My view is that you should first try as hard as you can to alleviate the harmful dynamics and revive the love in your relationship. If you're successful, congratulate yourself. But if the relationship is systemically unbalanced and can't be fixed to your and your partner's satisfaction, that *does not mean you have failed.* In fact, it means you've succeeded in freeing yourself and your partner from an unfulfilling relationship.

Expect to learn a lot about yourself and your needs as you do relationship work. If the relationship doesn't work out, you'll better understand the kind of partner you should seek (or avoid) in the future. When people are uneducated about relationships, they court emotional burn-out by jumping from one partner to another, never learning from their mistakes.

Some relationships cross a line of violence and abusiveness that make them poor candidates for rescuing. If you're in such a relationship, **please seek professional help as soon as you can.** If you feel threatened, or capable of causing injury, physically separate yourself from your situation. There are numerous helping agencies listed under "Social Services" in the Yellow Pages.

Planning Your Love Career

Experts on human behavior, from Freud to Dear Abby, agree that the psychologically healthy individual is the one who finds happiness in both work and love. When people seek therapy, it's almost always because they feel dissatisfied with their jobs and/or intimate relationships.

However, there is a distinct and curious imbalance between the ways people approach work and love. Consider the years of dedicated effort we devote to developing our careers. We go to college and graduate school, we get counseled and tested, we train and apprentice, and then we continue to hone and broaden our skills with hopes of advancement.

Now consider the way we approach the *other* part of life. We spend almost no time seeking the knowledge and skills necessary to build strong relationships. Instead, we "learn on the job," pursuing romance, getting involved, getting hurt, pulling back, retaliating, finding new loves, hurting new partners, and so on.

My point is to urge you to approach your relationship education as you would any new and complex skill. The noted therapist Jay Haley advises tackling love problems as a relationship researcher. As you work with the following strategies, some will prove fruitful, and some less so, as in any research program. There's no such thing as failure in this approach because you'll always be learning what does and doesn't work. Yet, your goals will remain clear: to fathom relationship dynamics and use them to create strong and lasting love with another person.

Chapter 8

Communicating

How to Talk Balance Back into Your Relationship

One of the first things Peg told me was that she didn't know how to talk to Bill anymore. If she told him about her day at the shop, it only made him feel more inadequate. Anything she said about the shape he was in—his drinking or the inertia in his life—caused a burst of defensive anger, a slamming door, and his disappearance for hours. Soon, she gave up. "I figured that if he wanted to talk, he could come to me," she said. In her heart, she knew he wouldn't, and she was almost grateful for that.

As a relationship falls apart, so does the partners' ability to communicate effectively. A wall of silence may grow between them, as it did for Peg and Bill. Or a couple may engage in plenty of communication, but of the wrong kind: shouting at each other, whining, accusing, or criticizing.

It's a cliché, but like most clichés it's true: The key to a good relationship is good communication. By believing in the healing powers of communication, I stand on the same ground as the vast majority of therapists. Where I differ from many is in what's communicated, and how.

What Imbalance Does to Communication

Relationships afflicted by the passion trap share one core problem: One partner needs the relationship more and more, while the other needs it less and less. But that doesn't mean all unbalanced couples share the same defective ways of communicating. In my practice, most problem communicators fall into three categories. If you're currently having communication problems with your partner (and everyone does at times), it's vital that you discover which category is yours.

The Wall of Silence

Imbalance silenced Peg and Bill. Peg was deeply ashamed of the unloving feelings she'd come to harbor toward Bill. The better part of her emotional energy was being spent on concealing these feelings, both from herself and from Bill. That left her with little that she really wanted to communicate to her troubled husband.

Bill's silence was more complex. To him, as to many one-downs, silence was a way to hide the depth of his need and pain. Men especially are prone to suffer in silence rather than admit their vulnerabilities (to themselves as well as others). To them, showing "weakness" is far worse than lonely suffering. But silence was a false source of strength for Bill.

Some one-downs get silent as an instinctive attempt to use passion trap dynamics. By *acting* distant, they hope to draw the one-up closer, just as the one-up's distance hooks them in.

Other one-downs censor themselves because of fear of rejection. They don't want to rock the boat or risk antagonizing the one-up. Many partners—and this can include one-ups like Peg—hate conflict and confrontation, subscribing to a "peace at any price" attitude.

Silence can also be used as punishment. Resentful one-downs may withhold communication as a retaliation, and with it any expressions of concern and tenderness. One-downs know how punishing it is to feel unloved, so they adopt a kind of pseudo-one-up stance, including distant, uncommunicative behavior.

The "wall of silence," then, is typical of a certain type of imbalance. The one-up is highly ambivalent and guilt-ridden about her negative feelings for the one-down. The one-down, like Bill, tends to a resentful, punishing withdrawal. Peg said what I'd heard on many occasions from partners such as these: "I felt helpless. I had no idea how to handle the situation without making it worse."

Noncommunicating couples are prone to occasional but frighteningly intense blowups. Often they fall prey to extreme but indirect forms of acting out their unhappiness, such as alcoholism, workaholism, and infidelity.

The Bad Communicators

Imbalance turned Beth and Miles into bad communicators. Beth recalled:

> We never stopped talking. But our talk was more like sniping at each other all the time. I'd be complaining and he'd be counterattacking. Or he'd be complaining and I'd be defending. And every couple of days, the snipes would turn into brawls. Then we'd cool out for a while until the pattern got going again.

Not all one-downs are shrinking violets. Beth, for example, habitually spoke her mind. But as a one-down, she often didn't like what she was hearing from herself.

> I think there were two things going on. First, my pride was wounded when Miles started pulling away. I didn't feel at all appreciated by him. That made me react by being a little . . . combative. Maybe I was compensating for feeling so powerless. And then, second, I wanted to hurt Miles. He could hurt me so easily, but *he* seemed invulnerable. I could get him angry, but I couldn't seem to hurt him. I guess that's wanting revenge . . .

Miles too felt plenty of frustration and anger. And, like Beth, he was bright and verbal. His problem wasn't one of keeping his anger bottled up.

> I was constantly blowing up about little things. A light left on could set me off. I felt like Beth was trying to irritate me. I'd lose control and say some pretty nasty, personal things. Basically, I was critical of who she was. I wanted her to be someone else, as if that would end the nightmare our life had become.

Miles's anger kept growing because he was dealing only with symptoms, not underlying causes. His barbs were meant to provoke Beth to change via the "Why Can't You Be More . . ." Solution. But solutions like that block good communication, fuel imbalance, and don't get the desired results.

Not surprisingly, bad communicators actively widen the imbalance between them. Her one-down resentment and demands make him feel angry and critical. His one-up anger and criticism make her feel less loved, less appreciated, and less powerful—and more inclined to express resentment and demands.

One Talks, the Other Doesn't

The third pattern has one partner growing silent while the other moves into a hyper-communicative mode. Paul found himself "communicating for two" as Laura became more involved with her big case (and with Nick) and less with him.

> Laura began to have this air of distraction. I found myself going through lists of things to talk about before seeing her. Nothing seemed to engage her. When I felt most anxious, I wanted to talk about "us," mainly to be reassured that she still loved me. But that seemed to fluster and annoy her the most. She'd turn the conversation to impersonal things like cases. Sometimes she'd get fidgety and make an excuse to leave.

Clearly, Paul was having a strong hypercourtship response to Laura's growing emotional distance. His attempts to instigate "open" communication carried the subtle demand that Laura be more responsive and loving. True to passion trap dynamics, Laura sensed the pressure, pulled further away, and felt guiltier for thwarting Paul's attempts to communicate.

Usually, however, it's the woman in these couples who verbalizes while the man withholds. Another couple in therapy with me fell into this pattern. Ron, a foreign-car mechanic, was emotionally aloof and communicated mainly with ironic one-liners. His wife, Marie, a hair stylist, was a vibrant, emotional woman—his temperamental opposite. He was the one-up who hated "scenes" and often walked out on their fights to take long drives or return to his auto shop. She was the one-down who blew up at him because he gave so little to the relationship. Adding to her anxiety was the fact that Ron was "gorgeous."

This type of pattern can be tough to break because it's rooted in sex-role conditioning and the partners' personality styles—subjects I'll be discussing in later chapters. Yet, when couples even in this much trouble begin to use new communication tools, dramatic changes can occur almost instantly.

Talking About the Passion Trap Is Hard

Talking about the passion trap is hard because you have to face the imbalance in your relationship. That means the one-up acknowledging his doubts and the one-down having to deal with it. It also means the one-down admitting her greater neediness and the one-up having to deal with that. Both partners must explore and disclose their most carefully guarded fears about their relationship.

I don't advise anyone to try such a discussion without first knowing *how* to talk about these volatile issues. Yes, it's very difficult to confront your greater vulnerability or power within a relationship. It's also necessary. But it needn't be torture. If it is, the method of communication is wrong.

People so fear revealing the "real truth" about their feelings that they get very clever about avoiding it. For most one-ups, it's a matter of kindness. They don't want to crush the one-down by saying directly they've fallen out of love. So they say something is wrong with themselves (i.e., they self-pathologize), or they blame their distraction on career concerns or other outside factors. These pseudo- or secondary issues often become the focus of relationship discussions *and* traditional couples' therapy.

One-downs have pride. Many, like Bill, will act like one-ups to avoid showing vulnerabilities. Others will join the one-up in blaming her character flaws—usually her "fear of intimacy" or commitment—for the relationship's trouble.

The partners feel protected by these avoidance techniques. While they do provide short-term ego safety, they jeopardize the relationship in the long run because core problems aren't being addressed.

If you talk about the painful truth in the right way, it will make you both feel better, not worse.

No-Fault Communication

Psychologists have discovered a way of communicating that minimizes pain, unites the couple in their effort to balance their stressed relationship, and fosters intimacy. It changes the way partners think as well as talk, and it helps them reach the underlying causes of their problems.

This method is called No-Fault Communication. Its goal is to get both partners to stop waging no-win accusation battles with each other and to shift their focus to problem relationship dynamics. It's composed of several key strategies. Using these strategies, you can actually talk balance back into your relationship. Even if only one partner uses No-Fault Communication, the benefits can be enormous.

Learning to use No-Fault Communication is a bit like learning a new language—it takes work and practice. I urge you to read these sections carefully and to perform all the exercises. Please do so even if your relationship isn't in crisis; it will help keep you on an even keel.

Strategy 1:
Rewrite Your Accusation Battles

We've all had the experience of trying to hold a civilized, calm discussion with a partner about things in the relationship that make us unhappy. Often, the discussion collapses into all-out verbal warfare, followed by icy silence. It's hard to stay calm and objective during these talks because, either overtly or subtly, they're almost always built on accusations. Soon both partners just want to defend their positions and prove the other one wrong.

In an early session, I asked Beth and Miles to discuss an episode that typified the relapse they experienced after Miles moved back home. Following is what they said, along with my notes on the accusatory, blaming messages they were hurling at each other.

Statement	*Accusatory Message*
Beth: I guess last night is a good example. You came home two hours late and didn't call. And I really think it proves my point that you care more about the restaurant and being a big shot than me and Chloe.	You're self-centered and thoughtless and you don't care about anyone but yourself.
Miles: I told you the dishwasher hose broke. What am I supposed to do? Let water squirt all over the kitchen while I run to call my wife so she won't have a fit when I get home? You know why I didn't call? Because it was so late by the time I got a chance that I knew I'd catch hell anyway.	You're possessive, bitchy, and suspicious, and you find fault with everything I do.

Statement	Accusatory Message
Beth: That's rich. I love these excuses that make you look good and me bad. But the truth is, you know how I hate the waiting game and you know that your track record is pretty weak. I just want you to act like I matter to you.	You'll stoop to anything to weasel out of the blame. I wouldn't be surprised if you had a new girlfriend.
Miles: If you'd stop acting *so* damn paranoid it'd make it a hell of a lot easier ...	You're incredibly insecure.

Note how easily and quickly this "discussion" evolved into a fight, and how very ordinary the fight seemed. The fact is that when a person feels hurt or threatened, he's far more adept at, and comfortable with, using language to injure rather than to heal. Even the most "ordinary" accusation battle is demoralizing because it looks like proof of a relationship's flaws.

Now let's learn how to "rewrite" accusation battles.

Spotting Accusations
and Other Hurtful Tactics

Our needs for self-defense and self-justification erect language barriers between us. We get into a "prosecuting" frame of mind and we don't fight fairly. We can tear down these barriers by sensitizing ourselves to the ways in which we hurt each other.

The next time you and your partner fight, sit down afterward and write it out. Try to reconstruct the fight as accurately as you can. Then put a check mark next to the statements that carried accusations — subtle or overt. Beth and Miles were shocked to see that every statement they made during their skirmish was accusatory. Most people are.

Examine your script to see if the passion trap is orchestrating your fights. You'll know this by the type of accusations you use against each other. The one-down's verbal arsenal includes labels like "selfish," "thoughtless," "insensitive," "uncaring," and "unloving," and epithets like "you jerk" and accusations like "you're incapable of making an emotional commitment."

Because of their guilt, one-ups may be somewhat less free in the name-calling department. But among their barbs are "possessive," "demanding," "nagging," "jealous," "dependent," "clingy," and the phrase "why can't you be more . . ."

Next, look for other ways in which you and your partner strive to "get" each other or to avoid real communication. Following are some hurtful tactics both one-ups and one-downs often use during periods of bad communication.

- Giving your partner "the silent treatment"
- Playing therapist by pointing out pathology in your partner that's disguised as helping (e.g., "It's your parents' fault you're so screwed up.")
- "Globalizing": accusing a partner of "always" acting a certain bad way when you know he acts that way only sometimes
- Guilt-tripping ("You love your work more than you love me.")
- Pushing your partner's "buttons" (e.g., dredging up past grievances that you know will hurt)
- *Acting* hostile but smiling and saying "everything's fine" when your partner asks you what's wrong
- Undermining your partner's confidence with criticisms

Of course, almost everyone uses at least some of these tactics some of the time. They are instinctive ego defenses and they make us feel less vulnerable. But the more familiar you become with your hurtful tactics, the more skillful you'll be in catching and tempering them.

Defusing

It's simple to grasp, difficult to do, but extremely effective. As your anger starts to build, make what Bay Area therapist and author Dan Wile calls an Overview Statement about your hurtful impulses.

Let's take Beth's first statement in her fight with Miles. She began by accusing Miles of failing to call when he was going to be late and of caring more about his restaurant than about her and Chloe. By referring to his weak "track record," she implied that he might be having another affair. Hit with all these overt and covert accusations the minute he walked in the door, Miles's natural reaction was to counterattack.

If Beth had made an Overview Statement about her impulse to get Miles, it might have gone something like this:

I have to tell you, Miles, I'm feeling like getting on your case because you came home so late and didn't call. And I don't want to start doing that again, so I think we ought to talk.

Note the difference. She didn't accuse. She said she *felt like accusing*. By making this Overview Statement, Beth would still be confronting the problem, but in a way that was less provoking and more likely to lead to a constructive discussion.

And Miles could have responded with his own Overview Statement:

I have to admit I was so worried about you getting mad at me for being late that I was psyched up for a fight too. But you're right. We have to talk.

Overview Statements can defuse fights while they're still brewing by putting a verbal buffer between the impulse to fight or hurt and the actual fighting and hurting. And that opens the door to healing communication.

Sometimes it's hard to come up with Overview Statements when you feel that first rush of anger. If this is a problem, try formulating and rehearsing the statements when you feel calm. A good way to do this is to return to the above list of hurtful tactics and practice defusing them with Overview Statements like these:

- I find myself wanting to give you the silent treatment.
- I'm feeling very critical of you.
- I'm so upset I feel like trying to push your buttons.

Then follow your Overview Statement with something like, ". . . and I think we need to talk."

Of course, Overview Statements aren't 100 percent foolproof in heading off fights. That's why it's important to learn the art of accepting and recovering from conflicts.

Accepting and Recovering

Our goal is to learn more effective ways of expressing anger and confronting problems. But it's almost impossible to have a calm, productive talk with your partner when you're bursting with anger. Anger, like steam in a pressure cooker, needs to be vented. When anger has built to a certain point, you're not thinking about "working on the relationship," or about some therapist's communication techniques. The anger is *there* and it wants out.

Paradoxically, couples who accept that anger and fights are normal are better able to recover from them. They ventilate their anger and get to the other side of it. Then they're ready to deal with the problems that caused it. When you know how to handle angry outbursts, they can prepare the ground for healing discussion.

By realizing beforehand that a relationship talk may trigger an accusatory fight, you won't feel so devastated if it happens. Once you calm down, you can use Overview Statements to start the recovery phase. A good opening line is, "I'm sorry for some of the things I said, but I think it was good we got those things off our chests. Now let's work on what's going on between us."

Strategy 2:
Talk about Problem Patterns

Problem relationships are marked by hurtful behavior and bad communication. A major focus of my therapy is to keep a couple's attention on their harmful patterns and in fact to encourage them to discuss all their "problems" as patterns.

When you begin to explore your patterns, remember that you'll be striving, above all, *to frame them in no-fault terms that don't accuse and do acknowledge their shared nature.* It helps to use the word pattern frequently when you talk about problems and also such phrases as:

"We seem to be caught in a cycle";

"We seem to be out of sync";

"There seems to be a 'push-pull' effect in our relating."

The basic structure of this type of No-Fault Communication is this: "We seem to have fallen into a pattern where you have this understandable reaction, which causes me to have an understandable reaction, which then causes you . . ."

When partners can isolate and objectify the pattern they're locked in, they're able to see its power. Then they can also see why blaming each other is a waste of time. This realization helps get partners working together to get out of their interactive ruts.

Isolating Patterns from Behavior

In discussing relationship problems, it's easy to get hung up on details. You talk about specific grievances and the way you're treating each other, but you miss the underlying pattern.

For example, when Miles and Beth first came to me, it was because they couldn't decide who was right and who was wrong. They had dissected their fights, and each passionately felt like a victim of relationship injustice. They were hung up on *details.*

We searched for their pattern by first defining their fights as being based on understandable reactions. Next, we defined the causes of their individual reactions. Then they were able to peel away the outer layers of their conflict pattern to see a common dynamic: When Miles was distant, it made Beth angry, and her anger made Miles more distant and angrier, and so on.

When you probe for patterns, try not to get sidetracked into a debate about which partner "started it." It's usually impossible, and always counterproductive, to try to pin the start of a pattern on one partner or the other.

Once you've sharpened your understanding of your problem patterns, you'll be ready to mount your first direct assault on the passion trap.

Talking about Your Patterns

After his reunion with Laura, Paul had a painful meeting with Daphne. He'd told her he was still confused about his feelings for Laura and needed to resolve them. Shortly after he'd broken up with Daphne, Laura's old doubts began to resurface — and with them her elusive ways. And Paul, despite all he thought he'd learned, felt himself losing control again. The passion trap had assumed its original position in their relationship because neither Paul nor Laura had really changed.

In a joint therapy session, I asked Paul to describe his insecurity about Laura as a pattern problem. He thought about it for a moment, then turned to her.

> Well . . . it seems pretty clear that we're falling back into our old pattern of me selling and you not wanting to buy. I'm always the one who's making plans and wanting to be with you, and I always have a sense you're edging away. I'm starting to feel like an insurance

salesman. I think we should step back and look into why this pattern has developed and talk about ways we can change it.

Laura knew instantly what he was talking about, and agreed.

What No-Fault Does for One-Downs

When the one-down employs interactive terms in discussions about emotionally charged issues, he gains instant leverage. These terms give him control by putting distance between his one-down impulses and actual one-down behavior. They also assuage the one-up's guilt about feeling distant, and that frees her to feel less one-up and closer. And No-Fault by its very nature means the one-down is taking responsibility for his part in the imbalance — and that strengthens him too. Finally, working on shared problem patterns gives the one-down concrete goals for changing the ways in which he interacts with the one-up.

What No-Fault Does for One-Ups

The one-up who uses interactive terms in relationship discussions will find himself finally able to speak honestly about his distant feelings without feeling like Vlad the Impaler. After Beth described their key pattern, Miles was able to explore the sensitive subject of his late homecomings without causing a fight.

> Beth, we seem to have this whole pattern that starts when I get delayed at the restaurant. You get upset, which I can understand. Then I start procrastinating at work because I don't want to face you. Then you get angrier. Then I don't want to call. And then we're almost guaranteed to have a fight. That's when I really want to back away. But we've got to figure out how to break this pattern.

Miles was able to express and explain one of his most trouble provoking one-up behaviors without blaming himself or Beth. When he invited Beth to help him correct the harmful pattern, he released the pressure of a volatile situation. Now Beth would be his partner in the project of working on the relationship.

Strategy 3:
Leave Love out of It

This is one of the unorthodox aspects of my therapy: I ask couples to back-burner the issue of love when they discuss their problems. Using the "L word" makes talking about relationship problems more difficult. Miles described how cornered he felt whenever Beth brought in the issue of love.

> When we first started having problems, we did try talking about them a couple of times. I remember Beth asking me, "Why are you acting this way? Don't you love me anymore?" And it stopped me in my tracks. I'd say, "Of course I do," then blame everything on pressure from my backers. And it would make me wonder what the hell *was* going on with me.

Beth's question put Miles on the spot in the most pressuring of ways. His options were to lie, hedge, or tell a painful truth — that he wasn't sure what he was feeling. The majority of one-ups, like Miles, are truly ambivalent: they don't know exactly what they feel for their partners.

The Problem with Love

One-ups naturally think along these lines: "I'm feeling less love for my partner, therefore I want more distance." This "logic" has the one-up blaming his desire to withdraw on the belief that he's falling out of love. Such thinking is dangerous because it turns the one-up's loss of love into the main problem that needs fixing.

I urge one-ups to reverse the logic of their thinking: "Something's going on in this relationship that's making me want more distance and feel less love." This reinterprets the "loss" of love as a *symptom* of relationship dynamics. It also brings new hope into the picture, because problem patterns are fixable, and they can be changed in a way that rekindles love.

When couples stop worrying about how much or how little their partner loves them, they can communicate more effectively about their harmful patterns. The yardstick should be how well they're interacting, not to what degree they feel love for each other.

Strategy 4:
Share Negative Feelings

Even in the most satisfying relationships, partners experience negative feelings — jealousy, depression, guilt, anxiety, anger — some of the
time. In unbalanced relationships, these feelings may prevail.

When a negative feeling takes hold, the person often wonders
whether he's just overreacting or if a "real" problem is causing it.
Often people end up obsessing over the validity of their negative feelings and not doing anything about them. And that thwarts good communication.

Observe the 50/50 Rule
of Negative Emotions

Please don't get hung up on whether your negative feelings are
appropriate or "off the wall." Instead, view them as roughly 50 percent reality based and 50 percent inflated. Using this rule, you can say
to yourself, "Sure, I might be overreacting, but something's going on
between my partner and me that's triggering these feelings." If I've
learned anything in my clinical work, it's that *every feeling occurs for an
important reason.*

Negative Feelings as Clues
to Harmful Patterns

In a private session, Paul told me:

> I'm finding myself feeling jealous about Laura again, even though
> I'm positive she's not having an affair now. So then I think it's just
> me, and I try not to think about it. But I can't seem to shake the feel-
> ing.

It's very difficult to talk about negative feelings such as jealousy.
If you bring them up, it's hard not to sound accusing or overly vulnerable. And often, like Paul, you're pretty sure that "nothing's going
on" outside the relationship, yet the feeling persists.

I asked Paul when he started feeling jealous again.

> The first time I remember being aware of it was a couple of weeks
> after our "reunion." I'd stopped by her office to say hi, and she

wasn't there. Instead of thinking, "Oh, she's not here," I thought, "Oh, who is she with?" Later, of course, I found out she'd been in a strategy meeting, and I had to know exactly who was there and all that ...

Since Paul really didn't suspect Laura of being in an affair, I suggested we look for reasons why his jealousy was so tenacious. In fact, it was occurring for a very important reason: it was his first clue that an unbalanced pattern of relating had returned to their relationship.

Negative feelings are barometers of subtle changes in relationships. Can you correlate such feelings with certain types of interactions you have with your partner? Do you see a pattern? Remember, we're not looking for villains. We're looking for the underlying dynamics that create toxic interactions.

I asked Paul if his jealousy could be a clue to a harmful pattern in his relationship. He said, "Definitely ... it probably has to do with my insecurity about keeping Laura." Once you understand what's triggering your feelings, you can turn your insight into communication.

Put Negative Feelings
in Their Proper Place

There's a way of sharing your most overwhelming negative feelings without blaming your partner or yourself. The key is to frame them *as symptoms of problem patterns.* For example, you can begin with an Overview Statement like, "Lately I've been feeling (jealous, guilty, depressed, anxious, angry, critical) ..." and immediately follow with "and I think it's because we're starting to fall into a pattern of ... What do you think?"

Knowing your feelings and letting them be known is an important part of healthy emotional intimacy. But in my system, this kind of communication isn't an end in itself. Consider that your feelings function most importantly as a window through which to view those crucial shared dynamics.

Strategy 5: Use Empathy to
Turn Imbalance into Intimacy

Empathizing partners come to share what each other is feeling, and that doubles their insight into the causes of their harmful patterns. In a session with Peg and Bill, I explained the importance of empathy. Bill was starting to work hard in therapy, and after a moment he decided to tell Peg how he imagined it must have been for her during their crisis.

> I know you felt bad about your shop's success just when I lost that promotion. But I can understand why you're so involved in your business. It was like me all those years, putting my energies into the bank and my career. It was more interesting and rewarding than problems at home, I guess. Also, I know it must have been frustrating seeing me drink and act like such a jerk. And every time you tried to help, I just pushed you away. See, I hated the fact that I needed help.

Then Peg spoke.

> I can't even imagine how it must have felt when they did that awful thing to you. For heaven's sake, I felt devastated when I lost the election for senior class secretary in high school. I saw how hard you worked all those years, trying to provide the absolute best for your family. I'm sure I would have taken it much worse than you did.

Relationship problems provide us with a rare opportunity to *deepen* the intimacy in our relationships. People who share a trauma and survive it — be it a shipwreck or a marriage crisis — emerge from the experience with empathy and a stronger bond. Granted, it's very difficult for partners in crisis to begin empathizing with each other. Usually they're both stuck in an accusatory, blaming frame of mind that's highly polarizing. Some are at a loss when I first suggest empathizing. But because it's so challenging, it's all the more meaningful when it works. Expressing empathy is an act of profound emotional intimacy, and it's a powerfully self-reinforcing experience.

Getting Started

Sitting down to discuss relationship problems, even in No-Fault terms, is a little like settling into a dentist's chair. You'd rather be doing *anything* else. Following are some guidelines that have helped my clients overcome their fears of communicating.

Step 1:
Agree to Talk About Talking

This is a little like two countries on the brink of war holding dialogues about whether to have summit talks. But if your relationship is in a crisis—actively tense and painful—a preliminary talk about having a relationship talk can break the ice and give you both time to prepare. Begin by acknowledging how difficult these talks are. A good opening line is, "I hate having to talk about these things, but we're having some problems and I think it'll be good if we can discuss them sometime soon." Then pick a time and place that's comfortable for you both.

Step 2:
Preface Your Talk by Predicting Strong Emotional Reactions

You probably know beforehand how you and your partner will react once you get down to the nitty-gritty. Making an Overview Statement about those reactions early in the conversation often tempers their actual occurrence. Peg, for example, prefaced her first discussion with Bill like this: "I realize talking about this will likely make us both upset. What do you think?" When partners are able to share their fears about talking, they're united in anxiety and in purpose: to help their ailing relationship.

Step 3:
Start Talking About Those Patterns
(and Stay with Them)

Convey your feelings, but frame them as reactions to the harmful patterns that exist between you (leaving love out of it). If your partner starts placing all the blame on you (or himself), don't criticize. Rather, try to reframe what he's saying by describing the problem in No-Fault, interactive terms. Sometimes it's difficult to express the pattern on the spur of the moment, but don't worry. You can bring it up later, when you've had a chance to think about it. If you both start accusing, remember the importance of recovering from fights, and of using Overview Statements to regain your perspective.

Once you get started with No-Fault Communication, expect to feel a pleasant sense of camaraderie with your partner. I've seen it often. Because "who's to blame" is no longer an issue, a couple's positive energies are freed to focus on solving their problem.

Fine-Tune Your Communication

We've covered the basics of No-Fault Communication. Now I offer some important tips to help you refine your communication skills.

Don't Be Afraid of
Talking Away the Mystery

Some couples worry that frank talk about their core problems will eliminate any chance of recovering the mystery and romance in their relationship. The truth of the matter is that mystery and romance die when couples fall into ruts of bad relating. When you explore your problems without blaming and accusing, you stir feelings of deep intimacy and trust. And if you've ever experienced such feelings, you know how exciting they can be. And when you succeed in changing your harmful patterns, the relationship feels new and fresh and, yes, very romantic.

When the Relationship Is New

The passion trap can strike a relationship at any time, even during a first encounter. But it's never too early to use No-Fault Communication. If you sense imbalance soon after meeting someone, try saying something like, "I realize we just started seeing each other, but it seems like we're already falling into a pattern of me (you) moving in too fast and you (me) backing off. What do you think?"

Beware of Harmful Patterns
Disguised as Solutions

The passion trap can sneak into a relationship even when the partners are wise to it. My favorite example of this occurs when imbalance strikes No-Fault Communication itself. One partner is forever wanting to talk about the couple's patterns, leaving little room for spontaneity in the relationship. The other partner resents the endless communicating, then feels guilty about her resistance. I tell couples in this situation to have a No-Fault discussion about No-Fault Communication. To wit: "It seems we're falling into a pattern of me (you) always wanting to talk about our patterns, and you (me) wanting to skip these talks. Do you see that too?"

Similarly, empathy can be misused. A one-up can use it in a condescending way: "You can't help acting clutzy because I make you feel so insecure." Or, a one-down can use empathy to guilt trip the one-up: "I can understand why you need to stay away so much because I'm no fun to be around. So please, go, I just want you to be happy." Watch out for these disguised "solutions," and if they crop up, use them to help define and defeat imbalance.

Don't Be Afraid to Call in a Referee

Breaking long-standing patterns and starting to communicate effectively can be a daunting task. If you can't get going or move beyond a start without backsliding, don't despair. It doesn't mean your relationship is a lost cause. It means you could use some professional help.

For Partners Working Alone

Some partners will automatically resist anything that smacks of therapy, especially "meaningful communication" about relationship problems. I urge you not to criticize your partner if he's reluctant. Your relationship still stands to gain even if you're the only one using No-Fault Communication. Once you become fluent in it (it will take time and work), you'll find it will usually draw out a silent partner or disarm an angry one.

A good way to begin with a skeptical partner is to explain No Fault Communication. Tell him that people are so used to speaking and thinking in accusatory ways that they often don't realize other options exist. Explain the difference between accusatory and nonaccusatory language by taking one of *your* recent accusations and reframing it as a pattern problem. Tell him that you're going to strive to discuss future problems in nonblaming terms and you hope he'll do the same. But also assure him that it's next to impossible to eliminate accusations entirely. What's important is learning how to *recover* from fights and resume negotiations.

Remember, your relationship may or may not work out. Your goal is to feel good about yourself for giving it all you can.

Use Humor

Miles and Beth came into one session saying they'd had a rough week. "How so?" I asked. "We had a lot of BPs coming down on us," Beth said. "BPs?" I asked, worried that it might be contagious. "Bad patterns," Miles said. We all laughed.

I was glad to see this couple recovering a sense of humor. Humor has been clinically shown to speed the healing of physical diseases, and it has a similar effect on problem relationships. You can't force it, because humor, like passion, is grounded in spontaneity. But if it happens, don't for a moment resist. And when you poke fun at passion trap dynamics (which can be comic as well as tragic), you're bringing them out into the open in a particularly benign form.

Formulate a Plan

Once you've spotted and discussed a problem dynamic in your relationship, formulate a specific plan that will involve you both in correcting it. Miles and Beth, for example, thought of the following plan to deal with his late homecomings. Miles said that any delay past a half-hour at the restaurant would mean he'd call Beth. Beth said she'd resist greeting Miles with complaints or bad news. "Maybe I'll even give him a kiss," she said.

If, after formulating a plan, you feel uncomfortable about it, express that feeling. Invite your partner to help you understand what it is about the plan that makes you feel that way. Regard each plan as an experiment that yields valuable information. If the plan works, congratulate yourselves. If the plan doesn't solve the problem, the experiment is still a success because it tells you that a different strategy is needed. No-Fault Communication is essential for evaluating the effectiveness of your plans and formulating new ones.

If your relationship isn't severely out of balance, No-Fault Communication may be all you need to get yourselves back in sync. But extremely unbalanced couples have more hard work ahead. While insight and open communication will always be needed, you may also need to learn how to think and behave in special ways to break rigid one-down or one-up patterns. Let's explore what one-downs can do.

Chapter 9

What One-Downs
Can Do

Seven Equalizing Strategies

Deborah was on the edge when she first came to see me. Staring out my window, she talked about her affair with Jonathan in a manner that strove too hard for nonchalance. But when she admitted she'd hoped they might marry, she broke down. All the pain, humiliation, and bitter disappointment of being a newly rejected one-down finally poured out. I handed her a box of tissues and told her it was okay not to speak until she felt ready. As she wept, I assured her she was doing some important and timely emotional work: facing her sense of loss.

Strategy 1:
Be Good to Yourself

One of the first lessons psychotherapists learn is the importance of timing. Working toward personal change is always hard. It's almost impossible while you're in the middle of an emotional crisis. If your world has been turned upside down by a partner who's thinking of leaving you (or who already has), I urge you not to attempt any major changes in your life just yet. Your first order of business is to get to the other side of your acute pain.

In a later session, Deborah realized she was lucky to have the moral support of her best friend Kelly.

> When Jonathan and I started getting really involved, I kind of let everything go, including my friends. I know Kelly was especially

hurt because I was always changing plans we'd made when Jonathan called. It was amazing she still cared enough to call. But then she seemed to sense from the beginning that there'd be problems.

Often people come to rely on their intimate relationships as their major source of emotional nurturance. But if the relationship is unbalanced, the one-down is caught in an obvious bind: she can't very well expect nurturance from the partner whose distance is causing her pain. And here we find the passion trap again: If she seeks it from him, she will likely drive him further away.

So friends become a major source of solace during a relationship crisis. For this reason, I always ask my one-down clients if they're taking good care of their friendships. Friends (and often family members) offer support and empathy, two essential recovery tools. A friend will affirm your sense of self-worth. You've probably nurtured a friend in need. Now it's time to let yourself be nurtured. Psychotherapy or spiritual counseling can also offer support and help you recover from acute emotional pain.

One last point. We rarely feel as alone as we do when our relationships are uncertain. And while it's important to seek support from friends, relatives, and helping professionals, I've found that people heal more quickly if they don't fight their feeling of aloneness, but rather harmonize with it. For some people, getting time alone is difficult, but for most it's possible. Now is the time to get what you need, so support yourself as you make sacrifices to have time to yourself. Take an afternoon off and spend it near the ocean, at a lake, or in a park or public garden. Nature can be uniquely comforting. If it's possible, spend an evening by yourself: Go to the symphony or a movie, read poetry, write in your journal, or cry as hard as you want.

Don't deny your sadness or try to avoid it through distractions, at least at first. Let yourself feel sorry for you, with no excuses or apologies. This is the fastest way to get through a bereavement period and start regaining emotional strength.

Strategy 2:
Get a Grip on Reality

An emotional crisis will cloud your perceptions. When you're not thinking straight, it's hard to act in your best interests.

With my one-down clients I work first on their patterns of thinking, then on their patterns of behaving. Let's look at the mental traps we all fall into when our relationships seem to be failing.

Catastrophizing

These are a few of the statements Deborah made in that first session:

- "I'll never find anyone I'll be able to love as much as Jonathan."
- "I don't ever want to get close to a man again."
- "I'll never get married or be a mother."

Deborah was catastrophizing, believing her life would have a negative outcome. From the one-down position, the relationship looms large in importance — so large that it seems vital to survival. That's why the prospect of losing it causes such pessimism and panic.

Those in the one-down position tend to fall into a kind of hypnosis that makes them deaf to reason. Friends, relatives, even their rational selves will plead with them to "wake up and smell the coffee." But they feel too threatened to listen to reason. And as the relationship becomes more unbalanced and toxic and less sustaining, the one-down paradoxically feels even *less* able to survive its loss. Caught in this contradiction, one-downs resist pulling away from punishing relationships.

Deborah came to realize that much of her desperate one-down behavior with Jonathan was due to catastrophizing. This charting exercise is how I show my clients the dangers of catastrophizing and other mental traps.

Deb's Perception: Jonathan backing away.

Deb's Initial Reaction: Normal anxiety and insecurity.

Deb's One-Down Overreaction: Panic and catastrophizing. She's 33, almost ready for the slag heap. Rejection anxiety and fear of "blowing it" with Jonathan become irrepressible. Suddenly, Jonathan is Deb's last chance for love, marriage, children, happiness in life.

Deb's One-Down Solution: Extreme one-down behaviors, notably echoing and hypercourtship. She parrots Jonathan and defers at every opportunity. She strains to look her best around him. She is self-conscious and unspontaneous. She attempts to elicit reassuring words.

End Result: Deborah's desperation becomes apparent to Jonathan. She's crowding him, not giving him the "space" he likes to have in a relationship. He backs off further and eventually ends the relationship.

Bouts of catastrophizing are built into the one-down position just as the paradox of passion is built into human nature. However, although we can't eliminate them, we can effectively deal with them.

When you find yourself saying or thinking things like, "I'll never love again," an alarm should sound. Write down those thoughts; seeing them on paper helps objectify them. Tell yourself your thinking has been distorted and negativized by the passion trap. Then attack the "logic" of catastrophizing your fears. Remind yourself that you've had these fears before, and so has almost everyone else. Have they proven true? Do you have any friends who didn't survive the end of a relationship? Who never again felt love or happiness? Before this relationship, were you ever left by someone whom you thought was the only person you'd ever, ever want?

Keeping this perspective will diminish the panicky, irrational quality of your crisis thinking. And that means not having to resort to desperate one-down solutions to save you from your "catastrophe." Remember, you *are* in a difficult situation, but if you view it as a cataclysm, you're catastrophizing.

Self-Sabotage

To be human is to feel insecure, at least some of the time. But many of us seem to have an "Internal Saboteur" who undermines our self-esteem and incites one-down behavior whenever we feel anxious. It is a powerful ally of the passion trap.

Bill received the most crushing blow of his life at a point when he'd expected to have reached his peak of success. The blow was sharpened by his wife's newfound success. Had Bill's self-esteem been more solid, he *still* would have felt great sadness, disappointment, and anger. But Bill, like many "traditional" males, had no coping mechanism for emotional crisis. Into that void stepped his Internal Saboteur, supporting his sense of failure, shredding his confidence, and pushing him toward alcoholism, self-hatred, abusive behavior, and severe depression.

With the support of Peg and his AA group, Bill began to regain his emotional strength. But it wasn't until later, after several individual sessions with me, that he was ready to face his career loss.

I asked Bill to think back to his point of greatest despondence.

I'd wake up in the morning and feel failure weighing me down, like an anvil on my chest. I'd think about the guys who'd made it. Obviously I had some big deficiency that everyone could see except me. I think I was feeling a lot of hate. I hated my company. I hated Peg. Most of all I hated myself. I didn't care if I lived or died. I didn't feel so bad about the hate when I drank, and I wouldn't have minded if it had killed me.

Then I asked him how he might have reframed his negative, self-loathing thoughts so that he might have been a friend to himself, not an enemy.

A lot of men in my AA group experienced major failures, and with the help of alcohol we did become our own enemies. I guess I could say that I'm a normal, fallible human being who's going to experience losses like everyone else. After all, Ford *fired* Lee Iacocca — they didn't just pass over him. I think the point is not to get back at the guys who hurt you by destroying yourself, or destroying your family, or even by destroying the guys who did it (though I've had plenty of fantasies about that). But it's to turn the thing around to your advantage. That's how you get back at them, and that's what I intend to do.

Bill's intention was, in fact, to turn his passion for sailing into a vocation. He was determined not to let his Internal Saboteur sink his dream.

The key to silencing your Internal Saboteur is to defeat its ego-crushing logic with thoughts that build rather than demolish your self-esteem. Think about recent episodes in which your thoughts eroded rather than supported your confidence, and write them down. Here are some common self-sabotaging one-down thoughts:

- I'm too . . . (fat, thin, tall, short, etc.).
- I'm no fun to be around.
- I'm not successful enough.
- I'm too old.
- I'm too insecure.
- I'm not smart enough.

I urge you to dispute your self-sabotaging thoughts by becoming a friend to yourself. You must accept that dynamics are behind your partner's distance, and stop blaming what you perceive to be your personal shortcomings. Realize that these dynamics have plunged you into a period of insecurity, making you feel unattractive and act in ways you may abhor. It happens to everyone. Don't make the mistake of believing this has to go on forever.

Take a bold stand: You are who you are, and if you're getting a reaction from someone that makes you feel bad about yourself, let it be their problem, not yours. Feel angry and motivated, not diminished and depressed.

The One-Down Reflex

The most basic panic reaction to a relationship crisis is the exaggeration of your one-down behaviors. Closely linked to catastrophizing and self-sabotage, these behaviors can surface in a flash—before you have a chance to stop them. But you can do the next best thing: Learn how to spot and counter your reflexive one-down reactions.

To develop this ability, first make a list of your most dreaded and familiar one-down reflexes. Here is what Paul wrote:

> Always agree with Laura's opinion.
> Never tell her when I'm upset or angry.
> Call her or stop by her office whenever I feel insecure or jealous.
> Do as many favors as I can for her so she'll like me more.
> Always do what she wants to do, even when I don't want to.

Paul told me he hated being "the boring, nice-guy jerk" around Laura. But he couldn't seem to stop those behaviors. I told him to study his list so that he'd be prepared to spot them as soon as they appeared. Then ...

Hold an internal dialogue. This is how Paul talked himself out of an episode with his one-down reflex:

> It was a Friday afternoon, and Laura called my office to tell me she'd just heard about a party. She wanted to know if I wanted to go. I'd been feeling bone tired and looking forward to a peaceful Friday night at home. But I automatically said yes. After I hung up, I was consumed with negative feelings about the evening and myself. I realized I'd done it again: gone along with Laura because I was afraid not to be there, "guarding" her, and afraid she'd think I was a stick-in-

the-mud. So I called her back and told her that on second thought, I really *didn't* feel like going, but it was fine if she did. And let me tell you, that felt pretty good, even though I honestly had some anxiety about her being on her own. The funny thing is that she wound up leaving the party early and coming over to my place. I felt a little smug about that.

I urge you to be prepared to catch unwanted one-down reflexes and then talk yourself out of them. With time, you'll get so adept at monitoring your reactions that you'll be able to nip them in the bud.

As you learn to control your overreactions and reflexive behaviors, your thoughts will gain clarity, and your impulse to act the one-down will subside. Don't expect total freedom from these mental traps; they're just a part of the human experience. But do expect to feel ready to start forming some healthy new attitudes about yourself and your relationship.

Strategy 3:
Have Brave New Thoughts

One-downs feel unnerved because their best efforts to make a relationship work seem to fail. They're faced with an imperative: to change their tactics. That means taking risks and making changes in themselves. Of course, such undertakings are not only difficult but frightening. They are also faced with urgings from the passion trap *not* to change their one-down tactics but to intensify them.

Following are guidelines for getting yourself into a positive and brave frame of mind that will help you alter your approach.

Why YOU Have to Change

You want your partner to change, to be more loving, attentive, and committed. But you're starting to realize that all the love, kindness, pleading, bribery, and nagging in the world won't do it. You can't change your partner, and the more you try, the more he'll resist. But you can change yourself—specifically, your one-down patterns of thinking, communicating, and behaving. It's a hard and scary prospect. But changing yourself is the most effective means you have to change your partner, because you'll be altering the relationship dynamics.

Not Being Afraid to Break Up Is a Good Way to Save a Relationship

In her catastrophizing frame of mind, the one-down irrationally fears that if she changes, she'll lose her partner. She's convinced that her unswerving love and devotion will eventually bring him around, despite mounting evidence to the contrary. When this fear controls your behavior, it will inhibit you and block spontaneity. Your neediness and desperation will be hard to conceal and damaging to your goal of regaining your partner's love. Perhaps most damaging, however, is that your fear of losing your grip on your partner will keep you from engaging in activities outside the relationship.

Paradoxically, of course, the braver you are about taking healthy, jeopardizing risks in your relationship, the greater the chance you'll save it.

I'm certainly not advocating that you play emotional doubledare with your partner. I don't want you to take risks for the sole purpose of jeopardizing your relationship. I want you to take them so that you'll have more power to be the person you want to be with your partner.

Whenever catastrophizing thoughts hold you back from taking helpful risks, confront and dispute them. What if your relationship *doesn't* work out? Yes, you will have to endure considerable pain. But you will survive, and you'll be stronger, wiser, and better equipped to find a balanced and fulfilling relationship—a relationship that makes you feel good about yourself, instead of the way you're feeling now.

When it comes time to take actual risks, remember that if you *didn't* feel anxious and tense, you wouldn't be normal. Keep in mind that tension is a companion of growth and should be viewed as a sign of progress in your life.

A New Source of Strength

It takes strength and courage to pull yourself up from the one-down position. I'd like you to turn to a source of strength you may not know you have: anger.

Most one-downs feel a great deal of anger because so many of their needs aren't being met. But they're reluctant to express it directly for fear of driving a distant partner further away. Sometimes they suppress their anger so effectively that they become oblivious to it. But inhibited anger will only build and harden into hostility and bitterness. In this form, it can be directed outwardly at your partner, inwardly at yourself, or both. Then, it's a wasted resource.

I urge you not to waste your anger by turning it against yourself *or* your partner. It should be valued as the great motivator of change. You can harness your anger by telling yourself: "Dammit, I'm sick and tired of being one-down! It's time to become the person I want to be in the relationship."

Let's now turn to the best way I know of accomplishing this.

Strategy 4:
Create Healthy Distance

The heart of my therapy program for one-downs revolves around a single premise: *A one-down's greatest chance for strengthening her relationship lies in her striving to shift her emotional energy away from it.* Her goal will be to gain what I call Healthy Distance.

This doesn't mean trying to stop loving your partner or playing hard-to-get. It does mean trying to get more balance into your own life. For some, this will entail reclaiming personal strengths that seem to have faded as the relationship problems grew. For others it might also mean building new strengths. In both cases it means making a conscious emotional withdrawal from your relationship.

You have two important objectives: to break free from the one-down position and all its demoralizing effects, and to add to your appeal to the one-up.

Healthy Distance will feel all wrong to you, at first. I'm asking you to pull away at a time when you feel almost helplessly connected to the relationship. You'll have a host of one-down excuses for not practicing Healthy Distance. But I ask you, at least on a trial basis, to reject them. You must also free your mind from the accepted notion that the only way to improve a relationship is to encourage intimacy in your partner. Healthy Distance is the best method of recapturing intimacy that I know of.

Reclaim Your Strengths

In an early session, Beth lamented the effect that her unsettled relationship with Miles had had on the quality of her life.

> When I used to feel secure about Miles, and, of course, before I married him, it was like I was free to be myself. I'd have dinners and go to the movies with friends, I'd shop, I'd travel, I'd read good books, I'd take the occasional night class. Of course, having a child has made a big difference in all that. But there's more to it. It's like life has shrunk from something large to a pinpoint. Everything feels "pending" because of this suspense about what's going to happen with us. My old, interesting life seems almost like a dream.

I told Beth that letting her worries about the relationship sidetrack her this way was natural but damaging to her and the relationship. You need to think about two things when you detect one-down symptoms in yourself: ways of reducing pressure on your partner, and ways of strengthening yourself. And the best means of accomplishing both ends is by working to reestablish your individuality apart from your relationship.

Take a Personal Inventory

Before formulating a Healthy Distance plan, I ask my one-down clients to take a personal inventory. Ask yourself the following questions:

- What are the activities I used to enjoy before getting involved with my partner (or before problems developed)?
- What are my personal goals outside of the relationship? Am I on a track to achieve them?
- How is my social life outside the relationship?
- What are my strengths? Are they being used right now?

The more specific you can be in answering these questions, the more helpful your inventory will be. For example, don't just write among your personal goals, "get another job." Write what the job would be, the steps needed to get it, and a timetable for achieving each step.

Make a Healthy Distance Plan

After taking her personal inventory, Beth found she was neglecting many areas of her life that had once been strong. Rebuilding her strengths formed the basis of her Healthy Distance plan.

- Keep my part-time PR job for now but shoot for freelance business. Put together brochure (April). Mail brochures to selected businesses (June). Do telephone and lunch follow-up (July).
- Forget aerobics and start swimming again at the "Y." One mile at least twice a week. Check into "Y" programs for Chloe (immediately).
- Make a weekly lunch date with a friend (immediately).
- Look into volunteering for Literacy Project once a week (immediately).
- Get out into nature at least once a month (immediately).

A month later, I asked Beth how her Healthy Distance efforts were coming along.

> It hasn't been all that easy. You know in your mind that you should be doing these things. But it's like relationship problems become an excuse to be a slug in the rest of your life. I'll get off to a great start in doing something, like the exercising. But it's so easy to get discouraged, and that feeds negatively into everything else. I'll lose it for a couple of days, but then I see things go downhill and get back on track.

I assured Beth that setbacks and backsliding were normal, acceptable, and no reason for having self-sabotaging thoughts. I encouraged her to stay with the plan. Two months later, I started to see a new Beth. She described the effect that Healthy Distance had come to have on her outlook and her relations with Miles.

> I'm feeling more energized, and best of all I have more of a sense that I'm controlling my life. I also feel a lot more relaxed about Miles. The things that used to bother me a lot don't so much anymore. I know this has helped us get along better. I sometimes feel it's a little like we're getting to know each other again.

Beth was feeling more fulfilled, busy, balanced, and sure of who she was, and less dependent, resentful, and victimized. Gradually, her narrow focus on Miles's behavior eased. The dynamics between them were changing in a positive way.

Build New Strengths

Bill felt that he'd made a mistake in his life by, as he put it, "being overly focused on what I thought was expected of me instead of on what really interested me." He admitted that banking per se had never really fulfilled him.

> I think one of the reasons I'd gotten so resentful of Peg was that she was loving what she was doing with the shop. My career never gave me joy, and maybe it showed. Maybe that's one of the reasons things didn't work out.

Bill had caught the sailing bug as a boy when his family summered on Chesapeake Bay. In college, he'd crewed in several races and done some mid-distance cruising, but he'd never considered turning his passion into a vocation. After marriage, he'd kept his subscription to *Sailing* magazine and occasionally taken Peg and the boys for weekend outings in rented boats.

But now, with his retirement pay, their savings, and Peg's new income, Bill realized that he had a chance to do something he could love, and draw a personal victory from a seeming defeat. With Peg's support, he bought a 33-foot ketch that needed work (he would do it himself). In the process, he made connections in the yacht business. He "really hit it off' with the broker on his ketch, another recovering alcoholic named Jack. Jack invited him to hang around the office and start learning the business.

I asked Bill how all this was affecting the rest of his life.

> It's like night and day. I love working on the boat, and Peg's in the spirit of it too. She helps me scrape paint on Sundays. We're planning some maiden voyage. In the meantime, I'm working part-time with Jack, unpaid at the moment, but I'm learning. We're taking out the boats he's considering and he's showing me some of the ropes of brokering. He thinks I'm "a natural." I can't tell you how much I'm enjoying myself.

When we develop new skills or talents, we mount a strong attack against one-down forces. In fact, the desire to meet a partner on an equal level is one of the great motivators of career success. It's the "I'll show them" response, and it's a constructive way of dealing with negative emotions.

Healthy Distance in Close Quarters

Shortly after we first discussed Healthy Distance, Beth called me for "a quick question." She and Miles were planning a weekend trip to a hot-springs resort (Chloe would be staying with her grandmother). She was wondering . . .

> how I should act around Miles in light of all this healthy-distance business. Should I try to be aloof? Should I take a couple of books, or work to do? Should I demand separate beds? [She laughed.]

I explained to Beth that the goal of healthy distance is not to *act* distant around your partner. In fact, you shouldn't try to act in any premeditated way with your partner — that only kills the spontaneity in the relationship. Rather, you should act however you *feel* like acting. Sometimes that may indeed mean reading a book around your partner, or doing work. And if you happen to be feeling very loving, by all means express that love. But if you feel loving and also anxious about what your partner is feeling, tell him something like: "I'm really enjoying being with you, and I want it to stay like this. So let me know if you want some private time, okay?" This kind of verbalizing combines intimacy and autonomy in a nonpressuring way.

I learned later that Beth and Miles's weekend was a great success.

Why Healthy Distance Works

Miles said of Beth's new activities:

> When I come home now I'm not gripped with this fear of "Okay, how did I screw up today?" I see Beth excited about what she's doing, and it makes me happy. She's really a neat person. I also like helping her when she encounters problems and frustrations in getting her business going, because that's what I'm good at. It's brought us much closer.

A consuming emotional investment in a partner is imprisoning to both partners. But Healthy Distance enables you to cultivate the following strengthening qualities.

- *Autonomy.* By emotionally easing away from the one-up, and at the same time enriching your life with other fulfilling pursuits, you're becoming a whole, balanced, autonomous person again. Autonomy — separateness and wholeness — is one of the most powerful countermeasures to the passion trap. And when it's balanced with intimacy, it's half of what makes great relationships great.

- *Spontaneity.* We've seen how the one-down's "Be Spontaneous" solution usually backfires by creating performance anxiety for the one-down. But you can regain your spontaneity when you don't feel that everything is riding on each move you make with your partner. When other parts of your life are rewarding, you'll feel more confident and less anxious and inhibited. And you'll be more spontaneous.

- *Self-esteem.* Self-esteem problems often lie behind the slide into the one-down position. When low self-esteem makes us feel unworthy of someone's love, insecurity is inevitable and hard to hide. The bind is that feeling less loved by a partner further erodes our self-esteem. A key aspect of Healthy Distance is finding new sources of self-esteem and confidence — that will offset your feelings of insecurity in your relationship.

- *Harnessing the paradox of passion.* Healthy Distance works because it uses paradox dynamics to fight the passion trap. We know that one-down pursuit creates one-up distance. When you shift the direction of your pursuit away from the one-up, you empower yourself.

There will be times when you'll feel no conviction about your Healthy Distance actions. Your emotions may be completely absorbed by the one-up, making any healthy-distance action seem fraudulent. But I urge you not to quit. If you keep at it, you'll begin to notice positive results that will reinforce your efforts.

Healthy Distance Isn't a Game

I've had one-down clients resist Healthy Distance because they thought it seemed like a game. But there's a big difference between Healthy Distance and game-playing.

I'm dismayed by the spate of recent self-help books and articles that recommend playing hard-to-get to snag a reluctant or ambivalent partner. Unfortunately, much of this advice is being offered by psychotherapists.

Game-playing is when the one-down attempts to manipulate the one-up's feelings with pseudo-one-up—that is, falsely distant—actions. Here are some I've seen recommended:

- Not returning messages left on the answering machine
- Flirting with others in the presence of the one-up
- "Disappearing" for a couple of days
- Dating others to "get" the one-up
- Giving the one-up "the silent treatment"
- Withholding sex
- Faking indifference to the one-up's behavior

The problem with these ploys is that even when they work, there's a good chance they'll add anger and distrust to the one-up's feelings. And they won't really improve the relationship because they won't alter your emotional investment in it. Games are Band-Aid solutions that, at best, can temporarily reengage the one-up by emotionally "zapping" him. Healthy Distance, on the other hand, is powerful medicine for your relationship, and, more important, *for you.*

Also keep in mind that games tend to be transparent to the one-up. Remember when Paul tried to get Laura jealous at the law-firm picnic? His attempt backfired because she easily saw through it. When you resort to games to save your relationship, it's because your investment in it is so high. And that's hard to hide.

Strategy 5:
Explain What You're Doing

It is vital that you keep communicating with your partner as you put Healthy Distance into effect. If you don't, you run the same risk as the game-player: Your partner may become confused, distrustful, alienated, and angry.

You may recall Marie and Ron, the couple mentioned in chapter 8. Their pattern was that she would rage at him for acting so distant and feel anxious because he was so attractive; he would take to the road. In individual therapy, Marie and I worked on a Healthy Distance plan for her. She was excited because it included two things she'd always wanted to do: take a modern dance class and do volunteer hairstyling at a home for the aged.

With characteristic intensity, she put her plan into practice. Only she wasn't communicating about her new activities. She told me Ron's initial reaction.

> When I started doing more things away from the house, *he* started staying out later, and coming home drunk, which is not typical for Ron. So I asked him what was going on. He said, "You tell me, you're the one who's seeing somebody." I told him that was ridiculous but he wouldn't believe me and it turned into a fight. And he left ...

Marie acknowledged that she'd neglected practicing her new communication skills in tandem with Healthy Distance. She said she'd felt her new activities might have more "impact" if she kept them secret, and she worried that Ron would laugh at her if she told him what she was doing.

I explained to Marie that Healthy Distance practiced without communication often led to the kind of backlash she'd experienced, and that could easily negate the benefits.

Because of Ron's reaction, Marie chose to write him a letter explaining her Healthy Distance.

> Dear Ron,
>
> I'm sorry for our misunderstanding. I assure you, I am *not* seeing anyone else — that's the last thing I want to do. You know I'm in therapy now and I've been trying to take the pressure off you. You see, I realize I've been driving you nuts with all my bitching about the way you don't want to do things with me. But now I see that one of the big reasons why you're not giving me very much is that I'm always wanting more from you. So I'm doing this thing called "Healthy Distance" (it's my shrink's term, not mine). That means I'm doing some things I've been wanting to do for a long time (like taking modern dance), and I'm trying to be a better friend to Sue and Delise, and a better daughter and sister, because I've neglected my family. I have to force myself sometimes, but the good thing is that I'm feeling better about myself, and that means I'll be taking the heat off you. Sound good? No more nagging, I promise.
>
> I hope this helps. And I hope we can talk about it sometime. I'm sorry I didn't explain this sooner.
>
> Love,
> Marie

She sent the letter to his auto shop. The next day when he came home, he jokingly asked if Healthy Distance meant he'd better not try to touch her. That night they went out to dinner and had one of their "most romantic times in a long time."

When one-downs communicate their Healthy Distance plans, they're transmitting some important messages to the one-up:

- That they're feeling confident enough to share credit for the relationship's problems
- That they're taking steps to ease the pressure for closeness in a way designed to foster love and trust
- That the one-up needn't feel guilty about his emotional distance (that takes him off the defensive)
- That the one-up isn't the center of their universe (which gives him a healthy jolt and a sense of the one-down's growing autonomy)

Strategy 6:
Face Your Fears of Distance

Beth admitted to a fear that Healthy Distance hadn't eradicated and in fact had fueled.

> I can't get it out of my mind that Miles will somehow use the fact that I'm busier now as an excuse to have another affair. He'll rationalize that I don't really care about him, or he's not being fulfilled, and use that as an excuse to mess around.

Good communication will minimize the risk that a one-up will have the reaction Beth feared. Nonetheless, there will always be an element of risk involved when a one-down starts cultivating autonomy. Letting such fears hold you back, however, is giving in to the passion trap. If the relationship is so fragile that Healthy Distance, presented in a loving manner, breaks it, then you've probably hastened an inevitable ending.

Still, these fears must be dealt with. Following is an exercise that helped Beth, and other one-downs, resolve their fear of Healthy Distance.

Step 1: Write down your biggest fear of creating more distance between yourself and your partner.

BETH: Miles having another affair.

Step 2: Imagine your biggest fear coming true. What is your reaction?

BETH: Feeling doubly betrayed. Extreme sadness, anger, disillusionment. And I feel like a fool for giving him another chance, and trusting him.

Step 3: Reframe your fear in nonaccusatory terms.

BETH: I know it's important that I give Miles and the relationship another chance. I still believe we belong together, and it will be best for Chloe if we can work it out. But this time I'm not going to fall into the trap of feeling angry and disgusted at myself as well as Miles. I'm on the right path now, and I'm feeling better and stronger, and if Miles has another affair, I'll know for sure he's not the one for me. I'll also know I tried hard to make this relationship work before giving up on it.

Now, the hardest and most crucial part of the exercise:

Step 4: Discuss your fears and your new "reframed" view of them with your partner. Be firm, however. Tell your partner that if he does what you fear most, he's choosing to jeopardize and possibly end your relationship.

Beth chose to do Step 4 in a joint therapy session with Miles. Miles seemed touched by her fear, and he respected her firmness. He assured her that he had learned the lesson of his life the last time around. He also admitted his own fears created by her Healthy Distance. In spite of himself, he still felt "a little worried about Kevin." Realizing that they shared the same fear made them both feel better.

What If the One-Up Opposes Healthy Distance?

Healthy Distance worried Miles. Some one-ups out and out oppose it. If you meet overt resistance from your partner, don't condemn him. But neither should you shrink from what may underlie it. The chances are good that your very resistant partner *needs* to control you out of a deep-seated insecurity. It may also be that you're in this relationship because you have an interlocking need to relinquish control to another person.

Needs to control and be controlled usually are found in people with limited interpersonal skills due to dysfunctional childhoods. (I'll discuss this issue in chapters 13 and 14.) Now, however, it's most important to bear in mind that bravely confronting even the least pleasant relationship realities offers the best hope for making things better.

Strategy 7:
Define the Limits of Your
Healthy Distance

Marie and Ron did make strides, but at a certain point her frustration returned.

> I feel lots better about myself, and we're getting along much better. But there's still a problem. He's just not the type to be all lovey-dovey. And that's something that means a lot to me.

Healthy Distance requires that the one-down make some compromises in closeness. But sometimes, for some reasons — in this case a deep personality style difference — Healthy Distance may be too depriving of a one-down's intimacy needs. If your one-up partner is rarely able to offer you closeness, even though you're getting along better, then your relationship may need serious reassessing.

Give Healthy Distance a good try for at least several months. Communicate in No-Fault terms about what you want from the relationship. And if it appears that situational or personality style factors are playing a part in your unhappiness, bring them into your discussions. Negotiate and be willing to compromise. Seek a balance that will meet at least your minimum needs for intimacy and your partner's needs for separateness.

If after all your efforts you still feel emotionally unfulfilled, you'll be faced with a hard choice. Before making it, have a nitty-gritty, No-Fault talk with your partner. Air your fear that perhaps you're not the best partners for each other. By taking this initiative, you're exerting control and bringing the relationship into greater balance. Sometimes, on this brink, a relationship is saved and goes on to flourish.

The Ultimatum

The ultimatum is the ultimate way to define your personal limits. It's a powerful tool often used — and often abused — by one-downs. Ultimatums should be given sparingly and with caution, to avoid the "boy who cried wolf" syndrome. They should not be used to gain leverage in a relationship or frighten the one-up.

Before using an ultimatum, a one-down should have a clear sense of what she'll no longer tolerate in the relationship. She should maintain her focus on dynamics and refuse to adopt a blaming attitude toward her partner. Her ultimatum might take this shape: "Unless we can *both* make some of the changes we've been talking about, and soon, I think it would be best if we break up." That is, make use of the ultimatum's strength to invite change.

Sometimes the shock value of an ultimatum will get positive results. But be realistic when an ultimatum seems to have worked. If a highly ambivalent one-up bows to your ultimatum, offering a commitment such as marriage, likely you will be thrilled. But an ultimatum is a "quick cure," not an agent of profound change. It may "win" you a commitment from a person who may not, over the long run, be able to give you the genuine love and closeness you want.

Marie eventually gave Ron an ultimatum. She began by assuring him that she wasn't blaming him — she just felt she wasn't getting her needs met in the relationship. She said that she hoped they could still work out their problems, but if things didn't change, she planned to move on. Marie felt devastated when Ron angrily told her to do what she damn well pleased, then left.' But the next day he agreed to start couples' therapy.

You now have a number of strategies to help you change your unbalancing one-down behaviors. Consider them a source of personal power, tools to use to get what you want out of your relationship. One-downs can make great things happen in their lives and relationships, if they choose to.

Chapter 10

What One-Ups Can Do

Seven Ways to Give Love a Chance

Ambivalent one-ups are experts at self-torture. Laura expressed classic one-up angst in our first individual session.

> I don't think I've ever felt so bad about myself. I've never thought of myself as being a manipulative person, but I'm starting to wonder. The worst part is I don't really feel I know myself anymore. I mean, first I think Paul is the man of my dreams. Then all of a sudden I feel irritated and antsy around him all the time. Then I cheat on him and dump him. Then I get dumped and the first thing I want to do is take Paul away from a woman who's probably much better for him than I am. All I want right now is to be able to feel love for him, not this horrible, nagging sense of doubt. Is there anything you can do to just, kind of, fix me?

Ambivalent one-ups like Laura question their innate goodness as people. They wonder how a "good" person could feel the way they feel, do the things they do, and think the thoughts they think. Of course, they already "know" the answer: a good person can't, only someone who's bad.

I told Laura what I tell most of my one-up clients: First, give yourself a break.

Strategy 1:
Empathize with Yourself

To empathize with yourself means to accept your one-up feelings and not to condemn yourself for them. These include your guilt, anger, feelings of distance and frustration, boredom and impatience, sense of confinement, and wish for more passion. Not only are these feelings normal given the imbalance in your relationship, but they're keys to understanding and correcting imbalances and very possibly to rekindling feelings of love.

The fact is, one-ups are passion trap victims every bit as much as one-downs are. They get confused because feelings stirred by the passion trap tell them they have the power in the relationship. They don't realize that their power renders them powerless to care romantically for their partners. One-ups' first task is to accept that they didn't start the relationship's problems by falling out of love. An imbalance grew between the partners, and *it* generated the unwanted feelings. The truth is that both you and the one-down are being deprived of love and intimacy.

When one-ups accept their feelings as normal, their guilt, anger, and frustration subside. Then the relationship begins to look better to them. So, it's of vital importance that one-ups learn empathy for themselves as a first step toward healing.

Learn Self-Empathy

Imagine that you have a good friend who shares your relationship predicament. She turns to you for help. What would you say to comfort her? Write down consoling words that you can imagine yourself saying. Drawing on your knowledge of the passion trap, link your friend's emotional state to the destructive forces spawned by relationship imbalance.

Peg, an accomplished self-torturer, badly needed compassion for herself. Following is her completed exercise.

> Listen, you didn't set out to hurt your husband. More than anything, you wanted for the two of you to be happy. But the timing couldn't have been worse. For the first time in forty-four years you were becoming your own person. You found something you loved doing and made you feel great about yourself. It wasn't your fault that your husband's company dealt him a devastating blow just when you'd started doing so well. What were you supposed to do? Give up the shop so he wouldn't feel so bad? That wouldn't have helped anything, and it probably would have made things worse. The two of you had been locked into the same roles for years, and neither of you knew how to adjust to the sudden changes in your lives. You both made mistakes, you've both been hurt, and you're both only human. And look at how much you've learned and how hard you're

working to make things better. You can't imagine how much I feel for you. I know the lonely hell you're in ...

When Peg read the exercise to me, the last line released a good, cleansing cry for herself. Peg's self-empathy had begun to free her from her need to punish herself. She was ready to work productively on her relationship.

Recognize the Role of Distorted Thinking

One-ups generally have just as many thought distortions as do one-downs. But there's a sharp difference between them. One-downs' distorted thoughts cause them to cling harder; one-ups' distorted thoughts leave them helplessly conflicted. For them, the unanswerable question is: Would leaving the relationship be a disastrous mistake, or would staying?

Ambivalent one-ups yearn for objectivity, but they find it hard to answer even the most basic questions about their feelings:

- Do I love my partner?
- Is this relationship right for me?
- Am I basically happy with moments of unhappiness, or am I basically unhappy with moments of happiness?

In searching for the answers, one-ups are chasing their tails. As important as these questions are, one-ups are better off leaving them and turning their attention instead to the dynamics behind them.

I urge one-ups not to make any major decisions during an acute attack of CAS (Commitment-Ambivalence Syndrome). My goal is to help you understand your distorted thought patterns and to correct them. Only then can you get a clear picture of your true relationship needs.

Strategy 2:
Learn from Your Guilt

When one-ups realize they no longer feel in love with their partners, they begin to feel guilty, especially so if their partners are very loving and/or very vulnerable.

Laura was plagued with guilt. It hadn't occurred to her that her guilt itself was playing a large role in her relationship's problems. She'd thought it was simply an unpleasant side effect of her negative feelings about Paul. Guilt made her resist the idea that wanting to get Paul back was an understandable, even predictable reaction. It felt more natural to her to condemn her behavior as maliciously controlling. Guilt made Laura want to punish herself with self-pathologizing thoughts.

Guilt is a complex subject heatedly debated in the psychological community. I sharply disagree with psychotherapists who believe that guilt is "the useless emotion." As I said earlier, I believe every feeling occurs for an important reason. Guilt in moderation can be a kind of moral beacon, warning us when we might be treating another person unfairly. It can also be a mentor, helping us learn from our mistakes.

But one-ups are prone to a special brand of out-of-control guilt, which I call "runaway guilt." It creates a kamikaze mentality in the one-up that can lead to extremely damaging behavior. One-ups with runaway guilt feel they're so bad that they have "nothing left to lose"; they're beyond redemption. Infidelity and cruel behavior often come from one-ups who've written themselves off for not loving their partners. Paradoxically, then, runaway guilt makes them prone to do the very thing that makes them feel guiltiest: hurt their partners. Often the intolerable pain of guilt leads to a one-up's most extreme action: flight from its source, the relationship.

The Guilt Exercise

Guilt tends to grind away hope for a relationship, so I urge one-ups to do this exercise whenever they feel a surge of it. This process actually turns guilt into a way to help *solve* core relationship problems.

Step 1: List Your Self-Pathologizing Statements

I asked Laura to list the ways in which she felt to blame for her relationship's problems. This is what she wrote:

1. I'm immature. I expected to find a perfect partner whom I'd find forever exciting and romantic.
2. I'm so emotionally shallow that as soon as I "have" someone I don't want him anymore. Maybe that means I'm afraid of commitment.

3. I can be really selfish about things like my career. If it's between doing something for Paul or for a case, I'll go with the case every time.

Step 2: Apply the 50/50 Rule to Your Guilt

For each self-pathologizing statement, write how it is *partly an exaggeration and partly a reflection of genuine relationship problems*. This is what Laura wrote:

1. At times I do get a little carried away with my romantic fantasies. But I guess I'm mature enough to have gotten a good start in a demanding profession. Paul is someone I can feel very affectionate toward, but sometimes he gets so possessive even my friends think I'm surprisingly tolerant.
2. I realize that someday I'm going to have to face my fear of commitment, especially if it's making me seek out a certain kind of guy. But at the same time, you have to be cautious. I mean, look at all the people who don't have enough fear of commitment. They rush into bad marriages and end up paying for years. I'm happy we're trying to figure out why I have trouble feeling romantic about Paul. It will give us a better chance of making the right decision.
3. That's more like 90 percent exaggeration. I know that professional couples who do best compartmentalize their work and personal lives to a pretty great extent. And that's really what I do more successfully than Paul.

Step 3: Confront the Core Problems

It's good to feel *some* guilt—as long as you don't self-pathologize. Use your guilt as a motivator to seek out harmful patterns and to communicate about them with your partner. Acknowledge that you play a role in your relationship's dynamics, but keep sight of the fact that your problems were spawned by an imbalance that may have eluded both you and your partner.

Even if you've done things that hurt your partner, you'll ultimately hurt him more if you condemn yourself. Tell yourself, "Yes, I've made some mistakes. Now what can I do to see if we can make this relationship work?"

Guilt gives a relationship a huge negative charge. But when one-ups gain control over their guilt, that negative charge loses its kick.

That's why I like to deal with runaway guilt early in my work with one-ups. Relieved of it, a one-up's attitude toward the relationship is often stunningly improved.

Strategy 3:
Harness Your Anger

On one hand, one-ups feel guilty and blameworthy; on the other, they feel a good deal of understandable anger. They're angry at their partners for disappointing them and they're angry because they feel so trapped and unfulfilled. But rarely do one-ups feel justified in their anger because the one-down is usually so loving and vulnerable.

Even under the best of circumstances most people have trouble expressing their anger effectively. One-ups are no exception. As their anger gathers power, they typically do one of three things: They slip into an accusatory mindset and blame everything on their partner; they turn it inward where it turns into guilt and self-pathologizing; or they find indirect ways of expressing it.

Displaced Anger

If you find yourself chronically feeling irritated or "blowing up" at rather insignificant actions from your partner, you're probably displacing your anger away from larger relationship problems. Miles, for instance, would occasionally "lose it" when Beth did the most trivial things, like leave a light on. Laura once lashed out at Paul for snoring. The problem with displaced anger is that it feeds directly into passion trap dynamics by eroding the one-down's self-esteem and fueling the one-up's guilt. And the one-up's anger will only keep growing because core problems aren't being addressed.

No-Fault Communication is the key to expressing anger *directly* and *constructively* at core problems. If you're harboring a good deal of anger toward your partner, please review chapter 8. I also offer my one-up clients an analogy that has helped them understand, accept, and rechannel their anger:

People who must care for a partner with a serious medical condition often feel angry and resentful. Suddenly they're burdened with heavy new responsibilities and restrictions. Commonly, they misinterpret the cause of this anger as *the ill spouse*. And that makes them feel self-condemning, because the spouse is so helpless and needy. People in this situation can be helped tremendously by the therapeutic suggestion that they reframe their anger so that the *changed life situation* rather than the partner bears the brunt of it. This approach promotes a "can do" attitude about making the best of the situation.

For one-ups, blaming the harmful relationship dynamics has the same effect. Reframing anger this way makes it justifiable and even energizing. One-ups can turn anger into a potent motivator by saying, "This situation is making me angry and I'm going to do anything I can to improve it."

Strategy 4: Learn to See Your Partner Clearly

When one-downs catastrophize, they imagine they can't live without their relationship. When one-ups catastrophize, they imagine they can't live within the relationship—that they'll be forever trapped with partners who don't attract or fulfill them. They lose sexual desire for their partners, and then in reaction pathologize about their "immature" need for romantic excitement. They begin to wonder if their standards are too high.

I urge you not to discount your negative perceptions of your partner. It could very well be that your partner's personality, intelligence, looks, humor, and so on don't mesh well with your needs. At the same time, remember that the forces of the one-up position cause you to magnify the bad and overlook the good in your partner. Be especially sensitive to distortions if your relationship was balanced, then slipped during a situational change.

The Objectifying Exercise

This exercise helps one-ups view their partners objectively and thereby defuses their confinement fears.

First, list the negative qualities in your partner that most bother you. Let your gut emotions dictate this list and don't put yourself down for anything you write.

Next, alongside these negative qualities list your partner's attractive features that imbalance may have devalued. It may help to think back to what first attracted you to your partner.

Here are Laura's lists about Paul:

Bad Qualities	*Good Qualities*
• He tries too hard	• He is very respected
• He's not athletic	• He is very bright
• His middle-aged looks	• His looks have appeal
• His social awkwardness	• He is loving and expressive
• He is possessive	• He is generous

Examine your list of negative qualities and think how the one-down position may *actually be causing them.* Laura realized that Paul's unattractive behaviors around her were likely due to his one-down insecurity. She also concluded that her perceptions of his negative qualities were enhanced by her one-up perspective. Next, imagine your partner in a situation, such as a party, in which his insecurity seems particularly acute. Visualize his insecure, one-down behaviors, like staying too close, wanting to leave, or trying to make you jealous by flirting with other people. Notice how your negative perceptions of him grow sharper.

Now, cast him in the role of a partner secure and confident in your love. You gaze across the room and there he is, having an animated conversation with an interesting-looking group of people; he winks when he notices you're looking at him. Or, an old boyfriend comes over to talk to you, and your partner gracefully excuses himself to give you time alone. When you excuse yourself from your old boyfriend to join up with your confident, secure partner, he squeezes your hand and says, "I missed you."

This is how Laura envisioned a confident, secure Paul. "It's funny," she said, "but this is the way he is in a work context." She realized why: because in his professional dealings he felt confident and secure; he wasn't a one-down.

I assured Laura that it was possible for Paul to feel truly secure in their relationship as well. Working on their harmful dynamics was the key.

Strategy 5:
Keep Your Freedom
Option Open

The Freedom Option is a very potent concept that has helped a number of my one-up clients deal with their feelings of confinement and resolve their ambivalence. It is the most direct way of tackling a one-up's feeling of being trapped in a relationship.

It doesn't matter what the source of this feeling is. It might be fear of not finding a better relationship, fear of independence, a sense of obligation, worries about what people will think, guilt and fear about emotionally devastating a partner or dependent children, and so on.

Holding the belief that you are truly trapped in your relationship, for whatever reason, guarantees three things: that you will be trapped, that you will be unhappy because you feel so trapped, and that you will feel all the more resistant to the relationship. Attempts to suppress your unhappiness will cause your feelings to grow more toxic. You may begin to act out your frustration by abusing harmful substances, having affairs, and emotionally starving your partner.

As we've seen, treatments for the passion trap often themselves hinge on paradoxical, or seemingly contradictory, ways of thinking. And so it is with the Freedom Option. Keeping your Freedom Option open means accepting that you can and should leave your relationship if your frustration continues to grow. It means telling yourself that you have *every right* to opt out if your needs aren't being met and if staying represents a serious personal compromise.

By assuring yourself of these things, you'll vastly improve your chances of reviving the relationship. In this mindset, you won't feel so trapped, so there will be less need to strain against the ties of your relationship. If you stop pulling away from your partner, your partner won't need to grasp at you.

Thus, the Freedom Option counters passion trap dynamics by:

- Freeing you of panic-based, distorted, negative thoughts about your partner
- Allowing you to assess your relationship more objectively
- Giving you greater incentive to improve the relationship
- Helping you to feel love again

The Freedom Option Exercise

When Peg first started individual therapy, she felt not only trapped but immobilized. Her "solution" — a persistent widow fantasy — was creating even greater problems. Often she found herself drifting into fantasies of Bill dying (of natural causes) and her own release-without-dishonor from the burdens of their marriage. However, she could not relish the sensation of freedom for more than a moment before beginning to feel extreme self-hatred and depression. When Bill drank or was abusive to her, she felt she had no right to stand up to him: After all, anyone who would fantasize about her spouse dying deserved to be abused. Thus, her fantasies ultimately fed her sense of imprisonment.

A major part of therapy is showing clients that they have many more options than they realize. While the focus of my therapy with Peg was on helping her to help her marriage, I felt it vital that she complete the following Freedom Option exercise early in our work together. I wanted to show her that if she could accept her right to leave Bill if his abusive behavior continued, she would feel more entitled to confront him about their problems. This is what she wrote:

Reasons I Must Stay	*Freedom Option Counter*
Bill needs me. If I leave him, he may actually wind up on skid row.	Bill is an adult who has to take responsibility for his actions. I have the right to be loved and respected.
Our shared history.	I cherish our past together, but it's no reason to live with abuse in the present and future.
The boys.	Each boy has privately offered support if I were to leave Bill.
I vowed to stay by Bill's side for better or worse.	Granted I need to learn better ways of helping Bill when he's down, but I didn't make a vow to endure abuse.
Fear of going through a divorce.	I would survive the pain and probably be happier over time.

Reasons I Must Stay	*Freedom Option Counter*
I'm too old to find a new partner.	Maybe, maybe not. But I might be better off alone than with the present Bill.

Because of her admitted "old-fashioned stand by your man" values, it was hard for Peg to feel comfortable with the Freedom Option. But as we worked on the exercise, she felt less trapped. Peg began to accept that she could stand up for *her* rights and needs in the marriage. And if Bill wasn't willing to do his part, she had the option to leave.

Confining Realities

The realities of dependent children and limited financial prospects may make the Freedom Option seem no more than a pie-in-the-sky fantasy. But it's not. The key is to set long-term goals that will bring you more freedom and independence, and to approach them realistically. This may involve waiting until the children are in school, slowly working toward a degree in the evenings, or taking part-time work. Any concrete effort to change your life will make you feel less trapped and will raise your spirits. As your feelings of confinement lift, you may find yourself feeling better about your relationship.

But Don't Feel You HAVE to Leave

The Freedom Option is not designed to give the one-up an easy way out of his relationship at the first sign of trouble. Rather, it is designed for one-ups who are subject to guilt and fear of leaving, or blocked by confining realities. The primary purpose of the Freedom Option is to give ambivalent, immobilized one-ups a sense of their options and an emotional safety valve. In my practice, I've seen the Freedom Option turn many despairing one-ups into effective problem-solvers.

Strategy 6:
Trial Closeness

This is the key intervention in my therapy with one-ups. Trial Closeness — the one-up's answer to the one-down's Healthy Distance — is exactly what it sounds like: the opposite of a trial separation.

As you know, when the passion trap locks in, your emotional distance compels your partner to pressure you for closeness. But her efforts backfire by making you crave distance all the more. Imagine what would happen, then, if you were suddenly to seek closeness from your one-down.

I have seen the results, and often they are startling. A one-down will quickly feel more secure and less needy. She'll regain confidence, composure, emotional control, spontaneity, and often her appeal to the one-up. Sometimes, of course, when imbalance runs very deep, the relationship still wont be right. But Trial Closeness offers the best way to make this decision and to resolve ambivalence about a relationship.

The critical word here is *trial*. The trial approach frees you from the *obligation* to feel closer and leaves your Freedom Option wide open. The goal is not for you to feel closer but to see if you *can* feel closer. This diverges sharply from the approach in traditional couples' therapy in which the one-up is viewed as avoiding commitment and intimacy and is pressured to overcome it. This "solution" offers only surface intimacy and does not correctly interpret or address the one-up's distant feelings.

When you try Trial Closeness, the result you seek is an end to ambivalence. Whether the outcome is renewed love for your partner or a greater wish for distance, you'll have gained perspective, insight, and greater certainty about your relationship.

You're feeling distant, frustrated, and generally negative about your relationship. Yet, I'm asking you to move closer to your partner. How is it possible for you to do that without feeling resistant, resentful, or hypocritical?

Start Trial Closeness with No-Fault Communication

The most important thing to know when you begin Trial Closeness is that its essence is communication. When you share your feelings in No-Fault terms—*even your negative feelings*—you're taking a step closer to your partner.

Laura was nervous about sharing her guilt and frustration with Paul. I told her to take time to think of the No-Fault terms that felt right for the task. As Paul had done before, she framed her remarks in an analogy. This can be a very effective way to maximize impact and minimize blame. Here's what she said:

> Paul, you remember how you said it was difficult for you to visit your mother because she'd be so thrilled to see you that she'd just wait on you and cater to you until you felt guilty. And you'd always come away feeling frustrated because you'd hoped you and she could just relax and be yourselves together. Well, sometimes I think we fall into a similar pattern. You can be so nice and giving to me that I start feeling guilty and frustrated. And then it's hard for me not to pull back, which is when you really start pouring it on.

Although it made Paul wince, Laura's analogy gave him a new perspective on his role in their problem patterns. And Laura felt unburdened of key negative feelings about Paul. As a result, she felt closer to Paul, and willing to try more.

Sometimes sharing negative feelings won't clear the air and make you feel closer — especially when you first try it. If one or both of you are threatened, you may wind up fighting or defensively withdrawing. Still, this sharing is a crucial step. You are, after all, offering the one-down genuine closeness — your true feelings delivered in a non-blaming spirit. You're also imparting important information to the one-down, who may lack awareness of the things that bother you.

Sometimes there's a delayed reaction to a one-up's No-Fault but negative disclosures. A day or two after such a discussion, a one-down will often approach his partner and say how glad he is that those issues have been brought out in the open. As Paul said later of Laura's disclosure:

> It told me she cared about our relationship. And it gave me a good sense of what I could do to make things better. I feel a little more grounded now.

Share the Little Things

One-ups tend to stop sharing with their partners the feelings, thoughts, and experiences that create the texture of intimacy between two people. This kind of sharing is what friends do, and this is what I ask one-ups to try with their partners: to reestablish their friendships with them.

When Peg was starting her business and Bill was still working, they'd had "fascinating conversations" about her discoveries and travails as a new businesswoman. But with Bill's career setback and personal decline came an end to their sharing and their friendship. Now Peg wanted to revive that aspect of their relationship.

> When the weather was nice, we used to like to sit out on the veranda late in the afternoon and watch the sun set and talk. So one evening I got home and invited him out there. I just wanted to tell him about my day. I mentioned something I'd heard on the radio coming home and seeing an old friend who'd come into the shop. He wasn't terribly responsive to begin with, but then I asked him about a problem employee I have. And he kind of perked up. What he said was simply astute, and I told him so. And then I asked him about his day. And he told me about a funny sort of debate he'd had with a Jehovah's Witness who'd come to the door. We sat out there until it started getting pretty chilly.

Peg showed Bill that she wanted to give him something of herself, even something as simple as her day. By soliciting his advice, she affirmed that she valued him and recognized a special strength in him. Peg was asking for Bill's friendship. For about a week, Peg reported, "we went in and out." But she stayed with it until new patterns of communication and positive sharing started to take root.

Experiment with Affection

When an ambivalent one-up feels favorable about the relationship, I suggest that he try an experiment with affection. Simply, he makes a concerted effort to express affection—more than he might normally. Many one-ups are pleasantly surprised to discover that showing affection enhances their affectionate feelings.

The dynamic that enables this is pure passion paradox. By expressing affection, one-ups help their partners feel more confident and less needy. That in turn loosens the grip of the one-down. The outcome is a better balance between the partners.

Think of affectionate gestures that would mean a lot to your partner. Miles came up with this list:

- Give foot rubs, which Beth loves
- Bring home flowers
- Arrange for just the two of us to spend a weekend together at a bed-and-breakfast or hot-springs resort
- Give her compliments
- Do more casual touching, kissing
- Surprise her by taking her to a movie, play, concert, etc.
- Tell her I love her

I suggested to Miles that whenever things were going well between them, he experiment with one of these ideas. After two weeks, I asked him how the experiment was going.

> At first, doing these things felt a little forced, even when Beth and I were getting along. But I kept reminding myself of what you said — that my goal was to *see* if I could start feeling closer. I even came out and explained that to Beth — how I wanted to feel closer to her. And she responded really well. She said, "In that case, why don't you come cuddle with me." We're still having ups and downs, but the downs aren't so low. And it's so nice when we get into an affectionate mode that I want to try to keep us in that place.

Although it wasn't an explicit goal, Miles found that bringing more affection to the relationship had led to very tender lovemaking. This pleased Beth too.

Experiment with Vulnerability

I ask my one-up clients to share with their partners some of their deepest hurts, fears, self-doubts, and secrets — things they may never have shared before. It may seem frightening, but it's a potent way of equalizing an unbalanced relationship. In a sense, your emotional risk makes you the one-down and your partner the one in temporary control. Again, the results can be powerfully reinforcing. It feels good to let down your guard and allow another person to share what may be a bigger emotional burden than you realize.

Laura tried this strategy. In a joint session, she reported how it went.

> The other night I told Paul something I've never told anyone. I mean the whole truth about something I've only partially told to people. Anyway, it was about my mother. She's had problems with depression. But she was actually hospitalized a couple of times, once after attempting suicide. They would tell us she was going to visit her sister. But I didn't learn the truth — including the fact that she'd had electric shock therapy — until I was in college. And I realized I was afraid to tell people for fear they'd think I was unstable too. But that makes me feel so guilty and disloyal, like I'm ashamed of this woman who loves me so much and gave up so much — she was her high school class valedictorian — to be a good mother ...

Laura broke off and took a deep breath, trying not to cry. She put her hand in Paul's and he squeezed it. Then she finished her thought.

> Anyway, when I told Paul, he said just the right things, and he held me. And I felt very safe and understood.

Sharing vulnerabilities with partners, and receiving emotional support in return, is a powerful source of intimacy. Some one-ups avoid such disclosures precisely because they don't want to lose their sense of control. However, when one-ups begin to take emotional risks in their relationships, they begin to feel more deeply. Laura said she felt so good after confiding in Paul that she wished she'd done it sooner.

A few cautionary words about this strategy: Don't feel you have to expose *everything* about your past to your partner. Start with something you feel comfortable discussing and see how that goes. And don't drop it on your partner out of the blue. Ask him if he'd like to hear something very personal about you. Plan a time to talk about it if the moment doesn't seem right.

Finally, be prepared to feel some anxiety—even welcome it. It's a sign that you're truly making yourself vulnerable, not simply going through the motions.

Explain What You're Doing

If you don't tell your partner about your Trial Closeness, its strategies will still aid your relationship. But when you choose to communicate about Trial Closeness, it lets your one-down partner know you care enough to work toward the relationship's improvement. And that invites the one-down to do his part to make things better.

When one-up and one-down coordinate Trial Closeness and Healthy Distance, the passion trap gets a therapeutic double dose: It loses potency as a negative force in the relationship. Then, the partners can break free of paradox-induced thought distortions and extreme behaviors. With greater clarity and calm, they can work as a team on core issues.

Trial Closeness Is Not a Game

Some one-ups don't want to discuss Trial Closeness with their partners because they think it sounds too much like an emotional game. After all, Trial Closeness does amount to the one-up putting his partner (and himself) through a "relationship test." That's likely to unnerve the one-down, so why tell her?

My response to this is that one-ups are already mentally testing their relationships, trying to decide whether to stay or to leave. One-downs usually sense this. "Relationship testing," then, is something that goes on naturally anyway. But it's more therapeutic to carry out this testing in a conscious, planned, results-oriented way. The one-up who can tell his partner, "We're having problems; let's see if we can make things better," has already made things better.

Quality Time

The emphasis during Trial Closeness should be on the quality of time you spend with your partner, not the quantity. If you feel obliged to spend every free moment with your partner during the trial, you may find it difficult to sustain a loving attitude. On the other hand, you and your partner may rarely be able to spend time together because of business and parental obligations. If this is the case, schedule regular times to be alone together.

Don't Set Conditions

Trial Closeness works best if your emotional closeness is offered *unconditionally*. For example, part of Peg's Trial Closeness involved making gourmet candlelit dinners for Bill on Saturday nights. But when she started this tradition she didn't tell Bill, "I'll make special dinners for you if you'll get a job tomorrow and stop sulking around the house." Peg's actions showed affection and acceptance of Bill as he was. And that ego boost helped him become someone she could fall in love with again.

Strategy 7: Be Patient

When Miles first experimented with closeness, he found that it felt "a little forced." But he didn't permit that feeling to foster panic, guilt, or blaming. He patiently persisted. And with time and Beth's help, he found his love for his wife growing, deepening, and becoming steadier.

I can vouch for the effectiveness of the strategies in this chapter, but the degree of their success hinges on your patience in using them.

The dynamics of imbalance are powerful, and sometimes it takes a while to determine whether they can be mended. Some of my clients worked up to a year before balance—and romantic caring—began to return. These one-ups persisted in trying different healing strategies and stayed with those that helped. They learned the art of recovering from conflicts and riding out the inevitable setbacks.

My "former one-up" clients agree that the renewed love and intimacy in their relationships were more than worth the efforts they made. When you invest hard emotional work in a relationship, you actually fortify the love in it and deepen the intimacy.

One-ups who are unable to recapture love gain as well, because their questions are finally resolved, their ambivalence ended. They know they tried their hardest to make the relationship work, and that can make its final stages a little easier on everyone.

Chapter 11

Seeking the Roots
of Imbalance

Situations, Sex Roles,
Attraction Power

You have learned how to talk to your partner about difficult matters and how to spot destructive patterns in your interactions. You have highly effective strategies for countering one-up and one-down thoughts and actions.

Now let's go deeper, to the very roots of imbalance in your relationship — what created the patterns, the trouble, and the pain.

In chapter 2 you learned about three causes of imbalance: situational, attraction power, and incompatibilities in personality style. I often see unbalanced relationships that harbor symptoms of more than one kind. But each relationship has a special area of vulnerability — the relationship's Achilles' heel — and it's important to know what yours is. Once you do, you can take care to shield it.

Situational Imbalance

Beth and Miles started out an evenly matched couple. But Beth's becoming a full-time mother around the time that Miles opened his restaurant put enormous pressure on them. Their roles changed and likewise their power positions. With the loss of balance came confusion, panic, and frustration. Beth said, "I was stunned when I realized things had really changed between us. What had seemed rock solid was suddenly delicate and fragile."

Situational imbalance forces people to appreciate the fragility of their relationships. It's a mistake to believe that relationships can be threatened only from within, by personal change or incompatibilities. External events can powerfully influence your intimate life by drawing on your emotional reserves. When emotional investments shift, so do interpersonal dynamics.

As a case in point, when Beth left work she deprived herself of the professional and personal validation she had grown used to. In the new arena of motherhood, she felt somewhat insecure and earned little validation. But her state of emotional neediness wouldn't have existed if her situation hadn't changed.

Miles too had changed his situation. He had never before been in such a pressured make-or-break situation.

> I was on the line. The backers were throwing money at me, but with the underlying message that my ass would be grass if the restaurant belly-upped. I made the wrong assumption that the home front would take care of itself.

So Miles's emotional focus shifted to the restaurant at the expense of the relationship. Had Beth still been working, this change might have brought only a slight imbalance. But given her new neediness, the imbalance was extreme.

Most of the couples who consult me are grappling with situational imbalance, but they don't know it. The human tendency to blame a *person* blinds them to the tremendous impact a stressful situation can have. Sometimes they make near-diagnoses: "Things just haven't been the same since Mother's operation," or (something I often hear in my part of the country) ". . . since we left Topeka" — or wherever. The liberating conclusion eludes them — that almost any couple in their stressful situation would succumb in a similar way to harmful relationship forces.

I usually feel relieved when I find symptoms of situational imbalance in my clients. It is the most tractable form of imbalance. Sometimes just explaining it to couples rather dramatically gets them back on track.

For most couples, however, it's not quite so simple. Experiencing imbalance is a little like opening Pandora's box. Emotional demons are set loose, and they need to be handled along with the unbalancing situation.

Spotting Situational Imbalance

Around the time your relationship developed problems, did you or your partner:

- Experience any change in job status?
- Go through a stressful transition such as moving, having a baby, getting married, or losing a parent or other loved one?
- Experience a family crisis such as a teen's rebellion or an elderly relative moving in?
- Take on a big task, responsibility, or project such as getting involved in a political campaign, becoming chair of the PTA, or winning a part in a community theater play?
- Have a disabling illness or accident?
- Gain or lose a substantial amount of money?

If you answered yes to any of these questions, your relationship probably suffers from situational imbalance.

By contrast, recall Deborah and Jonathan, the art teacher and the contractor. Their personal situations were relatively equivalent and relatively stable. Yet, passion trap dynamics developed between them, because they had unsynchronous personality styles (a subject we'll soon be exploring).

Beth and Miles, on the other hand, instantly saw their situation as imbalanced. This perception was good therapy for them because it rooted their problems in something external and tangible, not in some psychological shadowland. Of course, they would still need to work on the one-up/one-down patterns spawned by their unbalancing situation. But attacking those patterns along with the stressful situation itself would mutually reinforce their efforts.

Changing the Situation

Here's a step-by-step program for purging your relationship of situational imbalance. You'll notice that there's a natural meshing between this program and those of a one-down's Healthy Distance and a one-up's Trial Closeness. So don't worry about how to coordinate them. It will happen naturally.

First, Blame the Situation

Marcy and Steve, a fortyish couple, came to me knowing that a situation had created chaos in their relationship. But the way they saw it, this (not uncommon) situation had brought out the worst in each of them. Now that they knew "the awful truth" about each other, they didn't even like each other anymore.

Both Marcy and Steve were in sales: she in real estate, he in medical equipment. They had two young children. Things had been fine until Steve's newly widowed mother moved to California, where Steve and Marcy lived. Although she had her own condo (Marcy: "She wouldn't dream of living at our house, thank God."), her presence was strongly felt in the couple's household. Steve, concerned about his mother's adjustment, spent a good deal of time with her, taking her shopping and showing her around. Marcy was unhappy when her mother-in-law visited because she was openly critical of the housekeeping, the children's manners, "everything." Marcy tried to maintain a veneer of cordiality with her mother-in-law, but she was prone to fits of temper, crying, and rage before and after the visits. She also found herself . . .

> competing with my mother-in-law for Steve. One night the kids stayed over at their cousins'. I made a romantic dinner and dolled myself up in a silk wraparound number. And the phone rings just as we're finishing. It's Moms, panicking because she's just heard a prowler. Which is fine, except she hears them several times a week. Off dashes Steve. I drink the rest of the champagne and fall asleep on the couch. Steve comes home and goes to bed. I wake up on the couch the next day.

Marcy felt the problem stemmed from Steve's unhealthy attachment to his mother. Steve felt that Marcy was acting like a selfish child and had no empathy for his mother's situation. In other words, they were blaming each other.

Over several therapy sessions, I guided Steve and Marcy to the conclusion that they were basically a compatible, balanced couple suffering from situational imbalance. Steve's concern for his mother made him the one-up, while Marcy's pulling for more closeness made her the one-down. Their challenge was that the situation was so sensitive. Obviously, both had strong and very personal feelings about Steve's grieving mother, and the mother had her own complex needs.

Second, Empathize

The next important step is for the partners to empathize with each other's feelings. For Steve and Marcy, this proved a powerful exercise.

At the end of our second session I asked each to imagine the other's feelings and prepare to talk about them in the next session. This was Steve's response when we met again:

> From Marcy's point of view, I can understand that my mother's arrival has upset our way of life. It's true that I care very deeply for my mother, and I'm worried that she's still not taking the death of my father very well. But I know this has to be disturbing to Marcy because we're usually there for each other and suddenly that's changed. Unfortunately, my mother's not the most easy-going of people. If she and Marcy got along, there'd really be no problem. And I know, in all honesty, that Marcy's tried to make friends with Moms.

At the end of Steve's empathy, Marcy tearfully leaned over and kissed her husband's cheek.

> Steve has a strong sense of duty, and since his sister gets along about as well as I do with his mother and has been no help since their father died, he's kind of had to shoulder all the responsibilities. I think it runs really deep with Steve because his mother always loved him so much and gave so much, probably because his father was away from home a lot. And now he feels indebted to her. And I know that Steve is aware that this is a situation that has to give somewhere. But the pressure and frustration got to us before we were able to find a solution.

Now, their alliance strengthened, Marcy and Steve were ready to search for a solution.

Third, Negotiate Balance

If a situation is powerful enough to pull a couple out of balance, it's usually complex as well. That's why I urge my clients to avoid "vague sincerity" about making changes to improve a problem situation. Much better to devise concrete, action-oriented short- and long-term plans, as Steve and Marcy did.

MAKE SHORT-TERM PLANS

Steve and Marcy decided *not* to expect much change in the near future. Marcy's empathy encompassed the fact that Steve's mother, being elderly and by nature wary, couldn't be expected to adjust very quickly, and perhaps not fully, ever.

But Marcy volunteered to make a greater effort. As hard as it would be, she said she would reach out again to her mother-in-law, maybe take her out to lunch and antiquing, which she loved.

Steve said he would begin to set some limits with his mother; for example, he would designate times when he'd visit her or take her out. He would be loving but firm, reminding her that he couldn't very well have two separate family lives and inviting her to join in more with the rest of his family.

LONG-RANGE PLANS

Steve and Marcy realized that even if Steve's mother were able to strike a truce with Marcy, the situation wouldn't fully be resolved unless she had some activities and friends of her own. So, for the long-term, the couple would work toward getting Steve's mother into social activities.

At first Steve's mother adamantly resisted their efforts and spoke continually of wanting to "join" her husband. But by the time of our last session, three months later, she was beginning to find happiness with a bridge club for seniors, was coming to dinner at Steve and Marcy's twice a week, and had offered to babysit.

What If the Situation Can't Be Changed?

Let's say Steve's mother was shortly thereafter diagnosed as having Alzheimer's disease. Let's also say that it meant much to Steve to take care of her in their home for as long as they could.

I believe there are *always* things we can do to make a bad situation better. Any tough situation offers dozens of choices in its handling. In other words, you never lose all your options. But when you accept that you aren't a helpless pawn of circumstance, you must also accept the responsibility of working to make the best of a given situation.

It's most important to maintain your No-Fault Communication and to talk frequently about the feelings being stirred up by a stressful, unyielding, unbalancing situation. It's also important that the partners watch for harmful interactive patterns that may be widening their imbalance.

The worst situations can ennoble us when we rise to their challenges. For partners, they can be a rich source of empathy, intimacy, and mutual respect, all of which are powerful agents of balance.

Anticipate Situational Imbalance

Your boss has just declared bankruptcy, your doctor has announced you're pregnant with twins, and your husband's new assistant is a Britney Spears look-alike. Expect repercussions in your relationship. Talk to your partner. Discuss your feelings about the situation and deduce the harmful patterns that could develop. Forgive yourselves in advance for the inevitable moments of friction. Keep tabs on predictable one-up and one-down thoughts and behaviors and work together to counter them. Realize that it can take months or even years to fully overcome some situational problems. But each effort you make can speed this process and deepen your relationship.

Sex Roles

When we explore situational imbalance in romantic relationships, we must always consider one of the greatest outside influences any man or woman can know: society's rules and expectations for acceptable male and female behavior. I see these expectations as crucial factors in the formation of life situations *and* personality styles.

"Boy/Girl" Traits and the Passion Trap

The stereotypes of male and female roles have undeniably changed in the last twenty years. Yet, traditional notions about male and female characteristics still underlie our assumptions. For example, we still describe aggressive, high-achieving women as having *broken away* from the female stereotype, and men who stay at home with children as going against the male grain. It's helpful to see these tenacious underlying assumptions about men and women and some of the words associated with them.

Traditional Female	*Traditional Male*
Follower	Leader
Nurturer	Nurtured
Passive	Aggressive
Dependent	Independent
Submissive	Dominant

Mother	Provider
Home	Workplace
Financially vulnerable	Financially powerful

Obviously, the woman who embraces stereotypical female characteristics is positioned to be a one-down, just as a traditional man is expected to be a one-up. The man's emotional focal point lies outside the relationship, on his place in the world. For the traditional woman, the relationship and the family are the centerpiece of her emotional life. As the man's outer orientation increases, the woman feels a greater need for his fulfilling attention, and the passion trap cycle clicks into motion. Both come to feel stuck in this pattern, and both may bypass their partners to get important needs met. Friends, children, lovers, work, and outside interests become substitute sources of fulfillment when imbalance between two partners has eroded their bond.

Miles and Beth's case illustrates how powerful sex roles can be in triggering destructive relationship patterns. Before assuming her *temporary* role as a mother/housewife, Beth was a true contemporary woman. She had a fulfilling, challenging career, she was independent, confident, assertive, happy, self-sufficient, and financially secure. "But I also felt a lack in my life," she recalled, "and that's why I went for it when Miles came along." But later:

> I felt like I was turning into my mother on some kind of cellular level. My maternal instinct was really strong, and for the first six months or so the idea of anyone else taking care of Chloe almost made me panic. And I lost my sense of what I could feel righteous about. Housecleaning was a biggie. I feel women shouldn't have to do it all, even when they "aren't working"—a ludicrous concept when kids are part of the picture. But I was feeling guilty about asking Miles to help out, because I could see how hard he was working "for us." But then I'd realize he was doing something he enjoyed. Dirty diapers and dishes aren't exactly my idea of a good time. That's when the resentment set in.

Beth's desire to care for her child conflicted with her contemporary values. These conflicts cost her power within the relationship. Not knowing how to express her problems effectively, or to experiment with different problem-solving strategies, led to frustration and a needy, demanding one-down stance. Meanwhile, Miles, like many men, became so focused on his career success "for my family as well as myself" that he couldn't see the happiness slipping from their lives.

Surface Control Versus Deep Power

Because of the way traditional sex roles mesh with the passion trap, we're not surprised when we hear about distant husbands and needy wives. But sex roles can be smokescreens that *conceal a wife's power and a husband's neediness,* even from the partners themselves. In these cases, couples need to look beneath surface behavior.

On the surface, these couples fit the stereotypical picture of male-female relating. The man is domineering, controlling, and aggressive; the woman is passive, dependent, and submissive. But there's another factor that operates below surface behavior, and *it* ultimately determines which partner holds the most power. It has nothing to do with who makes or handles the money or who makes the major decisions or even who hits the hardest.

The deep power in the relationship belongs to the partner *who is less emotionally involved.* Surface control may belong either to the one-up or the one-down, but deep power lies only with the true one-up. And sometimes the true one-up outwardly appears to be the one-down.

The "Disguised" One-Up
and One-Down

For example, a woman may be passive, dependent, and subservient. But if she's less committed to the relationship than her partner is, she holds the deep power. Ultimately, she determines whether there will *be* a relationship. Often it's her partner's rigid, domineering personality that weakens her attachment. She is the "disguised one-up," her partner the "disguised one-down."

Their masks stay in place as long as she remains in the relationship. These masks are so effective that often the woman and man have no conscious awareness of her power in the relationship. But if she leaves — or if an adulterous affair is discovered — the masks suddenly fall. For the disguised one-up, there is often no turning back; her feelings of liberation may outweigh guilt. For the disguised one-down, there may be wild swings between punishing one-down retaliations and abject pleas for her return.

Hidden Balance

There are marriages in which the partners embrace traditional sex roles—*and both are happily and equally committed to the relationship.* Again, the *underlying* emotional pattern tells all. In this case, the partners' love, respect, and caring are balanced, though they may be expressed in very different ways by the partners. Often the wife has attraction power qualities such as intelligence, emotional strength, wit, beauty, self-respect, and so on. This wife's strengths may mirror the husband's or may compensate for his less developed areas. Again, this type of husband will *appear* to be the one who monopolizes the power and control in the relationship—the one who "wears the pants." But because he is as emotionally involved in the relationship as his wife, they equally share deep power and love.

The Sex-Role Risk Factor

Adherence to stereotypical sex roles greatly increases the risk that your relationship will fall prey to the passion trap. Fortunately, most contemporary men and women no longer actively seek traditional partners. A man seeks his female equivalent for love, companionship, nest building, and to share the financial burdens of chasing the American Dream.

By the same token, today's woman has no desire to be subservient to a powerful male figure. Her options have multiplied, and long-term dependence on a man is now the least appealing of them all. Her primary task will be weighing commitments to career and motherhood.

Unfortunately, there's still a good deal of confusion about what men and women really want from each other. Often, it appears that what people profess to want is at odds with what they seek (e.g., the man who wants his "liberated woman" also to happily assume all traditional domestic duties). This is why we should remain vigilant about the residue of traditional sex roles.

We live in a time that offers unprecedented opportunities for balance between men and women—a time when both are likely to evenly divide their emotional energies between career concerns and family concerns. And I do see among my friends and colleagues some very strong and dynamic romantic partnerships. But there are wrinkles, and they include phenomena like the "Superwoman" who tries to "do it all."

The Risk of Doing It All

Beth gave the traditional female role a try and slid into the one-down position. Many women attempt to handle it all — motherhood, home-making, and career — and confront a different side of the passion trap.

Consider one couple I treated, Hugh and Louise. He was a super-visor for a public utility, she headed the payroll department at a local university. They had two children, and they were busy, balanced, and happy. But then Louise, an active union member, was elected chapter president. Suddenly the demands on her time skyrocketed. She'd always taken the lion's share of responsibility for the children, and that didn't change much. Soon, almost all of Louise's emotional energy was being poured into kids, work, or the union. Little was left for Hugh, who began to feel neglected.

When Hugh wanted to make love, Louise either didn't have time or was too tired. When he suggested they go out, there was always something else she had to do. Like many women in this situation, the demands on Louise's time and energy had turned her into a one-up and her husband into a one-down. After a while, Louise. noticed that she wasn't feeling very loving toward Hugh anymore. He was simply a part of her life, and sometimes an annoying one. Hugh, on the other hand, was feeling emotionally neglected, needy, and resentful. They wound up in therapy after Louise learned he was having an affair with a secretary at his office.

Louise and Hugh's harmful pattern was co-created. Hugh didn't realize that the key to spending more time with Louise was helping her with the children and home chores. Ironically, Louise had a hard time asking for help because she couldn't accept that Hugh would or could do a good enough job.

Changing Gender-Based Imbalance

Like any other harmful relationship pattern, a gender-based imbal-ance should be defined, then attacked with No-Fault Communication and balancing strategies. But it's not easy for women to maintain a nonblaming perspective when it comes to the division of household labor. This is no trivial matter, because the domestic arena may be symbolic of the entire relationship.

There *are* hopeful signs of change, but recent studies of married partners with equal career demands and prestige have found that women still do 80 to 90 percent of the domestic and childcare chores.

The wives' combined career and household work load averaged eighty hours per week.

Men *aren't* wholly to blame. Many had mothers who picked up for them and didn't help them develop good habits. Some have a genuine fear of seeming unmanly, even in the eyes of their wives, if they houseclean. And some women enable men to get away with doing less than they should.

There are several strategies for dealing with gender-based labor inequities. One is to use No-Fault Communication to explain the problem and to ask for help in a positive yet firm manner. Another strategy involves looking at your financial resources in a new way.

Make Money an Ally

Money can be a powerful ally in fighting gender-based imbalance, when either or both partners work. Miles and Beth offered a good example. They had money in savings, but they were reluctant to spend in the areas that could have helped them when their situation changed. It was a matter of priorities, they said. Savings were earmarked for such things as an addition to their small home, a new car, and a vacation. To them, the benefits of Beth's staying at home with Chloe included saving on childcare and housecleaning expenses.

When an at-home wife has left a fulfilling career, the situation can be volatile. She comes to feel trapped and diminished by her situation and resentful of her freer spouse, and she becomes prone to one-down thoughts, feelings, and behaviors. As happened to Beth, such a situation can lead to a kind of identity crisis. Her loss of status may have her grappling with core self-esteem issues.

Given these facts, I explained to Beth and Miles how a cost-benefit analysis of spending on part-time childcare and housecleaning would support such expenditures. Regular, guilt-free time away from the child and housekeeping chores—when the husband can't or won't pitch in—can free a full- or part-time mother to keep up with her other interests and maintain her sense of identity. In addition, by using money to foster emotional balance in your relationship, you may be avoiding higher costs later on: those of therapy, lawyers, divorce, and the incalculable emotional price of a lost relationship.

When a stay-at-home wife (or husband) can't overcome her frustrations, she probably should return to part- or full-time work. If she doesn't get a high-paying job, this may mean breaking even when you factor in child care and commuting costs. But to the relationship it may well be worth it. By the time the children enter school, the wife's earning power will be greater than it would have been had she stayed out of the job market. That will help compensate for a few break-even years. But the main consideration, of course, is that her personal satisfaction will have buoyed the relationship.

Money Has a Downside Too

Having treated a number of "fast track" couples, I've seen how the pursuit of material and career success can lead to a dangerous emotional dynamic.

The drive for success and its rewards — money and power — cultivates in men and women a one-up orientation. Career success seduces because it offers a series of payoffs — raises, promotions, praise, accounts won, luxuries acquired — that directly feed the ego. But to earn it, men and women have to shield their vulnerabilities and maintain a guarded, controlling stance — that is, a one-up stance that can breed a deep discontentment.

For the financially independent "new woman," a one-up posture may translate to extreme choosiness and often deferral of serious partner-hunting until her childbearing years start to wane — at which point she may suddenly feel disconcertingly one-down. For the success-driven man, it may mean ongoing imprisonment in the one-up role and being labeled commitmentphobic or immature.

It's easy to mistake the payoffs of success for true happiness. Each career victory feels like a moment of perfect fulfillment. But it's a feeling that fades, pointing you toward new peaks to scale. Unfortunately, relationships may seem to offer more problems than payoffs, except at the beginning. They also tend to be harder to control than a career, so that area of life tends to get neglected. Sometimes fast-trackers don't even have time for closeness with others.

When you embrace success and ignore the importance of relationships, you begin to feel a creeping emptiness. That emptiness may spur you in a dangerous spiral toward yet new, ephemeral career "highs."

Because women bear children, they more easily escape the "success syndrome" than men do. But then they're often faced with a drop-out's loss of status.

When I work with people who've forfeited intimacy for success, I point out the emotional dynamics of their choice. And I assure them it's not necessary to renounce the fast-track in order to find emotional fulfillment. But it is helpful to strive consciously for a personal balance between the two areas. Otherwise, you may strand yourself in a one-up posture that limits emotional intimacy and keeps you running after increasing elusive tokens of success.

Attraction Power

I've found that the concept of attraction power causes many people to feel anxiety. This confirms my belief that the concept needs to be faced and explored. The obvious objection to attraction power is that it seems to involve surface issues. But in my view, attraction power has as much depth and complexity as any other force in a relationship—and often a good deal more mystery.

Like love itself, attraction power is not absolute. At different times, you're attracted to different "types." Sometimes people you've found irresistibly attractive at first glance turn out to be extremely incompatible with you. More mysteriously, some people continue to attract you even when there's no visible common ground.

As I discussed in chapter 2, there's a large subjective element to attraction power that's linked to our emotional needs and personal ideals. There's far more to attractiveness than a pretty face or a shapely body. That's why attraction power can be so mysterious. My friends Geri and Tom come to mind. She is overweight, but she carries it with flair and without apology. She has a wild sense of humor and a warmth that sets her apart. Tom shares Geri's love of good times, and he also happens to be classically handsome. But if there's any imbalance in their relationship, it's tilted in Geri's favor. In other words, in relationships, "beauty," or attraction power, is very much in the eye of the beholder.

Attraction Power and the Passion Trap

As I've discussed, passion trap dynamics can alter the balance of attraction between partners. When you feel insecure about your partner's caring, your partner may seem more attractive than usual; when you're stifled by your partner's caring, he or she may seem less attractive.

Conversely, a change in a partner's appearance or self-esteem may make that partner more or less attractive in *ways that affect relationship dynamics*. For example, a woman changes her hair color and suddenly looks better and *feels* better about herself — and that subtly changes the dynamics between her and her partner.

In other words, attraction power can be both a cause and an effect of passion trap dynamics. It poses the greatest problem when, over time, one partner is more attracted than the other — no matter what the cause. Yet, this needn't spell a relationship's doom.

When I sense this primary type of attraction power imbalance in my couples' clients, I know I face a challenge. The commonsense solution is for the one-down to try to become more attractive to the one-up. But the paradox of passion tells us that making the one-down more to the one-up's tastes doesn't create more love. The "Ornament Solution" merely invites one-down overcompliance.

There are steps you can take to deal with attraction power imbalances. These steps are designed to *use* paradoxical dynamics to your benefit. So. I urge you to tolerate your anxiety and read on about this sensitive issue.

The All-Important Role of Self-Esteem

There was a perceptible attraction power gap between Laura and Paul. It wasn't that Paul was unattractive. He had tremendous career success and prestige, key elements of a man's attraction power. He might not have been the life of the party, but he had a pleasing personality and was very intelligent. Although his looks might be considered average, he seemed distinguished because of his height. Their problems really stemmed from the fact that Laura was so unusually attractive. For Paul, and for all one-downs in his position, the key to finding balance lay in spotting and neutralizing insecurity and other classic one-down reflexes.

A one-down may not know exactly what's going on when an attraction power imbalance has struck. But he does know that he's feeling increasing anxiety that has an unusually unpleasant edge. He may be hypersensitive to potential rivals, and he may catastrophize about losing the relationship. His Internal Saboteur is chipping away at his self-esteem, making him feel unattractive, boring, and that he's out of control in the relationship.

Recall that office Christmas party where Paul first sensed the attraction power imbalance between Laura and himself. This is how Paul fell victim to predictable one-down thought distortions:

Paul's perception: Laura is paying more attention to these younger associates than she is to me.

Paul's initial reaction: Normal anxiety and insecurity.

Paul's one-down overreaction: Gut-level panic, extreme anxiety and self-doubt, pessimism, and self-contempt, culminating in self-sabotage: "Too bad, Paul, but these younger guys are much more exciting and attractive than you are. This *proves* that you're really a boring, unattractive jerk. Sooner or later Laura will discover this and leave you for one of these fellows."

Paul's one-down solution: I must try as hard as I can to always keep Laura's attention on me. I'll try to match wits with these associates, and if that doesn't work, I'll get her away from them, and this party, as quickly as possible, so I can have her all to myself. Tomorrow I'll buy her an expensive present so she'll like me even more.

End result: Laura begins to feel that Paul is lacking in social grace and that he's getting overly possessive.

Paul could have handled the situation differently. In an individual session, I asked him to imagine himself at another party where Laura seemed to be flirting with everyone but him. Then I suggested that he try to stop his self-sabotaging thoughts and counter them with self-supportive logic.

I'd tell myself, "Here I go . . . I'm starting to feel very insecure while Laura is talking to her friends." What I usually do in these situations is panic. I overcompensate. I try to crack jokes and compete on a level where I'm not really comfortable. What I'm going to do this time is listen, make contributions when they feel right, and see if I'm really engaged by the conversation. If I'm not, I'll politely excuse myself — trusting Laura not to elope with one of these guys — grab a canapé, and talk to Lars about the Butler case.

In this mindset, Paul could vicariously enjoy Laura's conversation or feel free to do something else. Laura, sensing that Paul was comfortable and confident, might have tried harder to include him in the conversation. She certainly wouldn't have felt guilty or pressured by him, and that would have freed her to feel love and respect.

Self-esteem is the strongest antidote for attraction imbalance. When you accept yourself as a worthy person, you're no longer so dependent on others' reactions to you as a source of validation (or invalidation). This means that you can relax. You won't panic when your partner pays attention to another person, because you have the confidence not to view it as a personal rejection. You'll resist hyper-courtship and other one-down solutions that weaken your position and widen the imbalance.

Apart from everything else, confidence itself is potently attractive, perhaps even aphrodisiacal.

More One-Down Weapons

Of course, cultivating self-esteem is easier said than done. While you work on it (see "Healthy Distance" in chapter 9), consider the follow-ing strategies to keep your footing when you feel unattractive to your partner.

Look good for yourself. A woman client told me that her ex-husband had talked her into having breast augmentation. She was opposed to the idea ("It's just not me"), but in her desire to please, she hid her true feelings. The surgery rekindled her husband's interest for a short time, but eventually he left her anyway. She still doesn't like her breasts. It was a hard way to learn the dangers of overcompliance.

Taking care of your appearance is considered a sign of emotional health. But it's best if your efforts are made first and foremost *for your-self*—as an expression of your basic self-esteem. That may include cos-metic surgery, if you're so inclined; I've had clients who underwent various cosmetic procedures and felt better for them. However, if you're beautifying yourself solely for your partner's sake, you're courting a passion trap reaction. Overcompliance in this area lowers your self-esteem and raises your partner's sense of one-up control.

Don't try to look perfect. You're in the bathroom primping before meeting your partner. You find yourself obsessing over your hair, clothes, and makeup. A ridiculous curl pops up and won't comb out. A smudge mysteriously appears on your shirt. Or, the ultimate one-down nightmare: a pimple on your face. Catch and dispute your cata-strophizing thoughts ("Oh my god, there's no hope for this relation-ship because I don't look perfect"). Tell yourself, "I'll try to look my best. But if my partner can't accept me for who I am, then he doesn't deserve to be with me." Realize that perfectionism in physical appear-ance fosters one-down inhibitions.

Interpret obsessiveness as a valuable clue. If you find yourself sud-denly obsessing about your looks and actions, start searching for harmful dynamics emerging in your relationship. Perhaps your partner has started acting more distant or less loving. Perhaps your situation is making you feel needier. Deal with those dynamics using the strategies in this book. Don't try to solve your relationship problems by trying to look perfect.

Attractiveness through Healthy Distance. Two of the most attractive features a one-down loses are autonomy and independence. I urge you to take the risks necessary to regain these qualities by carrying out the Healthy Distancing strategies outlined in chapter 9. When you successfully do so, you'll not only look more attractive, you'll *feel* more attractive — which is powerfully alluring in itself.

The One-Up Side of Attraction Power

The biggest challenge for one-ups is to figure out what's causing their diminishing feelings toward their partners, and not panicking.

First, it *is* possible that despite an initial attraction, you and your partner are unequal in important areas such as intelligence, creativity, and social skills. If your partner falls far short of your expectations, you'll naturally have a hard time getting excited about the relationship.

Second, however, it could be that relationship dynamics are really at the root of your partner's waning attractiveness. I've seen many couples who *were* well matched until imbalance dynamics set in.

So, attraction imbalance may be caused by problem patterns or it may reflect a basic mismatch. No matter which cause you suspect, I recommend that one-ups try the following balancing exercises:

Don't pathologize. It's the classic one-up reaction: "What a superficial, cold-hearted, immature person I am for wanting to leave my partner because he's unattractive." When you catch yourself having such self-pathologizing thoughts, dispute them. Tell yourself it's normal to go through phases of being less than charmed by your partner. When you don't feel so guilty and distant, you won't fuel the harmful dynamics that may be creating your negative perceptions.

Don't play Pygmalion with your partner. When you're in a relationship, it's normal to tell your partner when you think she looks most attractive. But if you attempt the Ornament Solution, urging your partner to beautify herself, you feed harmful dynamics in two ways: You make her feel more insecure and one-down, and her compliance will wind up making you feel more controlling and less loving.

Reframe your negative perceptions as valuable clues. The loss of positive perceptions is like the loss of love: If you view it as the main problem, you'll try to fix the wrong thing — that is, you'll try the Ornament Solution. Rather, I urge you to reframe your negative perceptions this way: "A harmful pattern has developed in my relationship, and it's causing me to view my partner overly critically." In this way your negative perception becomes a valuable clue to genuine problems in the relationship. And that will fruitfully focus your energies on correcting the harmful pattern.

Cultivate your self-esteem. Sometimes you're drawn to someone who your friends decide "isn't good enough for you." That colors your opinion of your partner, who may very well be just right for you in ways that may not be apparent to others. If you feel confident and secure in your own opinions, you won't let the opinions of others diminish your partner's appeal. When you're self-confident and emotionally secure, you'll be less inclined to judge your partner critically. Instead, you'll be more accepting and appreciative of his or her strengths. In a long-term relationship, those qualities alone can mean lasting attraction power.

Chapter 12

The Balanced Self

An Introduction
to Personality Styles

When couples come to me, usually they're in crisis. As I get to know them, I try to determine the source of their trouble as quickly as possible. If the problem looks situational or attraction-related, we stay in the present. But when one or both partners show signs of being chronically one-up or one-down, I shift my approach to a deeper level. We explore the partners' personality styles, examining their pasts to find problems and solutions — but not pathology.

Problems without Pathology

During my training, I had trouble accepting the standard theories of personality advanced in our texts. Each theory seemed to offer a very eloquent explanation of how *screwed up we all are*. Period.

Consider the most famous theory of all, Freud's psychoanalysis. Literally thousands of volumes have been produced by Freud and neo-Freudians telling how and why each of us falls into some psychopathological category. You can take your pick from the pathological cornucopia: hysteria, obsessive-compulsiveness, anal retentiveness, masochism, narcissism, melancholia — and these are only the moderate disorders. Unfortunately, psychoanalytic theory provides us with scant insight into what constitutes *healthy, adaptive behavior*. According to Freud, the best we can do is engage in continual struggle to minimize the "psychopathology of everyday life."

As I began to treat clients, I sensed that when I interpreted their problems according to psychoanalytic theory, a negative, adversarial note crept into our interactions. These interpretations kept my clients hooked on therapy, the way a cancer diagnosis would keep a medical patient coming back for treatment. In a subtle way, they also undermined my clients' self-esteem and dignity. Stripped of dignity, a persons internal strength is crippled and with it his ability to change.

It is for this reason that I have become so adamant about the dangers of pathologizing. Yet, there are people who, undeniably, have deep-seated problems that consistently lead to unhealthy relationships. How, I wondered, is it possible to acknowledge the seriousness of their personal problems without undermining their already fragile self-esteem?

Then, during my internship, I stumbled upon an early textbook written in the 1950s by Timothy Leary. As head of a project funded by the Kaiser Foundation, Leary had helped shape a new model of the human personality, called Interpersonal Psychology. This theory, based on the pioneering ideas of psychiatrist Harry Stack Sullivan, offers a revolutionary way of thinking about human behavior: It places as much emphasis on healthy functioning as on maladaptive behavior, and it offers a convincing "nonpathological" basis for personal conflicts.

Basically, the theory is that personality "problems" are really creative coping mechanisms developed during stressful childhoods. In response to a challenging family environment, a child will learn how best to survive emotionally by perfecting certain ways of relating — that is, certain "interpersonal styles" or strengths. But often this occurs at the expense of developing other, complementary strengths. I found this theory refreshingly therapeutic because it's not negative and fatalistic. Rather, it commends people's adaptive ingenuity in hard situations, and it points toward a solution: to balance overdeveloped strengths by nurturing underused interpersonal styles. It's an approach that preserves a person's dignity and gets results.

Leary's work was so highly regarded at the time that it landed him the ultimate academic honor: a professorship at Harvard. Unfortunately, the notoriety that was soon to follow his controversial LSD experiments cast a shadow over his brilliant theory of personality. In fact, it's only been in recent years that psychologists have rediscovered his groundbreaking work and begun furthering it.

The Interpersonal Styles[*]

Interpersonal Psychology starts with four core behavioral options that underlie our interactions with other people. Like yin and yang, they are paired:

control/yield: the options to lead at times and follow at others

separate/connect: the options to retain autonomy or to connect with people

From these core behaviors radiate eight interpersonal styles (or skills or strengths), *all of which are important for healthy relationships.* The eight styles are graphed on the following "Interpersonal Circle."

Ideally, all eight styles, in moderation, should play a part in your interactions with others. When a situation calls for nurturance (like comforting a child), you can nurture; when it calls for caution (like buying a used car), you can be skeptical; when it calls for decisive action (like closing a business deal), you can be assertive; and so on. If you have learned each of these interpersonal skills, you are indeed a "well-rounded," balanced individual. A key word is *flexibility.* We should be able to move flexibly from one style to another as warranted.

The Role of Childhood

Childhood is the crucial period when we forge our styles of relating. Starting in infancy, we instinctively tested a wide variety of ways of interacting with our parents. Some ways made us feel comfortable and secure, others elicited parental reactions that frightened or threatened us. These "experiments" were part of a learning process. What we learned was how best to position ourselves with others so that we could feel more secure and less anxious.

A home in which few styles of relating are used will hamper a child's quest for a healthy balance of personality styles. In such a setting, he'll instinctively mold himself to fit into the lopsided interpersonal world created by his parents. Consider the child whose parents are rigidly domineering. In the process of normal development, the

---

*I've adapted some of the terms of Leary's model to describe intimate relationships. But the basic ideas remain the same.

THE INTERPERSONAL CIRCLE

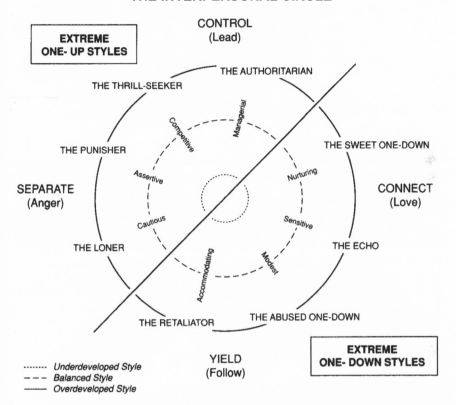

CONTROL
(Lead)

EXTREME
ONE- UP STYLES

THE AUTHORITARIAN

THE THRILL-SEEKER

Managerial

Competitive

THE PUNISHER

THE SWEET ONE-DOWN

Assertive

Nurturing

SEPARATE
(Anger)

CONNECT
(Love)

Cautious

Sensitive

THE LONER

THE ECHO

Accommodating

Modest

THE RETALIATOR

THE ABUSED ONE-DOWN

YIELD
(Follow)

EXTREME
ONE- DOWN STYLES

········ *Underdeveloped Style*
– – – *Balanced Style*
—— *Overdeveloped Style*

child naturally strives to stand up for himself, to exert his autonomy. But if his controlling parents react negatively, the child will begin to forfeit the important skills of assertion and leadership. Instead, he may become a virtuoso at yielding, accommodating, cooperating, and following, in order to ensure his emotional connection with his parents. He adopts what I call an unconscious *interpersonal motto* that tells him always to be as nice as possible. When he grows up, this motto will exert a powerful influence on his relationships.

If the child's authoritarian parents reject even when he yields, he may try more extreme interpersonal options. For example, he may find that aggressive counterattacks against his parents can neutralize their abusive treatment. Or he may simply remain in the family background, perhaps taking refuge in his bedroom. This "loner" strategy props up his sense of security by minimizing the chances of yet another painful rejection.

The factors that mold a child's particular interpersonal strengths are many. They include nuances in parenting styles, sex-role expectations, coping styles of older siblings, and the child's inborn predispositions. However, the basis of personality imbalance is provided by parents who themselves have rigidly unbalanced styles of relating.

Not surprisingly, most of us are at least mildly "unbalanced" in the ways we interact with people, meaning we favor one or two special strengths over other skills. But we can take heart in Leary's finding that mild or "normal" imbalances often work to our advantage. An individual with an overdeveloped nurturing strength, for example, might make an excellent therapist. An overly skeptical person could become a Pulitzer Prize-winning journalist. Only when a person has *very few highly overdeveloped* interpersonal strengths do real problems occur.

Factoring in the Passion Trap

People who carry into adulthood only one or two interpersonal strengths are at high risk for the passion trap. Usually those few strengths cluster on either the one-up or the one-down side of the Interpersonal Circle. Therefore, the person with very few skills will almost always be chronically one-up or one-down. The position will affect all his interactions with other people, but none so forcefully as those with intimate partners. Once a person begins to relate as a one-up or one-down, his or her interpersonal lopsidedness will be further skewed by passion trap dynamics.

The Interpersonal Circle offers a model of the inner workings of the personality. When any one of the eight styles gathers overpowering strength, the Interpersonal Circle will tell us which behavioral exaggerations are likely to occur. It shows how *controlling* and *separating* styles evoke one-up qualities, and how *yielding* and *connecting* styles evoke one-down qualities. Note how the exaggerated styles change around the circle depending on their position in the control/ yield and connect/separate sectors. For example, the Sweet One-Down's greatest strength is connecting with people. But she also possesses some skill in exerting control, evident in her nurturing ability.

You may have observed how the one-up and one-down styles mirror stereotypical notions of masculinity and femininity. To me, a compelling feature of this model is that it shows how a balanced blend of gender traits can produce a truly well-rounded individual.

Healing a Broken Circle

Every personality theory has its limitations. However, I've found the Interpersonal Circle to be a consistently valuable therapeutic tool. It will often very quickly yield the clue I need to understand why a client is having problems in his or her relationships. It also helps me formulate therapeutic strategies to help partners bring themselves into balance. When I position a client on the Interpersonal Circle, the information it offers enables me to do the following:

- Commend a client for his interpersonal strengths
- Identify complementary styles that may need buttressing
- Explain how the client's strengths and weaknesses may be fueling, and getting fueled by, bad relationship dynamics
- Help the client empathize with himself by explaining how in childhood it was emotionally necessary for him to cultivate few interpersonal strengths
- Verbalize the unconscious interpersonal motto that pegs the client in such a rigid one-down or one-up role
- Teach the client how to consciously dispute this motto, especially in anxiety-provoking interpersonal situations
- Encourage the client to gradually take more risks in expressing his underdeveloped interpersonal styles
- Show the client how to enlist his interpersonal strengths to help create a more balanced spectrum of skills

About the Cases

The next two chapters explore the most common one-down and one-up personality types and give strategies for achieving greater balance. As you read, you may find yourself identifying with aspects of not one or two but several of the cases. If you do, it simply means that you have a well-rounded personality and an ability to turn to a wide range of interpersonal styles as you need to.

However, if you identify very strongly with only one or two types, you may have discovered an interpersonal imbalance in yourself. Remember to view these styles as your *strengths*, and allow the insight to motivate you to change.

Learning new personality skills takes objectivity, emotional support, and other qualities elusive to the individual working alone. In other words, if you feel you need more than fine-tuning in this area, I urge you to seek professional help. Results come quicker and run deeper when you're guided by a good therapist.

Chapter 13

The One-Down Personality

Learning to Value Yourself

The nice term for them is "unlucky in love." They are chronic one-downs — the people who consistently find partners who either dump them or treat them badly. While there might be an element of bad luck involved in this, a much larger factor is personality imbalance.

True one-down personalities are underdeveloped in separation (independence) and/or control (leadership). Their energies are geared toward connecting with and yielding to other people. Of course, the shadings are many and varied, as we will now see.

The Sweet One-Down

The Sweet One-Down is friendly, generous, thoughtful, and almost eerily free of anger. Not one to harbor grudges, she's a cooperator and a pleaser. She gets along well with everyone. She would be upset to hear that someone didn't like her. She avoids "negative" things like violent movies and malicious gossip, preferring pleasant or uplifting things like romance novels and making cookies.

The Sweet One-Down's greatest pleasure lies in doing for others. She spends money much more freely on others than on herself. Her greatest ambitions are to be a good person and to help others. Her own career success is not high on her priority list. Her friends regard her as "the nicest person you'd ever want to meet."

Giving Too Much

A case in point is my client Ginny, a warm, motherly-looking woman in her mid forties. Her husband, Frank, was a police detective. Married in their early twenties, Ginny and Frank had never swerved from traditional sex roles. Frank was largely absent from the household, working long hours and spending much of his free time with "the guys." Over the years, Ginny had found evidence that Frank had affairs. Instead of confronting him, she threw her considerable energies into the mothering of their four children and creating a home that she liked to think was Frank's safe haven.

Liked by all who knew her, Ginny was always there when a volunteer was needed for a church dinner or school event. She had become an excellent cook because, she said, "it seemed to give people such pleasure." With her children, however, she felt she . . .

> might have been too lenient. I love them so much, and it always hurt me to see them unhappy. I guess I figured that they'd see enough unhappiness in life that I might as well do what I could to make them feel loved and accepted. And since Frank wasn't there too much, I wanted to make up for that.

The biggest negative factor in her life was, of course, Frank's womanizing. At first she tried to ignore it. In her mind, she made excuses for him, believing he was going through phases or letting off steam from his high-pressure, risky job. But over the years, Frank's philandering grew more blatant. Still, whenever he'd return from an out-of-town weekend, "working on a case," Ginny found herself nervously waiting on him hand and foot. She prayed that her steadfast love and devotion would make him come to his senses and everything would be fine.

Then one day their teenage son picked up the phone to make a call—only to hear his father making a date. He denounced Frank at the dinner table, and Ginny knew she had to take action. She turned to psychotherapy for help.

The Sweet One-Down's Childhood

By all appearances, the Sweet One-Down's family is loving and supportive, as Ginny's was. The hitch was that she had to act the "good little angel" to get the rewards of love and acceptance.

> My older brother and my father were always at each other's throat, and I couldn't understand it. Father was so sweet to me; we got along great. I thought my brother was trying to stir things up on purpose, and I told him if he'd just stop, everything would be fine.

In therapy, Ginny and I uncovered the fact that she'd been terrified by her father and brother's battles. Her loving feelings for her father thinly masked an abiding fear of him. Early on, she learned that sweetness, helpfulness, and agreeableness formed a shield against her father's wrath. As that shield hardened, she lost other interpersonal options: the ability to stand up for ideas and opinions, to assert herself, to be independent, and to feel confident.

The "black sheep," like Ginny's brother, and the "sweet little angel," like Ginny, often come from the same family. When asked to conform to the parents' rigid demands, the black sheep sacrifices connection (love) for separation (autonomy). The angel, on the other hand, forfeits separation for connection. Girls are far more prone to be Sweet One-Downs than boys because they're doubly reinforced by "sugar and spice" sex-role pressures.

Love and the Sweet One-Down

Sweet one-downs may have trouble finding romance. Their interpersonal style, so successful in protecting them from rejection in childhood, seems to invite rejection from romantic prospects. That's how it was for Ginny.

> I used to be the one everyone came to with their love problems, boys and girls alike. But in high school I didn't have any love problems of my own, or any boyfriends. My friends told me it was because boys thought I was too "pure" for them.

By cloaking herself in sweetness, Ginny had almost neutered herself. She wasn't exciting or challenging or interesting to the opposite sex. The Sweet One-Down finds easy acceptance as a friend, because she gives so much. This applies equally to her male counterpart, Mr. Nice Guy. He'd do anything for his friends and frequently winds up doing just that. Male and female one-downs of this type fall into the same trap: Their eagerness to please and to be liked drains away the tension vital to romantic chemistry. They forfeit the appeal of autonomy. After one or two dates, the Sweet One-Down comes to dread the words, "I really like you as a friend, but . . ."

When the Sweet One-Down finally stirs romantic interest, it's often with someone who's down-and-out, emotionally or physically or both, and in need of nurturance. That was the case with Ginny and Frank. He was recuperating from a motorcycle accident; she was his physical therapist. They married three months after meeting, and she stopped working when she became pregnant with their first child.

At first Ginny was ecstatic with Frank and the marriage. But theirs was a lopsided emotional arrangement, and it was only a matter of time before Frank, fully healed, began edging away. Ginny spoke for many Sweet One-Downs when she said:

> I almost felt like I'd served my purpose and now I should just be a good wife and not expect too much. I know he liked having me do everything for him. I *wanted* to do for him. But when you get almost nothing back, you start to wonder what's wrong with you.

When the Sweet One-Down's sweetness fails to delight her partner, as it did a parent, she's at a loss. Her primary coping strategy is sweetness. But compliant one-down sweetness actually sabotages her attempts to please the one-up, because it ignites passion trap dynamics. If the one-up's infidelity is a factor, the Sweet One-Down's desire to forgive and forget won't help curb it. In fact, it often *enables* her partner to cheat.

Balancing

If you see yourself in the Sweet One-Down, you probably share the unconscious interpersonal motto: *Please like me.* I suggested Ginny rewrite her motto this way: *People don't always have to like me.* Frequently reminding yourself of your new motto, especially when you feel anxious, will help you reclaim buried one-up parts of yourself. Your goal is to be firm and assertive when a situation warrants it, not reflexively sweet and giving.

I encourage you to educate yourself in the skills of assertiveness and setting limits. There are several excellent books that will help you (see the bibliography). Right now you may not even know when someone is overstepping your boundaries or taking advantage of you. A close friend or therapist can help you identify the situations that call for you to draw the line. They're probably much more frequent than you think.

It's vital that Sweet One-Downs accept their anger. Perhaps more than anything, the expression of anger frightens and threatens this one-down. Once you've learned when your boundaries are being crossed, permit yourself to feel your anger and express it.

Using No-Fault Communication will help you express your anger effectively. It'll also help you manage your partner's response. Be aware that he may react intensely. After all, he's not used to being challenged by you.

It takes time and patience to learn these skills. Don't expect mastery overnight or painlessly. Do expect increasing rewards. As you refine your one-up skills, you'll find your interpersonal strengths—friendliness and nurturance—working *better* for you. They'll no longer be turning you into a one-down enabler, because they're backed by balancing new strengths.

In spite of everything, Ginny still loved Frank. She wasn't prepared to leave him or split up the family. In therapy Ginny found the courage to begin taking a series of limit-setting steps with Frank. Before each step, she rehearsed with me exactly what she would tell him. After approaching him on small issues and surviving her terror of confrontation, she went for the big one. She expressed her hurt and anger over his affairs and bravely told him that if he didn't stop she would kick him out of the house. Frank didn't say much, Ginny reported; he seemed a little shaken, but afterward he treated her with more respect.

After six months in therapy and a strong start in Healthy Distancing (she took a brush-up course in physical therapy and found a part-time position), Ginny had reclaimed parts of herself that she hadn't known existed. I could see the change in her. She'd once been tentative and apologetic about almost everything, but now she was positive, vibrant, and attractive. Her marriage still had problems, but she managed to get Frank to join us in therapy.

The Echo

The Echo doesn't feel alive or whole unless she's in a relationship. Her interpersonal strength is her ability to let down her guard and share her most vulnerable feelings. Uncannily sensitive, she's deeply attuned to emotional nuance in her interactions with others. A risk taker when it comes to intimacy, she'll share all her perceptions with her partner. But she loses sight of where her feelings stop and her partner's begin. She seems to vanish into her relationships, losing her boundaries. Her qualities can make her a valued employee, as she anticipates the needs of superiors and carries out her duties with an instinctive sense of what's important. She can excel as a student. In romantic relationships, however, her Echoing is problematic.

Losing Yourself

Deborah, the artist, had strong Echo leanings. Before Jonathan, she was aware—as many Echoes are—that she was prone to "losing herself" in her relationships with men. Having been hurt in most of her involvements, Deborah was actively avoiding romance at the time she met Jonathan. But she admitted:

> Not a day went by that I wasn't thinking about finding someone. I've kept a journal for a couple of years, and practically every entry has something about men. Either I'm interested in someone or they're interested in me, or I've just started seeing someone . . . The rest is filler.

Obviously, trying to avoid relationships is not a real solution for Echoes.

The Echo's Childhood

In childhood, the Echo felt she *had* to remain in the "helpless child" role to win her parents' love. As Deborah recalled:

> My father kind of left my mother alone, and I think she turned to me for emotional nourishment. It was as if I always had to be her little girl. I could never make my own decisions . . . it always had to be her way. She was most loving when I had problems and needed her. In fact, she'd freak when I went against her. Once I tried to get out of going to the store with her. She got so upset that she locked me in my room and didn't come home until late that night. I was terrified she'd never come back.

Unless she's merging with another person, the Echo feels abandoned and alone. As an adult, it's hard for her to fathom why she dreads separation. She's not happy feeling she must continually barter her identity for closeness.

THE PASSION TRAP

Love and the Echo

We all lose our sense of boundaries when we fall madly in love. Fortunately, most of us have a core sense of self that guides us through the derangements of passion. (The poet W. B. Yeats observed, "The tragedy of sex is the perpetual virginity of the soul.") For the Echo, however, that core is less than solid to begin with. When she bonds, her core seems to disappear. Deborah said that her relationship with Jonathan seemed to "swallow" her.

> At first I thought I was going to be safe with Jonathan because I wasn't instantly attracted to him. But then he got under my skin. I didn't see friends, I didn't care about art. At school, I just went through the motions. I spent my free time reading up on subjects that interested Jonathan. I gave myself a lot of facials. When we started seeing each other, we'd go to art things, but gradually I went along with his preferences: used-book stores and garden centers. At the time, I couldn't see how systematically I was giving up pieces of myself.

Although Echoes in love may seem to lose themselves, they aren't always passive. Echoes learn how to position themselves to attract the partners they need in order to feel whole. Deborah noted that while the outcome of her affair with Jonathan was typical, the beginning wasn't.

> The truth is, there were a couple of other men at the party where I met Jonathan. In fact, I was tempted to make a move on one of them when Jonathan approached me. I don't exactly throw myself at men, but I seem to know how to catalyze things.

The Echo strives to anchor a partner by proving compatibility: she shares the one-up's tastes, interests, and concerns, and demonstrates how emotionally giving she can be. The usual result is that early love for an Echo *and* her partner is rapturous. Her partner feels he's found the love of his life, someone who seems to have known him forever and loves him for who he is. But as she continues to mold herself to him, the emotional climate changes. He begins to feel bored and unchallenged, then annoyed and suffocated. The passion trap takes over, causing the one-up to pull away and the Echo to increase her efforts to blend with him.

Depression commonly strikes the Echo at this point. Her interpersonal strength — sensitivity — makes her acutely aware of her partner's dissatisfaction with her. Since her self-worth has come to be defined by her partner's acceptance of her, romantic rejection offers unequivocal proof that she's *not* worthwhile. As Deborah said of her suicide attempt:

> When I lost control in my relationship with Jonathan, I concluded that I was truly incapable of being my own person. As strange as it sounds, I think suicide seemed like a way for me to establish my identity. I might be dead, but at least it would be me on my own doing it.

Balancing

If you have strong Echo tendencies, your unconscious personal motto is likely to be: *Without you I'm nothing.* Each time you feel rejection anxiety in a relationship, this motto compels you to cling tighter to your partner. Dispute this motto by repeating to yourself: *I can survive on my own.*

In trying to break her relationship pattern, Deborah had made two common mistakes: She had regarded her desire for closeness as "bad," and she had tried to suppress that desire by avoiding relationships altogether. I explained to her that emotional closeness was very important to her and shouldn't be sacrificed. In fact, her ability to get close was her greatest interpersonal strength; it simply needed balancing.

Together, Deborah and I defined a new goal for her: to build up neglected one-up skills that would enable her to find the right partner for *her*, someone who equally valued intimacy. Since sensitivity was one of her strengths, I urged her to focus it on a new partner's potential for closeness. If he seemed chancy, she would employ new one-up skills right away. Using No-Fault Communication, she would express the importance of closeness for her—a non-Echoing step because she would be revealing her true self at the risk of rejection. She would ask, in a nonblaming manner, if he too valued closeness. If his response and subsequent behavior failed to reassure her, she would confront the situation, telling herself, *I can survive on my own.* She would elect to pull back from an almost certain bout with the passion trap and another demoralizing one-down experience.

However, if balanced closeness seemed likely, she would consciously resist the urge to play the chameleon. She would retain her personal strengths—her art, her love for teaching, her friendships—

which would imbue her with more attraction power, and that would help secure the closeness she valued from her partner.

Like many Echoes, Deborah had only a flimsy idea of who she was. Much of our work—and it took much work—involved rebuilding her self-esteem. Accepting that she had many personal strengths, and deriving autonomy and assertiveness from them, helped her learn how to be intimate more effectively. Even her manner changed. Formerly high-strung and somewhat brittle, she now was calmer and more self-possessed.

The Retaliator

It may seem a contradiction in terms: a one-down who retaliates. But I see it often in my practice. Unlike other one-down types, the Retaliator *can* experience healthy levels of anger when she feels wronged. This ability is among her interpersonal strengths. Her problem is the way she expresses her anger.

Hitting Him in the Pocketbook

My clients Barbara and Stuart were another classic passion trap couple. Stuart was a political aide whose work entailed long hours and a passionate commitment. Barbara was a floral designer. They came to me to deal with Barbara's "problem" of running wild with their credit cards. Barbara explained:

> Every once in a while I seem to lose control with credit cards. I don't plan it. I'm out shopping and I buy one thing. And then I buy another, and then another . . . It's a little like an alcoholic having one drink and not being able to stop. But I only buy on sale.

To which Stuart added, "Yep. Like two-hundred-and-fifty-dollar shoes marked down to two hundred."

At one point, Stuart and Barbara felt they'd contained the problem. Stuart had canceled all the credit cards except one, which he kept himself. Barbara learned to live within checking account realities, while gradually paying off the heavy debt. After six months, Barbara was "reformed." Stuart rewarded her by giving her a duplicate of the one remaining card. Shortly thereafter, he went to a conference in Chicago. When he tried to check in at his hotel, his credit card was rejected. Barbara had charged it past the limit. This incident put the marriage in jeopardy and catapulted them into therapy.

They both assumed Barbara had the problem: compulsive shopping. But after we spoke awhile, it became clear to me that Barbara's charging sprees matched Stuart's periods of greatest distance: when he was involved in a major project or task, when "crises" arose on his job, and when he went to a conference without inviting her. Instead of expressing her anger directly, Barbara was hitting Stuart in the pocketbook — and assuaging her loneliness with the high of buying new things.

The Retaliator's Childhood

Barbara's childhood was typical for Retaliators.

> My mother was very competitive with me. She had a way of keeping me in line by saying things like, "No man will ever marry you if you keep that up." But it was like she didn't really want me to grow up. She wouldn't let me date until I was seventeen, and then I had a curfew of ten o'clock. Once I snuck out to a party, and when I got back in, around one A.M., she was waiting for me. She slapped me and grounded me for two months. But I adored my dad. He'd take me and my brother on little outings. But even he couldn't stand up to my mother.

Like most habitual one-downs, the Retaliator typically had one parent who was authoritarian and overly critical. But unlike other one-down types, she usually had another parent, or sometimes a grandparent, who was very loving to her. The authoritarian parent dominated the household, forcing the child to favor her one-down skills of submissiveness and accommodation. But the love from the more passive parent at least instilled in the child a sense of self-respect and dignity. It is from this sense of dignity that the Retaliator is able to experience healthy anger when she feels hurt or thwarted.

However, feeling anger is quite different from expressing it. The Retaliator must bring her half-developed skill of anger into balance with her one-down fear of noncompliant behavior. To do so, she must learn to express anger directly.

Love and the Retaliator

The Retaliator's personality may not seem overtly one-down. Many are very charming and vivacious in social settings; but that doesn't mean they're good at standing up for themselves in intimate relationships. The combination of sociability and compliance can be almost irresistible to certain one-up types, especially the Authoritarian (see chapter 14). He needs to control a relationship, yet wants a partner who can present to the world a pleasing reflection of him. Once the relationship is settled, the one-up assumes his partner is happily ensconced in her subservient role. Complacently, he turns to his own pursuits and concerns.

The one-up, then, is largely blind to his partner's unhappiness. She continues to offer one-down compliance, but resentment builds around her feelings of powerlessness, dependency, and emotional neglect. She can't find a way to navigate between her anger and frustration and the unshakable fear of standing up for herself. She may gain some relief by venting her feelings to others. But at the point when she can barely contain her mounting hostility, she reaches an unconscious compromise: She expresses her anger indirectly, so that she can maintain her veneer of compliance. Her main leverage is her keen sense of which indirect actions will "get him where it hurts."

Flirtation is a common Retaliator's tactic. In social situations, she may act blatantly seductive to other men in plain sight of her partner. Her partner feels embarrassed and humiliated. Afterward, he scolds her for her unseemly behavior. She says she was just being friendly. As might be expected, extramarital affairs are common for the Retaliator.

Barbara and Stuart's relationship shows how the partners' one-up/one-down pattern can destructively feed itself. Barbara's spending sprees provoked Stuart to more authoritarian actions: he felt "forced" to take away her credit cards, for instance. But his controlling actions only made her feel more dependent and powerless, and more likely to retaliate.

Balancing

Do you harbor resentments toward your partner, yet fear letting him know what's upsetting you? Are your resentments surfacing in the form of indirect retaliations? If so, you likely live by the interpersonal motto: *Don't confront*. Retaliators, believing that direct confrontation will cause emotional abandonment, stage covert actions against their partners, and that almost always creates bigger problems.

To begin changing, give yourself this new motto: *Stand up for yourself*, and think it often. Realize that you're halfway there. You have a healthy ability to feel anger. Now you must learn how to express it in helpful rather than harmful ways.

Spend time with chapter 8, learning how to use No-Fault Communication. Practice it in private, rehearsing what you might say to your partner the next time your anger flares. Barbara, for example, would have to learn to tell Stuart, nonaccusingly, when she was feeling emotionally short-changed. When you assertively attack real problems *directly*, you short-circuit your retaliatory impulses and foster balance in your relationship.

Barbara and Stuart were intelligent people. They quickly grasped the dynamics that were turning them against each other. It was rewarding to see each of them identify their weaker interpersonal skills and begin working to build them up—for Stuart needed balancing every bit as much as Barbara. While Barbara was learning to "stand up for herself" and express appropriate anger, Stuart was becoming sensitive to how his authoritarian "solutions" to their problems were fueling Barbara's frustrations. As they worked together to balance themselves, their relationship staged a remarkable recovery.

The Abused One-Down

Any extreme one-down is a candidate for emotional or physical abuse. That includes the types I've already discussed: the Sweet One-Down, the Echo, and the Retaliator. They are *not* masochistic. They don't enjoy abuse. But they do have two serious problems: their low self-esteem may make them overly accepting of abuse, and their strongest interpersonal skills tend to enable rather than counter their partner's abusive behavior.

For example, a Sweet One-Down will deal with abuse by tolerating it, hoping that if she's sweet enough and nice enough the abuse will end. An Echo will deal with it by trying harder to submerge herself and be the person her partner wants her to be. The Retaliator will find indirect retaliations, which will only make her partner angrier and more abusive.

The Abused One-Down is actually defined by her tendency to end up in abusive relationships. She'd love to find a "nice guy," but it never seems to work out. It's tempting to label her a true masochist—someone who "needs" punishment. But I don't believe this is the case. Abused One-Downs are as stuck and unhappy in their abusive relationships as anyone else would be. Where they differ from most people is in the extremity of the damaging lessons they learned in childhood.

It's Just Not the Same

My client Leigh, an attractive 40-year-old office manager, survived two abusive marriages. Her first husband worked in a sporting-goods store. Although he was "as charming as they get, he also had a real mean streak once you got to know him." Although never physically abusive to Leigh, he constantly belittled her.

> There were times he'd get into a kind of shouting frenzy. I couldn't do anything right. I was stupid. I was "like a cow." It was my fault he wasn't manager of the store because he couldn't get a good night's sleep with the baby crying. He didn't do much for my ego.

After having several affairs, he finally left her and their infant son for a "more athletic co-worker."

Leigh considered her second husband, a sales representative . . .

> to be my shining knight for taking in my son and me. But he had a bad drinking problem. And unlike Wallace, he did strike me at times, but only when he was drunk. I stuck with it for four years. When he was sober, I'd think things were getting better. But that never lasted more than a couple of days. I finally had to draw the line when he started to get after Richie.

Five years later, she turned to therapy because of her growing depression about a two-year affair she'd been having with a married man, an engineer at the manufacturing firm where she worked.

> I don't have any illusions anymore about Brock leaving his wife for me. He's not even spending that much time with me anymore, and I'm pretty sure he's seeing another girl at the plant. He denies it, but then he's hardly the trustworthy type. The bad thing is, I can't seem to stop wanting him. Other guys ask me out, but it's just not the same. I'm torturing myself about Brock instead of getting out there and finding myself a nice guy.

In my initial interview with Leigh, I learned that her involvement with men who abused or neglected her dated as far back as high school. Clearly, she was stuck in the most painful and destructive of all one-down styles.

The One-Down Personality

The Abused One-Down's Childhood

Most chronic One-Downs had one harsh, overpowering parent and one passive parent. What's singular about the Abused One-Down *is* the price she had to pay as a child to win the domineering parent's approval. Leigh had to pay such a price.

> My father was your basic tyrant. He was stuck in a pretty rough job — he worked in a shipyard — and he'd usually come home angry and drunk. I think it was a case where he took a lot of grief from his supervisor so he'd want to come and kick the dog — or whoever was there. No matter what went wrong, it was always somebody else's fault. Even if a tire blew out. The worst time I can remember was when he couldn't find a bottle of scotch he thought he had. First he blamed Mom. Then my sister said something smart-ass to him, and she paid for it. As he was thrashing her, one of my brothers tried to stop him, and he got thrashed too. Finally I lied and said I'd accidentally broken the bottle. He yelled at me but said I was the only decent one for telling the truth.

Besides being highly dysfunctional, Leigh's family was headed by a man who exhibited a key trait of parents of Abused One-Downs. He was an "externalizer." When something went wrong, it was *never* his fault. Someone else was always to blame.

A child trying desperately to win approval from such a parent often learns to accept the blame. In her emotionally dangerous and insecure world, the blamed child will probably come to believe that she really is to blame. The parent is, after all, an authority figure. He must know what's right and true. Like the other one-down types, this one-down learns that standing up for herself is asking for punishment, verbal or physical. But if she accepts blame, deserving or not, she will come as close as she ever can to gaining her externalizing parent's approval. And that's a reprieve from more punishment. The price of acceptance in this setting, then, is a guilty confession.

With this huge emotional millstone, it's difficult to imagine what the Abused One-Down's interpersonal strength could be. Often it's masked by the emotional tumult of her unhealthy relationships. But we have only to look at the outcome of her encounters with her abusive parent to see where her strength lies — and why she and abusive men so reliably find each other.

The Abused One-Down's specialty is *defusing*. In childhood, she is the repository of an irrational, volatile parent's anger. By taking the rap, she effects the end of a violent episode. Thus, she proves herself useful to her angry, externalizing parent. It is unfortunate that the very action that gives her a sense of competence—taking the blame—also makes her feel worse about herself, and more deserving of abuse.

On the Interpersonal Circle, the Abused One-Down displays an overdeveloped sense of modesty. Modesty without healthy self-assurance leads to a sense of unworthiness, a tendency to assume "it's my fault." An overly modest child believes she's causing the rage as well as defusing it.

Love and the Abused One-Down

The reason why many psychotherapists regard the Abused One-Down as a masochist is that she seems to avoid "nice guys" in favor of volatile, abusive partners. On the surface, Leigh's relationship pattern appeared to fit this mold; she'd even admitted that during her dead-end involvement with Brock, she was rejecting the advances of others.

However, in my view, masochism plays no part in this. There are several other powerful factors at work. First, the Abused One-Down's self-esteem is badly damaged. She's convinced that she's a bad person and undeserving of a "good" partner. (As Groucho Marx so aptly put it, "I'd never join any club that would have me.") This works both ways. Often, the Abused One-Down's lack of self-esteem is subtly evident to nonabusing men, and that lowers her attraction power for them.

Another dynamic comes into play as she seeks a romantic partner, and it's one that dovetails with the passion trap. The man who blames and externalizes can be very charming and exciting when he finds a partner he wants. He's a good salesman because he usually has something to hide, and that makes him all the more magnetic to the one-down weaned on emotional fireworks. But only slightly beneath the surface lies the hook—his need for a woman who can deal with his anger and frustration. The passion trap fits into this scheme because the Abused One-Down always feels out of control of her volatile partner, and that adds passion to her pain. It can be tragically addicting.

Balancing

If you are in an abusive relationship, I strongly advise you to seek professional help immediately. It's hard enough to deal with an unbalanced relationship when there's no abuse. But when it's there, the fears and *real* dangers can make you feel hopelessly stuck. I assure you, you have more options than you can imagine right now. A good therapist will help you find and act on them.

If you don't know whether your situation would be defined as abusive, ask a trusted friend, relative, or your physician. Or try this objectifying exercise: Consider how you would react to another woman in your situation. Would it seem to you that *she* was putting up with too much? If she was someone you cared about, would you be worried about her or even wish she would remove herself from the situation? If so, you should act. Several excellent books on how to identify and deal with abusive relationships are listed in the bibliography. I urge you to invest in them for your future happiness.

If you have a history of being an Abused One-Down, it is time that you reevaluate your approach to relationships.

First, be more cautious about fast-moving Romeos who sweep you off your feet and keep your head spinning with their unpredictable moves. These men can indeed be very romantic. But, as I'll discuss in the next chapter, they often lack the interpersonal skills of sensitivity and modesty. You may be exhilarated at first by the passion such a man inspires. But passion should never be the sole criterion for a relationship. Nor should it justify your tolerating neglect or abuse. The passion you feel from being out of control with an abusive partner is a dangerous side effect of the passion trap.

Second, give the "nice guy" more of a chance. At first he'll probably seem all wrong to you. You may feel undeserving of his niceness. You may have a strong sense of not "clicking" with him — as if he doesn't tap the best in you. But spending time with him will allow you to get more comfortable with him and start getting new interpersonal bearings.

If signs of abuse emerge in your relationship, dispute the interpersonal motto you learned as a child: *It's always my fault.* This motto makes you believe that you're solely responsible for the harsh treatment you're receiving; that *you* should try harder to fix the relationship; and that if things don't get better, you probably deserve this poor treatment anyway. Living by this motto will only *enable* your partner to be more abusive and make you feel worse about yourself.

It's *essential*, then, that you challenge your old motto with this new one: *I deserve love and respect like everyone else.* This new motto will help you build your self-esteem and rid yourself of your self-blaming pattern. It will help you to set limits on your partner's behavior, and to know when and if it becomes necessary to leave the relationship.

In therapy, Leigh learned to empathize with herself and to fight her tendencies to blame herself and seek emotional turmoil.

Learning about passion trap dynamics helped her see why "bad guys" seemed more exciting to her than nice ones, and why that excitement carried such a high emotional price. After several weeks in therapy and some planning and rehearsing, she decided it was time to face Brock about their affair. The next time he suggested they "get together," she used No-Fault Communication to tell him it was over. Her needs were not being met in their affair, she said, and she stuck by her guns despite his protests.

Afterward she told me, "It was one of the most difficult things I've ever done. But it felt great to stand up for myself."

Several months later, Leigh met a nice man and began dating him. It did feel a little strange to her, especially because her romantic feelings for him were developing slowly, but very surely. "I'm used to instant grand passion," she said. "But this feels much healthier. Does it mean I'm starting to like myself?"

Chapter 14

The One-Up
Personality

Learning to Be Vulnerable

The extreme one-up has many faces. He can be stern and authoritative, cool and aloof, aggressive, even abusive. He may come on passionate and strong, then swiftly reel in his emotions, leaving a partner confused and one-down. Or he may run from the very idea of emotional closeness with another person. He can be so absorbed by a personal pursuit that he has few emotional reserves left over for an intimate partner.

Many chronic one-ups had difficult childhoods like those of one-downs. But instead of yielding and connecting with a demanding parent, they resisted and pulled away. Some assumed one-up armor to deflect emotional pain; others learned that vulnerability was bad. All share interpersonal strengths that pull them toward separation and control in their love lives.

The Authoritarian

The Authoritarian is a leader. He conducts his life in an orderly, disciplined manner. He prides himself on his rationality. For him, the rules of life are black and white: there is a right way and a wrong way, and his life exemplifies the right way. Typically, he works in a managerial or supervisory position or owns his own business. He loves to preside over challenging, uncertain situations, and his solutions are often ingenious. Usually he attains career success, and he views its material rewards as proof that his way is right.

The Authoritarian believes there are two kinds of people: the weak and the strong. His interpersonal options are equally well defined: he feels compelled to control the weak and surpass the strong.

A Potentially Embarrassing Problem

When I think of the Authoritarian, my former client Marshall comes to mind. At 55, he was the director of a large medical center. While not exactly popular, he'd earned respect for his leadership and managerial abilities. The image of success was important to him, and his well-tailored suits and gleaming black Mercedes were conspicuous examples of this. He flaunted the politically conservative views that he felt had enabled his ascendancy. His social manner was somewhat stiff and awkwardly jovial. For example, his "icebreaker" at our first session was, "With all those kooks I read about in the papers, I imagine your business is booming."

Marshall had been married to Suzanne for twenty-five years, and they had three children, two in college and one in high school. Marshall liked to run a tight ship, both at home and at work. Suzanne won his approval with her smooth management of the household, socially correct community involvement, and utter compliance. The children went to private schools, had chores, and were expected not to get into trouble. By his own admission, he wasn't a "hands-on" father, but his high expectations were known to all. He meted out punishment when necessary.

A person like Marshall rarely enters therapy. Therapy requires the willingness and the ability to be vulnerable and introspective, to admit to weaknesses and mistakes. There is no place in the Authoritarian's world for the messiness and turbulence of emotions, and he has devoted a good deal of energy to avoiding them. Marshall never would have started therapy if personal tragedy hadn't occurred.

Three months prior to our first meeting, Marshall had found his daughter sprawled on their pool-house floor, dead of a cocaine overdose. The week before, he'd made a unilateral decision that he'd felt had corrected a "potentially embarrassing problem." His daughter had gotten pregnant during her junior year of high school. He'd insisted that she drop out of school and had made arrangements for her to live with his sister's family in Ohio until the baby was born. Now he couldn't get the image of his dead daughter out of his mind.

And his whole family, including his formerly submissive wife, had bitterly turned against him.

The Authoritarian's Childhood

The Authoritarian grows up in a family that rigidly embraces traditional sex roles. Typically, the father is an Authoritarian. His disdain for "weak" emotions is passed on to his son. This is how Marshall described his upbringing:

> Our home was like boot camp. If we didn't do things exactly like my father wanted, we knew it was time for the belt. No horsing around. I wouldn't call him a mean person. In fact, he could be quite proud of us. But we knew not to step out of line. I remember once when I was about four I took apart his flashlight and he spanked me. I started howling. He told me to grow up and stop crying or I was going to learn the lesson of my life. And I think that was the one time he left bruises on me. Needless to say, I learned to do things his way. But you know, in many respects I think his method of parenting was good. Unlike kids today, you really learned to be responsible for your actions early in life.

As a child, the Authoritarian is rejected and/or punished whenever he shows vulnerability. He soon learns that his worth is measured by worldly success, as defined by his parents. Whining, crying, and other "sissy" behaviors are simply unacceptable.

The Authoritarian's personal quest is to become "the hero." At play as a child, his fantasies revolve around military conquest, and in school he strives to excel athletically and academically. As an adult, his heroism is measured by the wealth and prestige he earns. Sociologist Warren Farrell has written that the traditional male is conditioned to be a "success object" in much the same way as females are taught to be "sex objects." The high price of this quest is a lack of emotional connectedness.

Marshall grew silent after voicing approval of his father's parenting methods. He had fallen into his typical my-way-is-right mode of thinking. But this rigid stance had collided with the image of his dead daughter, now frozen in his mind.

Love and the Authoritarian

Most people have at least one crushing romantic rejection in adolescence, but they recover. In a sense, the Authoritarian never does. His adolescent heartbreak shakes the foundations of his success-object self-image because it turns him into a wounded loser. From that point on, he will avoid women who are his equal in status, attraction power, or ego strength. Strong women unnerve him. He neutralizes his fear by mocking and criticizing them — strong women are "ballbusters" and the rest are "weak." Unconsciously he seeks involvement only with women whom he can safely control. Usually the woman he marries has pronounced one-down leanings and will either stay at home or work in a lower status job than his. The Authoritarian's wife and family are important to his success game plan. Although he may never feel passionate love for his wife, he will value her if she enhances his self-image and his worldly success.

Marshall's wife, Suzanne, was tailor-made for him. Her family was more socially prominent than his, which boosted his status; in addition, she was a model Sweet One-Down. But her daughter's suicide had changed her compliant posture. Now she was confronting Marshall with her anger. The stable imbalance in their marriage had turned chaotic.

Balancing

It takes a devastating emotional or financial loss to crack an Authoritarian's righteous stance. In fact, such a loss may undo him. The interpersonal skills that would help him navigate a life crisis are woefully undeveloped. He's never learned to let down his guard, to disclose emotional pain, to accept nurturance from others. He's the proverbial oak tree: He resists rather than bends with the wind and is more likely than the "weaker" willow to break in a storm. Not surprisingly, one of the highest suicide risk groups is men in their late fifties and early sixties who have failed for the first time.

Marshall couldn't rationalize away his pain over his daughter's suicide, and he had no place to "file" it. His stress drove him toward a heavier reliance on his primary interpersonal strength: leadership. He made desperate power plays. He clashed with Suzanne over the funeral plans, and at work he blew up at subordinates over trivial matters. Suzanne's ultimatum — "Please do something about yourself or we're through," — was the final blow to his Authoritarian sense of certainty. For the first time in his adult life, he cried. Also for the first time, he followed Suzanne's advice: he agreed to start therapy.

If you have Authoritarian leanings, I urge you to employ your strong rational thinking skills. Examine your relationship patterns and see how they may be linked to the way you interact with people. The interpersonal motto you learned as a child—*My way is the right way*—doesn't allow you the safety valve of being wrong. You force family members who can't go along with your way to resort to extreme measures. They may rebel or retaliate or become self-punishing (Marshall's daughter combined all three). Their stressful reactions will compel you to rely even more heavily on your top-heavy management skills. It's your fear of not controlling any given situation that is the problem. As Marshall later said, "I won the family battles, but we all lost the war."

You'll be a better leader if you learn to be flexible and empathic. Whenever you feel threatened and controlling, repeat to yourself this new motto: *Sometimes you win when you don't win.* In therapy, Marshall wept bitterly when he finally admitted the unbearable truth: If he had not railroaded his daughter and instead had reached out to her with understanding, the tragedy likely would not have occurred. It took several months for the acute phase of his suffering to begin to pass. Although he would probably never be free of guilt and bereavement, he came to realize that something good could come out of this dreadful experience. In fact, he was reshaped by it.

Marshall spearheaded a new suicide-prevention program at the medical center, and he and Suzanne joined a parents' group. At home, he was actively supportive of his college-age children and communicated with Suzanne about everything, from dinner plans to decisions about the medical center. His leadership skills, balanced with compassion, were coming into full flower.

The Thrill-Seeker

The Thrill-Seeker lives for challenge. If his life becomes too secure and predictable, boredom will drive him to find new perils and thrills. He is aggressively competitive because competition stimulates him. He needs great surges of adrenaline to reach his optimal performance level. His pursuits reflect his need for biochemical excitation: he is a race-car driver, a rock climber, a hang-glider. He is the athlete who performs best under extremely intense pressure. Arenas that tend to draw Thrill-Seekers include the military, politics, high finance, law enforcement, crime, and sexual conquest.

Sexual Adventures

Ginny's husband, Frank, the police detective, was a Thrill-Seeker. During an individual session, I asked him why he had chosen that occupation. His reply carried an ironic tone.

> I love the excitement and drama. I'd be bored to death in any other job. You're not cooped up in an office all day long. You get to mingle with the criminal element. You meet all kinds of people, damsels in distress being my personal favorites.

Like many Thrill-Seekers, Frank's excitement needs extended to the sexual arena. Not surprisingly, a stable, monogamous relationship isn't high on his priority list. Once a relationship becomes routine, the prospect of new sexual challenges may be irresistible.

The Thrill-Seeker's Childhood

The Thrill-Seeker's craving for stimulation can show up very early in childhood, which suggests a genetic component. Early sex-role conditioning for males to be heroic helps explain why there are more male Thrill-Seekers than female. It is likely that male hormones also play a part. In addition, some childhood experiences foster dare-deviltry and competitiveness. Frank's childhood included some of these experiences.

> My mother was divorced and had to work. She was a good, loving mother, but me and my brothers were a real handful. I was a smart-ass, independent kid. I did a lot of hanging out. I got my education, you could say, in the street. We thought we were cool, and we got into trouble. Not big trouble, but you know. But in my mother's eyes, I could do *no* wrong . . . She always believed my side of the story. I really got away with murder, so to speak.

An emotionally needy parent sometimes offers such uncritical love that the child becomes convinced that he truly "can do no wrong." The child gains the confidence to face extreme situations with minimal anxiety. But his confidence may not be balanced with normal levels of modesty and sensitivity. His competitiveness thus unchecked, he may overstep the emotional boundaries of others. But then, pushing situations and people to their limits is his lifeblood.

Some Thrill-Seekers are children of privilege whose parents were amply able to give materially, but were less successful at making their child feel warmly loved and accepted. Their flirtations with danger may come from an angrier place. Thrill-Seekers of all types share the feeling that the land of their childhood was at root hostile and unsupportive. There, modesty, shyness, and emotional sensitivity were liabilities. The adaptive child learned to bury these parts of himself. The question is whether a tough, risk-taking child will become a friend or an enemy of society. There's truth in the adage that cop and robber are basically cut from the same cloth.

Love and the Thrill-Seeker

The Thrill-Seeker brings a special fire to courtship. While many of us can barely stand the sweats and fever of new love, the Thrill-Seeker relishes them. He lives for everything courtship offers: uncertainty, challenge, risk, novelty, and pleasure. He feels alive and confident. He radiates excitement. The woman who finds herself the object of his attentions will rarely offer resistance. She senses that this will be a memorable encounter.

Frank described the rush he experienced each time he set eyes on an attractive woman.

> I can't put into words what it's like when you see a beautiful woman and you know you've got to have her. You look at her finger to see if she's married, and if she is, great. A challenge. If not, great too, but you have to be careful. At first you're all business, but you throw in a little surprise. A little joke about how great she is, but she's almost not sure you said it. A couple of days later, more business, and another teaser. Maybe you brush up against her, like it was an accident. And the next time you run into her, she's looking for you, but trying to act cool. By now you're burning for her. And you make the play, the gamble. It's the best part. Sometimes I ask them to lunch or coffee. Sometimes I come right out with it. You know what women like to hear? "I need you." You have no idea how great it can be in a Xerox room after hours. [He chuckled.]

Because Thrill-Seekers are so confident, independent, and hard to control — in other words, so exciting — their partners often fall in love with them. Predictably, the moment his passion begins to ebb, the Thrill-Seeker's eye will stray in the direction of a new sexual fix. It's not so much that he fears commitment per se. He just can't imagine life without romantic pursuit. His craving for excitement and novelty supersedes his need for intimacy and security. And it virtually guarantees that he'll be on the one-up side of the passion trap.

Like Frank, most Thrill-Seekers do wind up getting married. Some do many times. They are not immune to the expectations of society or to the desire to have children and a consistent female presence in their lives. It's not unusual for a Thrill-Seeker to marry after having a close call connected to his brinksmanship. Recall that Ginny had been Frank's physical therapist after a motorcycle accident. But once a Thrill-Seeker gets too comfortable, infidelity is almost inevitable. It takes an extreme one-down like Ginny to tolerate such an arrangement.

Balancing

Thrill-Seekers should first commend themselves for their strengths: healthy confidence, independence, charm, competitiveness, humor, and spontaneity. However, the very strengths that give them appeal can also trap them in self-destructive patterns. Their approach to life rarely succeeds indefinitely. When it does collapse, depression is the usual consequence. Moreover, when the Thrill-Seeker's risk-taking is sexual, he's now playing Russian roulette with AIDS.

It may sound odd at first, but the Thrill-Seeker suffers mainly from a malnourished sense of modesty. Modesty is an important interpersonal tool; it's a link with social realities. Immodest people tend to think they are, in a sense, "above the law." Their needs come first, and they don't fully take into account how getting those needs met might hurt others. Modesty helps people gauge the propriety or impropriety, the decency or hurtfulness, of their actions. Those who lack modesty live by the interpersonal motto: *I can have it all.* People who've internalized this motto run a greater risk of losing everything.

The Thrill-Seeker usually knows he's walking a tightrope and that he could fall at any moment. But recall that it's danger itself that so entices him. What you get, then, is a person who continually puts himself on the line, hoping to "get it all," including the charge from risk-taking.

A Thrill-Seeker's exploits can be shattering. When a spouse finally gets fed up and leaves, the Thrill-Seeker may be surprised by the devastation he feels. The charm and daring that brought him such success outside the primary relationship may then be consumed by depression.

Counseling Thrill-Seekers poses a dilemma. What gives their lives greatest meaning—especially when they're sexual adventurers—is so often hurtful to others. Yet, to advise a Thrill-Seeker to show restraint only imbues his indulgences with more challenge and excitement. My approach with Thrill-Seekers is straightforward. It supports rather than challenges their free will. Simply stated, I invite *them* to choose between short-term and long-term pleasures.

If you feel drawn to infidelity or some other injurious form of risk-taking, please consider this new motto: *I am prone to forget how much I stand to lose.* When short-term pleasures beckon, remember the long-term rewards you may be throwing away. This motto applies not only to your relationship but to risky short-term pleasures such as drug and alcohol abuse and gambling.

Frank candidly admitted that he didn't know if he could permanently end his philandering. He also said that the thought of hurting and losing his wife and children—a classic Thrill-Seeker's "close call"—had for now changed his priorities and dampened his desire for sexual adventure. He was spending more time at home and was surprised that he liked it. It was clear to me that Ginny's efforts to learn one-up skills were having an impact. She no longer enabled his exploits with accommodating sweetness. Their relationship had entered a phase of greater balance from which both reaped emotional rewards.

The Loner

When you were in school, you probably had a couple of classmates who didn't fit in with the group. They didn't try to, either. They seemed to be on their own separate track, indifferent to the social cliques, and often devoted to their own special interests. Sometimes they were nonconformist, maybe slightly "nerdy." In my class, the Loners turned out to be a concert pianist (the boy) and a molecular biologist (the girl).

Indeed, the ranks of Loners include artists, musicians, and writers. They also include people whose work involves minimal social contact: forest rangers, archivists, farmers, laboratory technicians, and long-distance truckers. The history of science is filled with accounts of major breakthroughs made by scientists working alone, sometimes for years at a stretch.

Jonathan, Deborah's lover, had a Loner personality style that had been reinforced by his painful divorce. Although he had occasional relationships, they tended to be few and far between. "I'm not what you'd call a compulsive womanizer," he commented. I asked him how he liked to spend his time.

> I read, listen to music, do some hanging out at bookstores and a couple of cafes where I like the atmosphere. I read philosophy and history, and I like jazz and classical music. I have an expensive home theater and the sound quality is incredible. In the summer I try to go backpacking by myself for a couple of weeks. And I do projects around the house and work in my garden, which I'm redoing in the Japanese style. I have some friends I see every couple of weeks or so. I like to have a lot of control over my time. It's not a bad life, really.

I asked Jonathan if he felt something was missing. He replied, "Sometimes, yes."

The Loner's Childhood

I think we tend to view Loners as being "just that way" due to a predisposition to shyness or introversion. When the Loner is also a creator, it's easy to believe his creativity has led him down a solitary path. While I think we do have certain inborn leanings toward one personality style or another, I've seen too much reliable data to accept this as the whole story. The evidence shows that most Loners were emotionally "burned" in childhood. Jonathan certainly was.

> My father was an alcoholic and I never knew how he was going to act around me. Occasionally he'd be jovial, but usually he was just very drunk and mean and bitter. He'd start yelling at me for no reason at all. I don't know why *I* always got the brunt of things. He never seemed to yell at my sister or Mom. What really bothered me was that Mom would just sit there as if nothing was happening. Once in a while I'd get fed up and yell back at him—which was always a mistake. Then he'd get physical, and he was big. The only place I felt safe was my room. I was always handy, and I installed a deadbolt on my door when I was about eight.

The Loner child naturally feels rage for being emotionally excluded by his family. However, unlike most extreme one-up types, *he doesn't feel he has the right to be angry.* Being the only child exempted from his parents' love has the predictable effect of making *him* feel somehow at fault. In essence, the Loner assumes a one-up adaptive style because he feels so vulnerable, like a one-down. Rather than using forceful one-up strategies, he withdraws, attempting to control his situation by absenting himself. He forms the unconscious belief that he'll be safest in isolation from other people. Adopting a distant interpersonal style, he rarely offers or seeks emotional closeness with others. His behavior reflects the sad lesson he learned as a child: "When you get close to people they hurt and reject you."

For some Loners, the most traumatizing rejection comes from their peers. Singled out on the playground, they're harshly ridiculed and excluded. But even these Loners usually fail to get the emotional support at home to revitalize their self-esteem.

Like Jonathan, many Loners had unpredictable and inconsistent parenting. Jonathan never knew when his father was going to blow up at him. To survive, he was forced to rely on the *interpersonal skill of caution* — which in its extreme form is distrust. He grew hypervigilant, alert to subtle clues signaling one of his father's outbursts. Whenever Jonathan saw his father's jaw muscles twitch, he'd slip away as quickly and quietly as possible.

To ease the pain of rejection, many Loner children fantasize brilliant careers for themselves, lives of attainment that bring them love and adulation. Sometimes these fantasies become reality when the child directs his rage toward the attainment of high goals.

Love and the Loner

The Loner feels pulled in opposite directions. Loneliness and sexual urges push him toward romantic connection, while his deep-rooted fear of moving close and getting burned again holds him back. He compromises by adopting a passive interpersonal strategy. Typically, he sits back and lets potential partners make the first move. The resulting aloofness enables him to start a relationship in the emotional power position by deliberately giving less than his partner. Unfortunately, this stance often backfires. Jonathan described an episode that illustrated a common Loner pattern.

> A couple of times a week I run. And, you know, there are always a couple of people you see every time you go out. There was one woman who started getting friendly, a really fine runner, and I got interested in her too. She started coming on to me a little, like suggesting that sometime we should get together for coffee. I was pleased but held back a little. Anyway, this went on for about two weeks before I finally worked up the nerve to ask her out. But wouldn't you know, that very day she was running with another guy. I had this sense that I'd really blown it on one hand. But I also felt kind of relieved ...

When the woman moved toward him, Jonathan instinctively held back. Likely she interpreted his distance as rejection and gave up on him. Jonathan, in turn, felt hurt when she took up with another man. For him, it was further proof of his vulnerability and the wisdom in staying aloof most of the time.

When a Loner actually initiates romantic contact, his needs are usually strong — and often his confidence has recently gotten a boost. When he met Deborah, Jonathan hadn't been with a woman for almost a year. He'd also just won the biggest remodeling contract of his career. Deborah had seemed to him a kindred spirit, hence a good risk. Yet, recall that he didn't initiate sexual contact for several weeks. He was infatuated with Deborah, yet the signals he sent for more closeness were mixed. Even the strong forces of courtship couldn't overcome his self-protective reflex.

Unable to penetrate Jonathan's shell, Deborah grew anxious. Bowing to the forces of the passion trap, and to her own strong Echo tendencies, she then closed in on him. By this time Jonathan had realized she'd be a safe, nonrejecting partner. But now he was gripped by a new fear, an emotional claustrophobia. Deborah was crowding him. Not only did this one-down response cool his feelings for her, but it left him with a Loner's primal dread of losing his privacy and his control over his time and his life.

Balancing

If you identify with the Loner, first accept your need for privacy as valid and important. There are things you can do to increase your interpersonal options, which may now be few.

It's likely that your insulated life has proved, in a sense, too successful. Alone, you may accomplish much that fulfills you, and you may feel safe from the hazards of emotional entanglement. However, all but the most extreme Loners come to feel at least somewhat imprisoned by their isolation. By clinging to the interpersonal motto that protected you during childhood — *Never get close to people* — you keep yourself in emotional exile.

Most Loners have no problem accepting their need for privacy as valid. Now I ask you to accept, as well, your natural, healthy, biologically based desire to share part of your life with another person. With prolonged disconnection, your valued privacy may be darkened by depression, the usual consequence of emotional isolation. You're also statistically prone to develop health problems.

When a Loner finds a partner who makes few emotional demands — in essence, another Loner type — his contentment and productivity are optimal. But such partners are rare. Women generally tend not to have the Loner's dread of emotional risk-taking and not to share his behavioral patterns.

If your Loner tendencies are an issue right now, communication is the most important new skill for you to learn. Tell your partner you enjoy your privacy. By disclosing your need for distance, you paradoxically deepen your connection with your partner. This also helps her not to misinterpret your distance as rejection.

Next, talk about the patterns that have harmed your past relationships. You needn't go into painful details, but do say that your distance tends to be misperceived as rejection. Explain how that misperception can lead to people withdrawing, and how that reaction makes you warier. Explain too that sometimes people start putting on the pressure when you hold back, and that reinforces your impulse to disappear. Then ask your partner what level of closeness she wants, and try to determine when her intimacy needs may clash with your privacy needs.

Partners needn't have identical intimacy/privacy needs. But those whose intimacy needs differ must be careful not to set off passion trap dynamics. Again, communication and negotiation are the keys to reaching mutually satisfying interactions. I've worked with many partners who had unequal intimacy needs and were able to negotiate successful compromises.

When you feel an urge to run from your partner — and periodically you will — challenge the impulse with this new motto: *I need closeness too.* This attitude will help you balance your Loner tendencies with the normal desire to connect and to take emotional risks.

Sometimes you'll think you have everything negotiated to a tee, but in practice one or both of you continues to feel emotionally shortchanged. Perhaps that will be the issue on which your relationship hinges. But at least you'll have had open and direct dealings with your partner. You won't have bailed out precipitously, as Jonathan did with Deborah.

Like most one-ups, Loners can benefit tremendously from therapy but are highly unlikely to seek it. The same issues that block them from connecting with others — distrust, fear of disclosure, giving up privacy — make therapy an unappetizing prospect. Paradoxically, these are issues that respond very well to therapy, which is unconditionally accepting and nonrejecting. Especially if you feel acutely lonely and isolated, I urge you to consider therapy.

The Punisher

For years I led a therapy group for Vietnam veterans at a V.A. medical center. Bob was a 32-year-old patient in my group. He grew up in a small farming town in central California. His adolescence was marked by aggressive behavior and fighting. But by his town's standards, he was just a normal, healthy boy. In fact, he was quite popular. He starred on the football and wrestling teams, and his steady girlfriend was a cheerleader.

Bob graduated from high school during the height of the Vietnam war. His father had been a Marine and all of his friends were enlisting. The thought of staying behind never crossed his mind.

On his second day in Vietnam, his best friend was killed. He went numb, he said. The numbness grew over his nine-month tour, helping him survive the horrors of Vietnam. He estimated that he killed over 30 Vietcong. In a battle near a village, the deaths of several friends drove him "berserk." He attacked the village with machine gun and grenades, killing a couple of women and even one child. His rampage ended when a piece of shrapnel sliced into his abdomen, an injury that brought an end to his tour of duty.

When he got home, he tried to resume a "normal" life. He got a job as a tractor mechanic. His high school sweetheart had married and moved away, but he married Kate, a girl who'd always had a crush on him. They had two boys. However, Bob was merely going through the motions of a normal life. He was feeling estranged from the people around him.

> There was a bitterness eating inside me, like a poison. At first I tried to drink it away. Like a case of beer each night. But things just kept getting worse. You know, the nightmares and everything. I started hanging out at bars. I got into this game of looking out for hippies. You know, the ones who blamed us, the Vietnam veterans, for the fucking war. I'd wear my old Marine hat, and as soon as one of them made the slightest comment about it, I'd deck him. But the worst things I did were at home. I blamed Kate for everything. I'd come home drunk as a skunk and slap her up for no good reason. And the worst part was she'd just take it. And the more she'd take it, the more I dished it out.

The One-Up Personality

Bob had fallen into a vicious Punishing pattern. The aggression he needed to survive the Vietnam nightmare couldn't be turned off when he returned to his hometown.

One night Bob came home to find that Kate, the boys, and their belongings were gone. There was no note. In a drunken frenzy, he tore up the house, then drove around town shooting his gun in the air. He was arrested for disturbing the peace—actually his fourth such arrest. This time, the judge gave him an ultimatum: six months in jail or treatment at the V.A.

The Punisher's Childhood

Most Punishers become well acquainted with violent aggression during a critical period of their youth or adolescence. Bob's upbringing involved a good deal of traditional "men must be tough" conditioning, and he had interpersonal leanings toward aggression. But there was also plenty of love in his family.

For Bob, the delicate balance between angry aggression and loving connection was toppled by the Vietnam war. He entered the war during a crucial period in his life, when adolescents make their final passage into adulthood. How well they negotiate this passage affects their lives for years to come. Bob was 18, still more boy than man, when he landed in Vietnam. The horrors that met him there demanded an extreme adaptive response. That was the numbing he spoke of, and the eclipse of the connecting skills he'd learned while growing up. Only the aggression and anger remained, and they became his salvation in the jungles of Vietnam.

There are, of course, many Punishers who were never in a war. But if you examine their childhoods, many had upbringings that to a young child would be equivalent to pitched combat. The 3-year-old who sees his drunken father beating his mother, and then realizes in terror that he's next, will view the world as a cruel, vicious, life-threatening place. An extreme case of this was a Punisher client of mine who, at the age of 7, saw his father repeatedly stab his mother to death. Unbalanced by love, acceptance, nurturance, or a sense of emotional safety, traumas like these often mold a child into a hostile, aggressive, volatile person who believes that if he doesn't get "them" first, they'll get him. He grows up to be the proverbial powder keg, ready to explode at the slightest provocation.

Love and the Punisher

Most women instinctively back away from the Punisher. His appearance and manner often express the anger churning inside him. When he does elicit avoidance, he gets angrier and more bitter, which make him even less approachable. It's a vicious circle.

Of course, he needs and wants a woman for all the normal reasons. When his needs get very strong, he is quite capable of turning on a kind of rough charm that will appeal especially to one-down women. They seem to sense his need for nurturance, but they also may be drawn to the aura of masculine danger that often surrounds him. Kate recalled that when she ran into Bob after he returned from Vietnam . . .

> he was kind of cute and shy, almost like a little boy. I was working at the bank, and he'd make a point of waiting for my window to be free. He asked me out about the third time I saw him. I sensed something was wrong, that he wasn't happy, but of course I thought I could fix all that. Mainly, he seemed very dashing to me.

Kate was a Sweet One-Down. It pained her to think of the horrors Bob had experienced, and it meant a lot to her to be the supportive, loyal wife. But even before they married she realized she'd have her work cut out for her. Like most Punishers, Bob didn't stay charming for long.

> I could see that he had a problem with alcohol, and that he seemed to have a lot of demons inside him from Vietnam. And as soon as we got engaged, I started getting some tastes of how they could get the better of him. I got pregnant pretty soon afterwards, and I sometimes wonder if he'd have followed through with the marriage if I hadn't.

Committed to helping Bob "work it through," Kate never swerved from her sweetness and support, even when he became physically abusive. Of course, unknown to both, she was enabling him. When the pattern and the abuse got worse rather than better, she finally left. That action saved them both by precipitating the crisis that brought in helpful intervention.

Balancing

If you've fallen into a violent Punisher's pattern, *seek professional help immediately.* Your pattern is one of the most difficult to break. At some point in the past, you probably felt you had to rely on physical aggression to ensure your survival. But now that aggression is turning the world against you. And that compels you to fight back more fiercely. Any help offered in a book will only scratch the surface of this pattern.

Although you will likely resist the idea of turning to a therapist for help, I urge you to examine your alternatives. Your life is probably far from what you'd like it to be, and it's highly unlikely that on your own you'd be able to turn it around as quickly as with guidance and support.

Bob's emotional breakthrough came in our group. As other group members courageously faced their Vietnam nightmares, his wall of hostility began to crumble. During one session, he listened as another man castigated himself for killing a young Vietnamese boy. Bob began yelling at him: "It wasn't your fault, man. They were trying to kill you! You couldn't trust no one over there." He started to say how he had done the same thing, and then it happened. All the memories and emotions he'd dammed up behind his anger began to break free. He buried his face in his hands, and his body began to shake violently. He got up to leave the room, but the man who'd spoken first put an arm around him. These two men, conditioned from childhood to deny their vulnerabilities, trained as killers, and witnesses to unspeakable horror, were finally, ten years after the war, beginning to find a healing balance they'd *never* known.

At the end of the group, Bob said that facing those emotions was in a sense more frightening than any combat mission in Vietnam. It was a real turning point. In subsequent group meetings and in couples' therapy with his wife, he forced himself to let down his guard and deal with his emotional agony. In essence, he was using his interpersonal strength of aggression to tackle the challenges of therapy. He said that after each painful session, he always felt an unburdening. He was feeling less estranged and numb, more "alive." By the end of his treatment program, he had assimilated balancing one-down skills that gave him a sense of personal equilibrium. He no longer felt the need to turn his home and his town into battlefields.

Chapter 15

When to Leave

I have a good friend who married his high school sweetheart. They had been each others' romantic "firsts" at every step of the way: first date at age 14, first kiss, first "steady," first "I love you," first lovemaking. They married right out of high school. A very deep and loving bond existed between them.

Yet, when my friend started graduate school, an imbalance began to build. His wife worked as a nurse and idolized him. He valued her stability, nurturance, and love. But there was something missing in his marriage that he shared with women friends in his graduate program: wit, common interests, and intellectual parity. They had a child, and that brought them closer for a while. Indeed, he still felt surges of satisfaction and tenderness in the marriage. But other feelings began to prevail: discontentment, guilt, frustration — the feelings of a true one-up.

He spent several years trying to make things better. He initiated couples' and individual therapy, and he tried to hold his attraction to another woman in check. Sometimes things seemed to get better, at least on the surface. At those times, he would think, "Yes, it will work if only I stay with it." But beneath the surface, he couldn't stop his unhappiness and dissatisfaction. The iron grip of ambivalence had seized him and wouldn't let go. The turning point came when he acted out in an affair. He knew a decision had to be made.

The Hardest Choice

Life holds many hard choices, but none is harder than the one you face when a relationship isn't working. So much of your life, and the lives of others, will be affected by your decision.

The problem is, there aren't any rules to guide you. I've seen too many highly stressed relationships recover to say there is an absolute point of no return. I've also seen the splitting of partners who truly seemed "made for each other." So many factors come into play, and for each couple each factor is weighted differently.

When you understand the passion trap, you have an advantage. You can avoid the blind alleys and find ways to ease the pain and uncertainty of making your decision.

How Not to Make Your Decision

At several points, my friend sat down and tried to be logical about his dilemma. He used the old Ben Franklin technique of listing the pros on one side of the page and the cons on the other, to see which list winds up longest. But he found it of no help. In fact, it made him more confused.

If you're in the market for a dishwasher or weighing Europe against Tahiti for your vacation, you might want to rely on this venerable decision-making method. But when your choice involves something as emotionally charged as the fate of your relationship, Franklin's method usually collapses.

One reason, as we saw in chapter 4, is that the same factors often wind up in *both* pro and con columns. For example, "safe, available sex" versus "boring, predictable sex."

More vexingly, each factor carries different weight. You wind up comparing things like "good cook" on the pro side with "avoids sex" on the other. Moreover, the relative importance of the factors may shift from day to day.

However, the main reason why this technique can actually add to your confusion is that there are so many crucial variables. Things like tastes, intelligence, job, sex, looks, religion, humor, money, and so on. Yet, even a one-for-one match-up on these points is no guarantee of a great relationship. It boils down to interpersonal dynamics, with these other factors playing supporting roles.

For example, my friend could say of his wife that she was attractive, kind, a wonderful mother, successful and well paid in her career, loving, supportive, loved by all, a gracious hostess, neat, thoughtful, and well organized. He valued all these qualities, but they didn't matter much in the larger scheme of things. The woman he thought he was falling in love with was attractive, but she was strongly absorbed in herself and her career and decidedly messy in her personal habits.

She was blunt almost to a fault and tended to be late and forgetful. He didn't particularly value these qualities, but they didn't matter to him as negatives. She was bright and dynamic and exciting to be with. Their give-and-take felt very natural, spontaneous, and balanced.

This is why trying to be logical about a relationship decision is unlikely to give you an answer.

Making the Decision

First, be understanding of yourself as you struggle with this question. Don't condemn yourself for being indecisive or erratic. In other words, don't pathologize yourself and add another negative charge to the situation. Realize that you're trying your hardest. Realize that any decision to stay or to leave will involve gains, losses, and painful trade-offs. It is one of the most important decisions you'll ever have to make. Therefore, it *shouldn't* be easy. Although it's painful, at least you're confronting the problem, not running from it.

Take an Action-Oriented Approach

If you try to resolve ambivalence by thinking it through, a la Franklin's method, you wind up chasing your tail. But an *action-oriented* approach can help give you answers. Taking action means trying as hard as you can to correct the harmful patterns in your relationship. The goal is to make every effort to improve your relationship, to give it its best shot, before you make your decision. This way, you'll have confidence in the wisdom of your choice. You'll also learn more about your true relationship needs.

Following is a summary of the most helpful action strategies:

- No-Fault Communication, the single most healing action you can take
- Disputing self-sabotaging and catastrophizing thinking patterns, and harnessing your anger in positive ways
- Fighting passion trap dynamics, with the one-down using Healthy Distance and the one-up Trial Closeness
- Addressing situational, sex-role, and attraction power imbalances
- Developing a more balanced self by learning new one-up or one-down skills
- Predicting and recovering from the inevitable setbacks

It takes hard work, courage, and maturity to use these strategies. If you feel very pessimistic about your relationship, it will also take an act of will. In the context of marriage, and especially when there are children, I recommend trying these strategies for a year or even two. That's really not so long when you consider the profound effects your decision will have on your life, your partner's, and children's. No matter what the outcome, you'll be grateful that you tried your hardest.

Then Trust Your Instincts

For years my friend was tortured by Commitment-Ambivalence Syndrome. One minute, he desperately wanted out of his marriage, the next he felt like a fool for even considering leaving the love and security his wife offered. But as his thoughts careened from pros to cons, one thing never changed: "an almost physical gnawing sensation right in the middle of me—a real gut feeling." His *deepest* feeling, the one constant, was that chronic ache that never left even when he was focused on the good things in his marriage. Finally he could no longer deny that pain.

He slept with the woman he was so attracted to and he realized he had to end his marriage. It was a traumatic time for both him and his wife, and self-doubt dogged him every step of the way. Despite the deep bond he felt with his wife, the pain of letting her go and breaking apart the family, and the guilt of making her suffer, he trusted his intuition and followed through with a divorce.

Now, ten years later, they're both remarried and both much happier. She realized that, despite her passion for him, his emotional distance in the marriage had left her lonely and frustrated most of the time. He realized that he needed a more exciting, fulfilling, equal relationship. Because of their child, they still see each other on a regular basis, and they have remained good friends.

In the final analysis, *you must trust your instincts*. But trust them only after you've made every effort to restore balance to your relationship, and taken your time doing it. Indeed, sometimes these crises do pass if you can ride them out.

Focus on the Long Term

It's one of life's cruelties that we can cherish someone and still feel desperately unfulfilled by that person. My friend told me of his many "dark nights of the soul," when he cursed life itself for allowing a situation like his to occur. Sometimes life offers two unpalatable choices, and either one will cause tremendous pain. How do you negotiate such a choice?

When my friend finally accepted that his marriage must end, it was with the certainty that over the long run, prolonging it would be unfair to *both himself and his wife.* It's always best to focus on the long term when making a major relationship decision. Many people do prolong moribund relationships because they can't face the short-term agony of breaking up. But by enduring that agony, you opt against the punishment of long-term suffering.

The Problem of Young Love, Early Marriage

The critical variable in my friend's case is obvious: the young age at which he and his wife married. In high school, he'd yet to formulate his career goals. He didn't know that as his ambitions crystallized, he would encounter people different from any he'd known before. His wife remained consistent, but he changed.

This type of situation is always fertile ground for passion trap dynamics, and few can cause as much self-blame, guilt, and frustration. If you are in my friend's position, some empathy for yourself is in order. You are not to blame for pursuing your ambitions. Sometimes people grow and change equally, but in different directions. That can be problematic. More difficult is the situation when one partner grows and changes and the other remains the same.

My friend did everything right. He gave the relationship chance after chance. He tried therapy. They tried therapy together. He conducted what I consider an exemplary Trial Closeness period that lasted for several years. He shared child care and housework with his wife. He tried all the strategies that have helped so many of my clients. But for him, the match that was so perfect in high school could not be regained.

Laura and Paul

When Laura first left Paul for Nick, she had no idea that she would want Paul back. Yet, she went to near-degrading lengths to get him back after her affair with Nick had failed and Paul had taken up with Daphne. Laura was needy at a time when Paul had seemingly left her sphere of emotional control. And that made her feel even needier. She found herself filled with passionate longing for her rejected lover. She began to rewrite emotional history. She had been a fool to leave him. He was the best and only partner for her. She didn't know exactly what had gone wrong, but now she was going to make it right.

Factoring in the Paradox of Passion

Most one-ups who leave one-downs go through a period of wanting their partners back. They'll agonize that they've made the mistake of their lives in leaving. If an exciting partner awaits them, that time may not come for years. But it may come very quickly, within days or weeks, depending on how well the one-up and one-down are faring on their own. If the one-down is doing well and the one-up is doing poorly, a passion trap reversal is highly likely. Suddenly, the one-up, like Laura, remembers only the good things, not the bad.

The question is, where does the paradox of passion stop and where do our "true" feelings begin? When we want a partner we've left, is it mainly because we've lost control of them and feel passion stemming from their unavailability? Or, have we gained perspective on the relationship that allows us to recover positive feelings that were there all along but hidden behind harmful patterns?

By the same token, when we want to end a relationship, is it because the passion trap is magnifying our partner's flaws and our feelings of confinement? Or, do we want to leave because objectively we know the relationship isn't meeting our needs and won't be able to?

Time Will Tell

I saw Laura and Paul over a four-month period. They were exemplary clients. Both worked hard and mastered No-Fault Communication, and both came to a clear understanding of their interactive patterns. They managed a good balance between Healthy Distance and emotional closeness. Neither was acting out in a one-up or one-down way.

But in the fourth month, we had a decisive session. Laura confessed that despite her great affection for Paul, she still wished she could feel "just a little more something."

> I know I'm supposed to use this vague feeling to interpret an underlying pattern. But isn't it possible that I just have some little hang-up that, oh, maybe a few individual sessions could clear up? Because I really think Paul and I have something special, and he's such a good man, and I don't want something so superficial to be a problem. Or at least I *think* it's superficial . . . In any case, I think it's very important that we be able to *accept* certain things in our relationships that may not be perfect, because nothing's ever going to be absolutely perfect. Right?

Laura, obviously confused, was starting to self-pathologize again. I glanced at Paul. Not surprisingly, he looked troubled and sad. He said:

> It's okay, Laura. We both know what you're talking about, and I don't want you to start feeling bad again. The fact is, I'm wrestling with something too.

Laura looked surprised. Paul continued:

> This is hard to say. I trust you implicitly, but I can't shake certain feelings, either. When you have lunch meetings, just you and some guys, I suffer the whole time. When I walk by your office and you're not there, it's like I feel a stab. I have these dreams about you and other men that shouldn't bother me, but they do. And having to deal on a daily basis with this *anxiety* . . . it's just wearing me down. And I know it means something, just like your feelings do.

Tears had started to form in both their eyes.

> We've worked so hard, Laura. And I think we've found something very wonderful. But I'm afraid it's . . . more like friendship. I guess sometimes you have to face what's there . . .

Laura took Paul's hand and squeezed it. For several moments she couldn't talk. Then she said:

I do love you, Paul. I've never felt so close to anyone. But, I don't know, it's like sometimes we do seem to be forcing it, and I know we're both aware of it. And now I feel so guilty, like I led you on a second time and made your life miserable again . . .

Paul quickly interrupted: "Listen, Laura, sometimes it just takes time to find these things out."

We spent the rest of that session, and another, exploring their feelings. The more they talked, the more it made sense to them to bring their relationship to an end. They shared their sadness and discussed the practicalities of how they would manage at work. Paul said it would be difficult for him to be "active friends" right now, but he hoped he and Laura could have a strong, friendly connection after he recovered. She said she wouldn't have it any other way. They held hands as they left their last session.

The Role of Acceptance

Laura had raised an important point in their pivotal session. She wondered whether she should simply accept that Paul didn't inspire the kind of romantic feelings she valued. Given all his other attributes, maybe it would be a reasonable trade-off.

Indeed, acceptance is a key ingredient in all successful relationships. It also requires a balanced perspective. It is possible to be *too* accepting of a relationship that simply can't meet your most basic needs. Unfortunately, it's not always easy to spot overacceptance.

Again, it's best to look to your instincts, to heed to your deepest feelings. Had romance not been very important to Laura (it was), and had everything else about Paul closely met her needs and her ideals (almost, but not quite), then accepting the relationship wouldn't have posed such a challenge to her. But Laura was young and she had high expectations for her career and personal life. She wasn't ready to compromise or settle down. In accepting this about *herself,* she realized that she would be hurting both herself and Paul if she tried to force the relationship to work for her.

Paul's nagging anxiety was the one-down side of Laura's acceptance dilemma. Should he have chosen to tolerate it, or was it too great an emotional drain? One-downs in this situation most commonly choose to accept their anxiety because it also happens to foster passion and attachment. But when one-downs are overly accepting, feelings of weakness and self-contempt begin to fester inside them. Paul burned out on these feelings and chose not to live with them.

Breaking Up Isn't Failure

Keeping a No-Fault perspective through a breakup allows you to appreciate how lucky you are and how proud you should be of yourself. After all, you had the courage to take risks. You *did* have joyous times. You bravely endured the pain. You became a wiser, more compassionate person. And you learned that emotional agony isn't a necessary companion of love.

Laura and Paul had arrived as closely as a couple can at a no-regrets, bilateral decision to break up. They were happy to have shielded their feelings of closeness and affection from the ravages of the passion trap. Most of all, they were thrilled to have avoided, as Paul put it, "an emotional *Jaws II.*"

It's been two and a half years since I last saw Laura and Paul. Recently I tracked them down to see what they were doing. Laura was dating a surgeon: "My appendix ruptured six months ago, and guess what?" Paul had returned to Daphne not long after breaking from Laura. They had married a year later, and now she was expecting. "We're very happy," he reported, "and very well balanced."

Laura and Paul also expressed the fondest of feelings for each other.

A One-Down Wife Who Left

Marie, the hair stylist, worked hard to bring Healthy Distance into her marriage. As you may recall, when Ron, her mechanic husband, didn't change, she issued an ultimatum. Fortunately, that jolted him into action. He agreed to start couples' therapy. They began negotiating a better balance between her closeness needs and his privacy needs. They spent more time together—including one day a week when Marie got to plan their day—and Marie promised to give Ron a couple of nights a week and one day each weekend to do what he wanted. (She still had *her* separate interests to pursue.) Their friction level fell dramatically. For a while, it looked like they were balancing their relationship.

Five months later, however, the picture wasn't so bright. When they did things together, Ron was usually sullen and uncommunicative. He thought most of Marie's weekend jaunts were a waste of time. He wanted to go to sports events or fishing, which were not of great interest to her.

Then Ron started finding excuses to avoid therapy sessions. Gradually their couples' sessions again became her individual sessions. During one of these sessions she told me:

> I feel like I'm making all the effort. And some of it really is paying off. I'm feeling stronger. It used to be when Ron would leave me alone I'd feel ugly and undesirable, even though everyone's always saying how "cute" I am. Now I'm kind of getting the feeling that the problem isn't so much me as it is us. He's still the most attractive man I've ever been with. More than anything in the world I want things to work out between us. But I think we're just very different people. It's so simple. He's not the affectionate type, and I am. His idea of affection is sex. I just want some hugging and kissing and to be told once in a while, "Hey, babe, you're great." Like he did when we first dated. But I have to stop banging my head against the wall and decide whether to stay with the Ron I've come to know, or move on.

Why One-Downs Leave

Three factors, often in combination, can motivate a one-down to leave a chronically unbalanced relationship: emotional burnout, a new partner, or a resurgence of self-esteem (which is what makes Healthy Distance such a potent program). For Marie, it was a combination of burnout and renewed self-esteem. She stayed with Ron for another four months, and during that time she realized she would never feel truly loved by him the way she wanted to be. She didn't blame him. She realized that *she* was as unable to give him the distance he wanted as he was unable to give her the closeness she wanted. Looking back, she also realized that their two-month courtship before marrying was just too short a period for them to learn about each other's very different personality styles.

Finally, Marie left Ron. She moved in with her sister and began to look for her own place. At first, Ron called and came around, trying to persuade her to come back. She was tempted, because now he was acting like the Ron she really wanted. But she suspected that the passion trap was playing a part in his sudden courtship behavior. They had dinner together, and Ron didn't really have much to say. Marie sadly kissed him good-bye for the very last time.

If It Must End

If all your efforts fail to forestall the downward spin of your relationship, realistic action is in order. Here are some further thoughts that may help clarify the issues and blunt a little of the inevitable pain.

"Emotional Cold Turkey"

Prepare to go through a period of "emotional cold turkey." It may be rougher for the one-down, but the one-up is not at all immune. After all, even problem relationships breed deep attachments, and losing a partner is like an emotional amputation. A period of adjustment is necessary.

You will feel deep insecurity, doubt, loneliness, and regret. You will have catastrophic thoughts, the most common one being that you'll never find another lover. This is *not* a pathological reaction. It is a normal consequence of an ancient, biological reaction that originally evolved to ensure mate bonding and species survival. The acute phase of this reaction period usually lasts about six weeks. (Interestingly, this is the same recovery time that surgeons tell their patients to expect.) Emotional tenderness can persist for several months (or more) thereafter. During this period, bolster yourself with emotional support from friends, relatives, spiritual counselors, and possibly a therapist. Empathize with yourself. (And please review the "Be Good to Yourself" section in chapter 9.) By facing up to your pain, accepting it as normal, and grieving your loss, you will recover and gain strength more quickly.

The Yo-Yo

Sometimes a yo-yo pattern develops when a couple tries to break up. The one-up leaves, then returns, then leaves, then returns. Or the one-down does the same thing. If you quickly resume old one-up/one-down patterns after reuniting, especially if you're working to fight those patterns, you'll probably have to conclude that the passion trap motivated the reunion. It's painful to face this fact. But *not* to draw a line when a chronic yo-yo pattern develops is to permit the passion trap to take destructive control of your life.

On the other hand, leaving may indeed have been the wrong move. But you'll still have a hard time distinguishing between a passion trap reversal and a resurgence of true feelings of love unless you're able to give the relationship another chance. If you're able to return to your partner, and you do experience a strong sense of relief and happiness that clearly outweighs your doubts, your intuition is probably telling you to stay.

However, don't assume that all your problems are behind you. Go to work as soon as possible on those harmful patterns. If they cropped up once, they're likely to crop up again. Your renewed happiness in the relationship will motivate you to nip the bad dynamics in the bud this time around.

When There Are Children

Divorce is always hard on children. They give us perhaps our most important reason to put everything into making a relationship work. But, as the wisdom goes, it's a bad idea to preserve a chronically toxic relationship for "the sake of the kids." Children experience a devastating combination of anxiety and depression when their parents are fighting or alienated. These symptoms often improve when the parents separate. Ways to minimize their short-term hardships caused by divorce are:

- Always strive to keep your displays of conflict with your partner away from the children
- When children need to know something about the trouble between the two of you, always use No-Fault, nonaccusatory terms to explain
- Never enlist children as allies against a partner
- Channel your normal guilt over hurting your children *constructively* by maximizing their time spent with both parents and supporting them with love

Beware of "Let's Be Friends"

After a breakup, the leaving one-up will often try what I call the "Let's Be Friends" Solution. Even though the relationship didn't work out on a romantic level for the one-up, he wants to maintain a friendly connection with the one-down—on his terms. The one-down, after all, knows him intimately, and cares. She's probably closer to him than any other human being. This arrangement helps ease the one-up's insecurity about suddenly being alone and appease his guilt over hurting her. The one-up often finds it easy to switch roles from lover to friend, since his romantic feelings may have long since fled the relationship.

For the one-down, however, the switch is often emotionally difficult if not impossible—at least immediately following a breakup. She may try to convince herself that she should be mature enough to handle friendship with her former lover. She may try her hardest to act out that role. She may even wind up being the one-up's confidante about his new romantic adventures. Subconsciously, however, the friendship role often is her last ray of hope for reclaiming her lover. Sooner or later, her emotions will betray the fact that she's only *role-playing* friendship. Eventually, expressions of love or jealousy or both will spill out. Then, the one-up may be forced to take the bull by the horns and cut off all interactions with his former partner.

The lesson in this? If a romantic relationship has truly ended, both partners need to be apart from each other for a time. This period enables the one-down to grieve her emotional loss, put it behind her, and begin restructuring her life. It allows the one-up to face his insecurities without turning his former partner into an emotional crutch. Of course, it's not unusual (even though it's not the norm) for former partners eventually to become close friends. But before this happens, a period of separation is usually necessary to ensure that both partners have begun adjusting to life without each other.

Dealing with the Anger

A normal and important part of the recovery phase, especially if you're the one-down, is a period of anger. You'll feel enraged at your former partner for all your pain and at *yourself* for having been "such a fool." However, lashing out vindictively never helps and usually only prolongs the agony. But there are effective ways of dealing with your anger.

Ventilating anger in benign and sometimes humorous ways can make you feel much better. Recall, for example, Beth's "fuck off and die" letter or Nora Ephron's "I want him back dead" fantasy from chapter 6. Many rejected one-downs have channeled their anger into the "I'll Show Him" reaction, and become career successes or amazing physical specimens. Others have transformed anger into artistic creation or good deeds to benefit others.

As always, I urge you to *value* your anger—it will energize you to make the most of your life. Tell yourself, "Yes, I've had a major setback. But dammit, I'm going to learn from this experience and move on to find a better partner for me."

Finally, let's explode the myth that there are any right or wrong decisions when it comes to choosing whether to leave a relationship. We still nurture the belief that the "right" decision will bring magical happiness forever, the "wrong" one endless misery. The happiest people I know courageously make their choices, relish their gains, accept their losses, and move on to make the most of their lives. In this spirit, the decision you make is the right one.

Chapter 16

Embracing the Paradox of Passion in Love and Marriage

The passion trap may be a harmful influence, but insights about it teach us how to keep love alive and fresh. Embracing it means accepting that bad times are normal, and not panicking. It means looking for signs in the way you and your partner treat each other and listening for messages in what you say to each other. It means searching out causes of relationship imbalance and working to correct them. It means *acting* on new knowledge and tapping its power to create deep, vital, lasting love and happiness. Here are some of the challenges my clients faced as they put the lessons of the passion trap into practice — and the rewards they reaped.

Seesawing

Even the most compatible and balanced of partners have ups and downs. Their healthy autonomy keeps them attracted to each other, but either partner may nurture occasional feelings of insecurity. The result is "seesawing." In seesawing relationships, the partners often trade the one-up and one-down roles. When seesawing gets extreme, they also swing between feelings of love and pain. For the most passionate of these couples, there's a link between the love and the pain they feel. The more they love each other, the more it hurts when they can't get along. I see these couples when seesawing locks them into a no-win power struggle.

The plus side of seesawing is that the partners don't take each other for granted. They're capable of feeling one-down lovingness and vulnerability. And because they're basically balanced, they respond well to couples' therapy. As with Miles and Beth, the passion trap is most likely to be tripped by situational factors.

Seesawing and Setbacks

After four and a half months, Miles and Beth were almost ready to make the break from therapy. They were communicating well and had become expert at spotting and dealing with bad patterns. They knew they should expect the occasional setback, and they knew that situations held the power to unbalance them. But when they walked into my office for their next-to-last session, I could tell they'd hit a big one. There were no smiles of greeting as they entered my office and took their customary seats. I asked what was wrong. Beth said:

> You know how we'd been getting along so great? Well, I'm thinking it was just for your benefit. Because now we're back to square one.

I asked her to elaborate.

> It's kind of like the tables have turned. I have this new account, a guy who manufactures fashion footwear — denim high-tops. He wants to launch his new line in a big way, and I'm working on a campaign for him. It's taking time, but he has the bucks. Two nights ago we had a dinner meeting that went late. Miles was frothing at the mouth when I got home. You see, that never happens, me getting home after he does. He said I should have called and that I was being very inconsiderate of the babysitter, who had school the next day. I said I'd knew he'd be home at a reasonable hour so I didn't worry …

Miles broke in:

> She *was* being inconsiderate. You should have seen the look on her face when she came in. Like the new Miss America. She reeked of fine wine. And this "guy" is no ordinary guy. He was profiled in the business section the other week. "The Entrepreneur of the Year: Young, Smart, and Very Rich."

I asked if they'd been using No-Fault Communication. Beth answered:

> Yes, but it's not working. I told Miles I can understand how he's feeling, because that's the way I felt for all those months. I even admitted

I might have been trying—just a little bit—to "get" him. But he's still angry and so am I.

I told Beth and Miles I was pleased that this setback had occurred before their therapy ended because it raised several important points.

First, I told them, it's perfectly normal to feel anger even when you're using No-Fault terms. The main thing is that you're communicating, and you're not making things worse by communicating only in accusations. One of the prime functions of No-Fault Communication is to help you get to the other side of a problem without lashing out and doing major or even irreparable damage to your relationship.

I told Miles and Beth that they were doing better than they thought. Such an incident four months earlier would have had them coming to counseling in separate cars.

Love and Amnesia

Sometimes, when things have been going unusually well, a setback will feel all the more severe and ominous. It may seem to point to horrible, encrusted, deep-rooted problems that you've merely been glossing over. A kind of amnesia sets in, making you forget that your partner is lovable most of the time.

Love plays with our memory. I told Miles and Beth that there is scientific evidence that strong emotions powerfully influence our mental processes on every level. The same region of the brain that transmits our memories—the limbic system—also mediates our emotions. The result: when we feel loving, we tend to remember only the good and blot out the bad. When we're angry at our partners, we have no idea why we're in such horrible relationships.

Giving Beth and Miles this physiological explanation was helpful. Beth said:

> That explains why the No-Fault Communication felt unreal. It was seeming like the progress we'd made with you had been fake—and why go through the motions anymore?

I told them that major setbacks weren't uncommon for couples nearing the end of counseling. Some anxiety about breaking free from a therapeutic relationship is normal, and often that anxiety renews stress between partners. I also reminded them that their great progress made the setback, by contrast, seem a nearly crushing blow.

Rewards and Risks of Seesawing

Lasting passionate love in a balanced relationship is not a myth. It's the upside to seesawing, and I've seen it often. But in all the cases I've seen, the partners had to earn that passion. They had to learn how to manage those I-hate-my-partner pain phases so that they'd end in happy reunion rather than divorce court. Sometimes a couple will burn out on the pain, or one partner will and the other won't. And sometimes the pain will drive one or both partners to infidelity or substance abuse or bitterness about the relationship, and then the problem is vastly compounded.

The prototypical seesawing couple would be Elizabeth Taylor and Richard Burton during their headline-grabbing heyday. Their fights were shouting matches heard round the world. But when they kissed and made up, they shared the ultimate in attraction power and passion; no diamond was too large for Elizabeth's delicate hand. Their legendary extremes included two marriages and two divorces.

Noisy seesawing relationships like the Taylor-Burton liaison can benefit greatly from patience. Patience reduces the risk side of seesawing and plays an important role in any strong relationship. I urged Miles and Beth actively to cultivate patience, as I do anyone in a close relationship.

The Role of Patience

Using patience means adding a cooling-off period to a pain phase. It means not acting out in your relationship when it goes from good to bad. It means avoiding extreme one-up or one-down solutions. It means trying not to react or attack in fear or rage. It means holding an internal dialogue to objectify the situation: reminding yourself that you're in a pain phase that is causing amnesia about your partner's lovable qualities and doubt about the worth of the relationship. It means telling yourself that everyone has problems like yours. They're universal. It means *thinking* about acting out, but not doing it. Of course, it's perfectly normal to slip up. There will be talk that gets accusatory and actions that are retaliatory. Everyone backslides, but acting out in serious, intentionally wounding ways during a pain phase is making a choice to inflate and prolong the pain. Patience means giving yourself time for your emotions to subside so that you can regain a No-Fault perspective. It means realizing that during an acute pain phase you're naturally prone to feel self-righteous and to take a *fault finding* perspective. It means accepting that it's only normal *not* to draw on all the helpful strategies you read about in relationship books like this.

Prepare a Game Plan

I invited Miles and Beth, as I do all my couples' clients, to think of ways to handle the pain phases. Having a game plan gives you a bridge between the good times and the bad, and it can be an emotional life preserver when the pain is pulling you toward despair.

A good first step is simply for the partners to acknowledge that they're in a pain phase. Miles and Beth did so. I asked them how it felt. Beth said:

> Better. I especially like the word *phase*. It says this is just a temporary thing. We're going to get through it.

But beyond this acknowledgment, couples differ in the strategies that work for them. Following are some that have been helpful to my clients.

- Agree on a time to verbally "fight it out" — a time alone and out of earshot of children. But don't approach each other like contenders for the heavyweight crown. Instead, allow yourselves to fully express your points of view. Acknowledge that anger is blocking your empathy for each other. If you keep talking, you'll start gaining control over your emotions.
- Agree to avoid each other as much as possible until you both feel calmer. Or, separate by one or both of you going to a neutral place, like your parents' or a friends'. (But catch yourself if you spend this time making mental propaganda against your partner.) Then talk. This strategy shouldn't be confused with a cold-shoulder treatment; the avoidance period should be mutually determined.
- Make love, even if it seems awkward. Sometimes actions can make peace more effectively than words.
- Socialize with friends as a couple.
- Watch a comedy together.
- Say you're sorry.

Talk about these options and come up with some of your own. Then agree to try as hard as you can to *act* on your game plan during bad times. The key, of course, is to let down your pain-induced defenses and actually put the plan into practice.

One Cannot Love and Always Be Wise

Miles and Beth had intellectually accepted my suggestions, but emotions take longer to change. When they came back the following week, they were able to laugh about "Beth's night out." They had agreed to wait until that evening to talk about the episode. By then they'd gained control over their strong emotions and could really start communicating. Miles said:

> Of course I knew I was "getting a taste of my own medicine" from Beth, but in my mind what she was doing was worse because we were in a period of trying to make our relationship better. Also, I assumed she was up to something, which was an unfair assumption. When we talked about these things, we realized Beth still had resentment about my affair, and I was afraid she'd try to retaliate if given half a chance.

Beth took up the story:

> Then we talked about the situation behind all this, and it became very apparent that my renewing my career somewhat successfully was creating stress. Once we started focusing on that, the pressure decreased. I was able to assure Miles that I wasn't the slightest bit attracted to the high-top king—I mean, sneakers are like a religion for this guy—and he dates teenaged models.

Just knowing that it's normal and inevitable to be somewhat irrational some of the time is the best way to get back to being rational. Once you regain your equilibrium, you can focus on restoring loving harmony between you.

Sturdy Love

At their last session, Miles and Beth held hands and radiated closeness. I told them they looked very happy. Beth said:

> It's so nice to feel this way again. It almost makes it seem worth having the occasional battle, just so we can clear the air and get close again. I used to think each fight was going to be the last, in the sense that we'd never recover from it. But now I'm starting to have confi-

dence that our fights are survivable, even though they feel terminal at the time.

Miles added:

I feel more and more in love with Beth. She was the one who initiated communication this time, and I was impressed. I'm starting to feel like we can trust each other to do the best thing for the relationship.

Clearly, Beth and Miles were in a phase of exceptional intimacy, love, and affection. We should expect our relationships to bring us luminous moments like these. Intimate partnerships should offer a bedrock of comfort, trust, companionship, and support, along with peaks of strong romantic feeling. We can have all this and still fight once in a while.

Beth and Miles would continue to seesaw and to throw off sparks in the process. Of that I was certain. But now that they'd fully accepted this fact — meaning they'd genuinely embraced the paradox of passion in their marriage — I felt confident that they'd be able to survive their spells of disharmony. Seemingly in affirmation of this feeling, I heard from them recently, two years after the end of their therapy. They sent me a card announcing the birth of a little boy.

When You're Single

After six months of therapy, Deborah had regained her emotional bearings. No longer fixated on Jonathan, she felt relief that she hadn't gotten more deeply involved with someone who was on such a different emotional wavelength. She accepted that their personality styles simply didn't mesh, and that both were better off apart.

Now her goal was to get into the kind of emotional shape that would, among other things, minimize her chances of having another Jonathan-type episode in her life. She realized that meant building up her personal strengths, working on her self-esteem, and gaining insights about herself and relationship dynamics. She was focusing on her art to accomplish all three ends. But as she said in one session:

I know I have the technical skills, but I just can't seem to shake my "painter's block." I still need to find my own "voice." It's frustrating, and I have a hard time keeping my concentration. And guess what I start thinking about? The cute guy in the camera shop or the new history teacher. Kelly and I go out together a lot, and we always seem to wind up at night spots where it's possible to meet people. Why can't I just forget about guys and turn into another Georgia O'Keeffe?

Deborah was facing the biggest challenge for single people who want to be romantically involved.

The Paradox of Finding
Happiness in Love

Love relationships, especially new ones, can be so exciting that they become an emotional holy grail. They seem like the only true source of happiness and fulfillment, the only thing worth pursuing. Work, friends, family, and interests may fill our lives, but there's still an overpowering feeling of emptiness. We can't be happy until we find a partner.

When our lives revolve around finding a romantic partner, we tend to appear emotionally needy — that is, one-down — to others. Acting *slightly* one-down signals availability, and that's good. But if we seem desperate for involvement, the emotional dangers are obvious.

When relationships are the focal center of our lives, we also tend to neglect the very thing that can make us most attractive — building our personal strengths. This explains why people who are blatantly "on the make" often seem less appealing than others who have interests apart from mate hunting.

When the search for love rules your life, you may also come to expect so much from love that potential partners who are attracted to you never quite make the grade. These unreasonable expectations can make you highly sensitive to perceived shortcomings in a new, attainable partner. You're then likely to slip into a one-up distancing mode before you've given the relationship a fair chance. That engenders one-down behavior in your new partner, throwing the relationship out of balance.

The paradox, then, is that if you put all your efforts into finding romance — and if you expect romance to be your emotional salvation — you'll lessen your chances of finding lasting, satisfying love.

Paradoxically too, building your strengths for *yourself* is the very thing that will add most to your appeal to others. But even in this area it's wise not to go overboard. People who get too wrapped up in their own pursuits may put off potential partners by seeming too self-involved, distracted, or inaccessible. A flicker of attraction needs to be met by a corresponding flicker. If that's not forthcoming, most people will set their sights elsewhere.

The most attractive people are those who strike a balance between one-up and one-down behaviors, autonomy and availability. They're the ones who project both confidence and emotional openness.

Deborah knew she had a strong tendency to put all her eggs in a relationship basket. She also knew that that didn't leave her enough emotional energy to make the kind of art she wanted to. Moreover, she was having a hard time convincing herself that her conscious efforts to channel energy away from relationships and toward art would work. It's that old feeling that plagues almost everyone when they take Healthy Distance actions in a relationship: the feeling that they're just "going through the motions." I reassured Deborah that it didn't matter how it felt to her. When you work on building your strengths, it's going to have an effect no matter how you're feeling. You will be changed, maybe subtly, maybe in very noticeable ways. Because when you change your behavior, you are changing the way you interact with others. You're actually altering interpersonal dynamics.

Dealing with Loneliness

Deborah felt most alone when she came home after work to her empty apartment.

> I don't even like TV, but the first thing I do is turn it on. It keeps the walls from closing in on me. My mother says I should get a cat, but I don't know. Sometimes I start crying and can't stop, because it feels like no one cares or ever will. I doubt a cat would.

The pain of loneliness reminds us that people are social animals. On its most basic level, loneliness is another biological impetus to find a partner.

Obviously, some of us have a greater tolerance for loneliness than others. Those who have the hardest time with it are people who think it's *abnormal* to feel lonely. By feeling this way, they increase the normal unhappiness of loneliness by pathologizing themselves. They think that because they're alone, they must be social misfits, or, as Deborah did, that no one will ever care. Every life has periods of loneliness, and, like a pain phase in a relationship, loneliness can create a kind of amnesia. That is, during lonely spells, your whole life may seem meaningless and empty.

Again, the key is accepting that loneliness is not only normal but biologically based. If you didn't feel lonely some of the time, you wouldn't be normal. A good thing to say to yourself during bouts of loneliness is: "Well, here I go again. I'm feeling isolated and alone and hopeless. That means it's time to take really good care of myself so it won't get me too down."

Using Loneliness

Some will deal with loneliness by stepping up their social lives, others by working harder and longer hours or pursuing new interests. Because she was artistically gifted, Deborah was trying to turn her loneliness into art. In the process, we hoped she would overcome her "painter's block." She decided to confront her feelings in a series of paintings that shared the theme of the loss of self in love. She was calling it "Echo, Echo," and from the beginning it went well.

> This is kind of a breakthrough for me. You know how I told you that when I wrote in my journal, I felt I should be putting down my thoughts about weighty things like life and art, but I always wound up writing about guys and relationships. In my art, I had the same feeling that I *should* be painting a certain way, so that my art would look the way contemporary art is "supposed" to look. And that was a problem, because my paintings didn't have any life in them. So I'm not fighting myself anymore. My art is like my journal, no apologies.

Deborah brought in some preliminary sketches, and, though I'm no critic, I was impressed. One sketch was especially striking: a woman's figure fading into a man's. Deborah's expression told me she was particularly proud of this picture. She was embracing her greatest fear, and in doing so was winning control over it.

Once Again into the Breach

It takes courage to get involved again after a major rejection. But once Deborah had put her fears into her art, she'd begun freeing herself from their tyranny. Her artwork was no longer filler in a life dominated by wishful thinking about relationships. She was thinking about her art and feeling passionate about it.

Deborah was thrilled when her new paintings were accepted by a gallery to be part of a three-woman show. "It's not the most prestigious gallery in town," she said, "but it has its own niche as a showcase for new talent."

At the opening, Deborah met an interesting man. Significantly, she told me about him *after* giving a lengthy report of the show and her feelings about that. She agreed that six months earlier she probably would have started with the man.

Jack was a friend of one of the other artists in the show. He was a soundman who worked on independent feature films in Los Angeles. Deborah said:

> He's a real sweetheart, and *very* attractive. He commutes between here and Los Angeles, and right now he's in between shoots. He really likes my art and thinks I should try to get a show in L.A. We saw each other the next night, and we had a great time. We really seem to get along well. We're seeing each other again tonight. I'm trying to keep my head, but I'm pretty excited. I sense the time is almost right to ask him what he wants out of a relationship. My hunch is that we have compatible personality styles.

I congratulated Deborah on her plan. She'd come a long way.

Do I Want to Join This Club?

Two months into her new relationship, Deborah had good news and bad news. The good news was that Jack shared her attitudes about relationships. He'd been in one stormy long-term relationship that had ended by mutual agreement. He didn't like being alone and told her he wanted someone to come home to, or someone to come home to him. He wanted to spend all the time he could with her before returning to Los Angeles for his next job.

Meanwhile, three out of four of Deborah's paintings had sold. She said:

> It's like two great things are happening at once, Jack and my art. Jack is coming on strong, and he's seemingly perfect for me. But if he's taking up every free moment, like he wants to, I can't get enough time to paint. So that's becoming a problem for me, and it's confusing my feelings about him.

Deborah's increased autonomy had given her a new experience of love. I confirmed what she suspected: that she had become the one-up in the relationship and it was cutting into the passionate feelings she'd expected. She thought she might be in love with Jack, but at this point she wasn't feeling the same kind of delirium she equated with falling in love. A habitual one-down in her previous relationships, her response wasn't surprising, nor was it unusual.

Give It Time

I suggested that Deborah resist her impulse to cool the affair with Jack after two months. It was still too early to tell if the relationship could work for her. Fortunately, Jack was secure enough not to fall into the hypercourtship trap. He tipped the scales in his direction when he told Deborah that he sensed her conflict; he knew he was coming on too strong and crowding her.

After Jack left for his next film assignment, Deborah found herself missing him intensely. She realized that he had the sensitivity and flexibility to help iron out their conflicts. Best of all, his actions matched his words. He'd started making it a point to preface his invitations with, "After you're through painting, let's ..."

Comfortable Love

Six months later, Deborah told me that she and Jack were talking about marriage.

> This is an extraordinary feeling. I love Jack and I know he's crazy about me. You know how when someone loves you so much you don't have to worry about getting hurt? Well, that's how it is with Jack, and it feels really good. I wouldn't say our relationship is the wild, passionate type, but it has its moments. I'm happy when I'm with Jack, and it feels much better than the gut-wrenching stuff I had with Jonathan, and others.

Deborah had found a comfortable love that offered her the emotional rewards she'd been seeking for so long. Did she feel she was making an unacceptable sacrifice by forfeiting the passion she'd valued so highly? Some habitual one-downs like Deborah find it hard to adjust to life without "the gut-wrenching stuff." Deborah said:

> Sometimes I miss it, but I've gotten to the point in my life where other things matter more. I've had my fill of relationship agony. Jack and I are talking about children. Who wants to bring a child into a crazy relationship? I can accept what I have, and don't have, with

Jack because overall it's so good. It makes me happy to think about spending the rest of my life with him.

Deborah said she felt strong enough to leave therapy, and she was. I felt that the lessons of the passion trap would stay with her.

Finding Balance for the First Time

Peg and Bill also found a comfortable love after the tumult of their crisis. Their rebirth as a balanced couple followed two decades of *stable* imbalance. Before, they'd had an arrangement. Now, they have love and intimacy that often surprises as well as fulfills them.

In some ways, Peg and Bill's former relationship was easier. It followed the predictable, traditional path. Their complementary roles were well defined. Because they were on the road most traveled, they had little need for an emotional road map. They could stay on course with few relationship skills.

While traditional marriage can be satisfying for the partners—especially when "hidden balance" is at work—it can also hold a very real danger. Traditional married couples are highly vulnerable to changes in the balance between them—especially when the change involves a one-down wife who starts building her strengths, as Peg did.

> I never really liked being a housewife. I think I first realized this when my youngest boy started school. I'd dedicated my life to giving to others, yet I was finding myself more and more alone. I knew that was the natural course of things as far as your children go. But I also felt isolated from Bill, even though we were living under the same roof. Still, for years I didn't do anything about it. Partly because it felt safe not to change, and partly because I really didn't know how to change.

When a one-down wife begins to assert herself, she creates a whole new set of dynamics between herself and her husband. If her husband is not very secure in his own life, the effects can be drastic, as they were for Peg and Bill. Traditional marriage hadn't equipped them with the complex relationship skills needed to negotiate this balance shift.

How Crises Can Deepen
Our Relationships

Near the end of our work together, Bill reflected on their crisis.

> At the time I thought it was the end of the world. But now I thank God I didn't get that promotion. It forced me to face things about myself I'd always run from. If I'd gotten the promotion, I'd feel great, sure. But I'd still be stuck in the rat race, and I'd still be miserable. Only I wouldn't have known it because I was too close to it. Now I'm about to close my first boat deal. And our boat is a gem. I can honestly say I've never felt happier. [He turned to Peg.] And I'm the luckiest man in the world to have you in my life.

The storm that almost blew this marriage apart had actually produced a stronger union.

If your relationship is acutely troubled, you may be wondering whether it will survive, or even if you want it to. It will be difficult, but I urge you to ponder the therapeutic potential of your crisis. In fact, you and your partner may be struggling through a critical stage that will free you from rigid patterns of relating to find deeper levels of intimacy. But relationship crises more easily do damage than good. So I urge you to seek professional help if your conflicts seem beyond your control.

Two Pros

Near the end of their therapy, I saw Peg and Bill once every two to three weeks. I wanted to maintain at least minimal contact for a couple of months, to see how they'd handle the inevitable setback. It came soon after Bill had finished restoring his boat. He described what happened.

> I invited this lady here to take a little sailing trip with me. After all we've been through, I think we deserve it. Just a week or two sailing up and down the coast. Nothing too ambitious. I thought Peg would go for it, but she didn't. And I'm starting to wonder what's more important to her: me or her business.

Peg countered:

> I'd love to go with you, Bill. But I really can't right now. I'm in the middle of so many things at the shop. I'm afraid if I took off now, I'd

be thinking so much about the business that I wouldn't be any fun at all.

Bill turned to me.

It's ironic, huh. All these years I was saying these very things to Peg, and now I'm getting it back.

I invited Bill to share what was most upsetting about that.

Oh, I suppose it's that for so many years I was used to having Peg always there for me. Her life always revolved around mine, and not the other way around. I'm just not used to this new Peg. But I *am* really proud of her. I sometimes think I'm just an overgrown baby.

By acknowledging how difficult it was for him to adjust to Peg's new autonomy, Bill had activated their new empathy skills.
Then Peg said:

No, no, honey. When I think of where we were six months ago and where we are today, I think I'm living in a dream. I feel just like a young girl in love. I'm really very annoyed with myself, and I'm very proud of you. You are right, just like you always used to be. We really do need to take this trip together ...

Bill interrupted:

Now hold on. Remember, I used to be in your shoes. I know what it's like to have that kind of pressure on you. How 'bout I take the boys this time around. They've been hounding me about it anyway. Then we can plan a trip of our own in a couple of months, during your off season.

Peg said, "You've got yourself a date."
I was impressed. Within minutes, Peg and Bill had resolved their episode of imbalance. I wouldn't be seeing them again. They were prepared for the challenges of equal, dynamic love.

You may have noticed that none of the couples I worked with had an uncomplicated "happily ever after" ending. In fairy tales, cheery endings are not what interest us. What's absorbing about them are the challenges — the evil witches, the conniving magicians, the bramble forests, the dragons, the curses — that keep the lovers apart and keep them struggling to reach each other.

Now let's consider the real-life equivalents of the fairy tale obstacles—the emotional challenges we face. Instead of a dragon or a wicked stepsister, we must deal with things like insecurities, faulty communication, and sometimes the unwelcome attentions of sexual rivals. In fairy tales, the obstacles are overcome, never to be revisited. In life, they are permanent features of our relationships. Sometimes they loom large and close together, sometimes small and far apart. But they will never go away. Only dealing with them, facing them head-on, will keep a couple's life dynamic.

This is why I feel the paradox of passion should be embraced, both realistically as an inescapable presence in our lives, and warmly, as we'd embrace someone close who complicates our lives but also enriches them.

Bibliography

Annotated titles are especially recommended.

Alberti, Robert E., and Michael L. Emmons. *Your Perfect Right.* San Luis Obispo, CA: Impact, 1986. A popular book on how to be more assertive.

Bach, George R., and Peter Wyden. *The Intimate Enemy.* New York: Avon Books, 1968. A classic book on how partners can deal effectively with their anger.

Beck, Aaron T. *Love Is Never Enough.* New York: Harper & Row, 1988. Explains how to use cognitive therapy for improving relationships.

Branden, Nathaniel. *The Psychology of Romantic Love.* New York: Bantam Books, 1981. Provides wise advice about our expectations in loving relationships.

Cowan, Ruth S. *More Work for Mother.* New York: Basic Books, 1983.

Ellis, Albert, and Robert A. Harper. *A Guide to Successful Marriage.* North Hollywood, CA: Wilshire Book Co. Explains how to think more rationally in relationships.

Farrell, Warren. *Why Men Are the Way They Are.* New York: McGraw-Hill, 1986. This book is helpful for taking a no-fault perspective to problems caused by gender differences; it explains why men are conditioned to be "success" objects much as women are conditioned to be "sex" objects.

Forward, Susan, and Joan Torres. *Men Who Hate Women and the Women Who Love Them.* New York: Bantam Books, 1986. Provides helpful advice for women involved with abusive men.

Haley, Jay. *Strategies of Psychotherapy.* New York: Grune & Stratton, 1963.

Halpern, Howard. How To *Break Your Addiction To a Person.* New York: Bantam Books, 1983. If you're having difficulty leaving a no-win relationship or getting over a former partner, this book will help you.

Bibliography

Leary, Timothy. *Interpersonal Diagnosis of Personality*. New York: Ronald Press, 1957.

Masters, William H., and Virginia E. Johnson. *The Pleasure Bond*. New York: Bantam Books, 1976. Discusses the importance of equality between partners for enhancing intimacy and sexual pleasure.

May, Rollo. *Love and Will*. New York: Norton, 1969.

Milkman, Harvey B., and Stanley G. Sunderworth. *Craving for Ecstasy*. Lexington, MA: Lexington Books, 1987.

Scarr, Sandra, Deborah Phillips, and Kathleen McCardney. "Working Mothers and their Families." *American Psychologist 44* (1989).

Singer, Irving. *The Nature of Love, Vol. 3*. Chicago: University of Chicago Press, 1987.

Stendhal. *Love*. New York: Penguin Books, 1982.

Sternberg, Robert J., and Michael L. Barnes. *The Psychology of Love*. New Haven, CT: Yale University Press, 1988. A good resource book on psychological studies of love and relationships.

Tolstoy, Leo. *Anna Karenina*. Tolstoy's classic novel offers the most poignant illustration of passion trap dynamics that I have read. Levin and Kitty's relationship begins with an imbalance in love and grows equal; Vronsky and Anna's relationship follows the opposite pattern.

Watzlawick, Paul, John H. Weakland, and Richard Fisch. *Change*. New York: Basic Books, 1974.

Wile, Daniel B. *After the Honeymoon*. New York: Wiley & Sons, 1988. A valuable book for helping partners resolve conflicts.

About the Authors

Dr. Dean C. Delis is a clinical psychologist, Professor of Psychiatry at the University of California, San Diego, School of Medicine, and a staff psychologist at the San Diego V.A. Medical Center. He has more than 100 professional publications and has served on the editorial boards of several scientific journals. He is a diplomate of the American Board of Professional Psychology and American Board of Clinical Neuropsychology. Raised on his family's farm in the central valley of California, he lives near San Diego with his wife, Meg, and three boys, Patrick, Drew and Miles.

Cassandra Phillips' background includes literary criticism, newspaper reporting, and film industry script development. Currently she lives in Hawaii, pursues free-lance writing, and works with her husband Bob Burkey in their commercial orchid nursery. They have two children, Billy and Keely.

9396876R00175

Made in the USA
San Bernardino, CA
13 March 2014